A Bad
Beginning
and the Path to Islam

A Bad
Beginning
and the Path to Islam

Gai Eaton

This first edition published in 2010 by
Archetype
Chetwynd House, Bartlow
Cambridge CB21 4PP, UK

www.archetype.uk.com

ISBN 978 1 901383 32 4 hb
ISBN 978 1 901383 33 1 pb

All of the pictures are the author's own with the exception of:
frontispiece portrait of Gai Eaton courtesy of emel magazine, 2005;
pictures of René Guénon and Martin Lings © Mrs Lesley Lings;
picture of Frithjof Schuon © The Schuon Estate.

Pictures at chapter headings:
Chapter 1, p. 13 *Muddock*; Chapter 2, p. 35 *Gai as a boy*;
Chapter 3, p. 53 *Francis*; Chapter 4, p. 66 *Francis at 85*;
Chapter 5, p. 83 *Francis & Gai*; Chapter 6, p. 98 *Gai at Cambridge*;
Chapter 7, p. 117 *Military*; Chapter 8, p. 138 *Ruth at 50*;
Chapter 9, p. 157 *Kay*; Chapter 10, p. 176 *Guénon*;
Chapter 11, p. 198 *Flo*; Chapter 12, p. 219 *Young Gai*;
Chapter 13, p. 235 *Martin Lings*; Chapter 14, p. 253 *The Island*;
Chapter 15, p. 275 *Corah*; Chapter 16, p. 295 *Corah with Judy*;
Chapter 17, p. 313 *Maurice, Ann & Corah*; Epilogue, p. 328 *Packing up*

Pictures in text: p. 286 *Corah painting*; p. 323 *Christmas card*;
p. 345 *Leo, Maurice, Judy, Gai, Ann & Corah*; p. 348 *Frithjof Schuon*

A full CIP record for this book is available from
the British Library
A full CIP record for this book is available from
the Library of Congress

Book design by Shems Friedlander

Printed and bound in Great Britain by TJ International Ltd, Padstow, Cornwall

for my children
Leo, Judy, Maurice and Corah Ann
and for Margaret to whom I owe so much

That which hath been is now
and that which is to be
hath already been; and
God requireth that which is past.

Ecclesiastes 3:15

I on my side require of every writer
a simple and sincere account of his
own life, some such account as he
would send to his kindred from a
distant land, for if he has lived
sincerely it must have been in a
distant land to me.

Henry David Thoreau, *Walden*

INTRODUCTION

I was sixteen when I decided that, one day soon, I would write my autobiography. Time has passed, as it tends to do, and I am now eighty-four. I had better get on with the job. There is, however, a problem. As a Muslim of a particular bent, I have to find excuses for wallowing in the past and revealing shameful secrets. In Islam such self-exposure is, if not a sin, certainly ill-mannered. I am not sure that my excuses are valid, but they will have to do.

In the first place, the story ends in 1959 when I was thirty-eight. That year was a watershed, the end of the 'bad beginning', the beginning of something better. This man of long ago is, in many ways, a stranger to me, so I call this story a 'biography' rather than an 'autobiography', which is why it is written in the third person. That stranger is 'he'—'Gai'—not 'I', and it is based on the documents rather than memory. At the age of eleven I started to keep a personal diary, thinking that a life recorded in detail from childhood to the end might be of interest. If I can try, more than seventy years later, to articulate what was in that strange child's mind, I can only think that he wanted to stop time in its tracks, to conquer time. In any case, the diary has continued ever since, running by now to some eighteen million words, and it soon became, if not an addiction, at least an ingrained habit and a safety valve.

For the diary writer nothing has 'really happened' until it is recorded, and only the diary writer knows how unreliable memory is, how it falsifies both objective facts and subjective feelings. There is no point in writing one's personal history unless it is true, and I cannot escape the truth since it is on record. By writing my story in the third person I have attempted to distance myself from the person I was and to achieve at least a measure of objectivity. Am I, perhaps, comparable to a schoolboy who, when accused of some offence, says: 'It wasn't me, Sir. It was another boy of the same name'?

7

A diary offers an opportunity to relive the past. When I read a particular passage written fifty or sixty years ago, the emotions of the time are rekindled. At an early stage I began to record snatches of conversation, usually scribbled on the backs of envelopes while fresh in my mind and copied into the diary later. These, more than any other entries, bring back the moment and recapture from long ago a tone of voice, a personality. So it is that not only images and faces but also patterns of speech, lost in the whirligig of time, emerge from the dungeons of memory and I hear again the voices of the dead. The past is brought back, as though mirrored on the shimmering surface of a lake, assembling the scattered events of one man's life in a kind of unity. But into what historical framework does this life fit?

My maternal grandfather, 'the Old Man', was the dominant figure of my childhood. At the age of fifteen, newly arrived in India, he had been through the Indian Mutiny which broke out in 1857. Seventy years later he was able to tell me stories of that imperial catastrophe with all the eloquence of a born story-teller (he was the author of more than sixty novels). He told also of his experiences in the Australian gold rush, in China under the Dowager Empress and in the American Civil War. These events, so distant in time for most of my contemporaries, were incorporated into my memory archive. But my sense of connection with the past stretches even further back.

My father, Francis, was born in 1854 during the Crimean War, his father—my paternal grandfather—in 1806, nine years before the Battle of Waterloo, when the younger Pitt was Prime Minister of Britain and the President of the United States was Thomas Jefferson who, thirty years earlier, had drafted the Declaration of Independence. Only in my old age has this come to seem significant. If both had started their families at the age at which I started mine, I might now be preparing to celebrate my 155th birthday. I was born out of my time, a survivor from another age living now in a world changed utterly by two World

Wars and by the universal collapse of traditional structures. I have often felt myself to be an alien amongst people whose culture and mindset are strange beyond belief, but I have also been a fascinated observer of a dysfunctional civilisation adrift in time. Unlike so many who are 'out of synch' with their own period and have no voice, I have been able to express my unfashionable beliefs in four books, published over the course of fifty years. Not long ago a stranger visited me in my office in the Islamic Cultural Centre holding a book behind his back. He read me a paragraph. 'That's good', I said. 'I must make a note of it. What's the book?' It was my first book, published in 1949. It may be that I have not changed as much as I supposed, at least in my way of seeing the world.

In telling my own story, I have written at some length about my childhood — Gai's childhood — because it was so extraordinary and because, from today's vantage point, I detect in it the roots of so much that happened later. Today I would probably have been taken into care by busy social workers, if only to have me educated and socialised. They would have thought my situation as a child who met no other children until he was nine — and then only as creatures who might have come from another planet — fatal to my future wellbeing. I survived none the less and had more happiness than I could possibly have deserved, though never forgetting the saying: 'Call no man happy until he is dead'. There is a balance of advantages and disadvantages in most human situations and, for my part, I regret nothing, but that is not to say that this upbringing did not complicate my life. The complaint — 'I'm just no good at living' — in the 1939 diary might seem like a typical adolescent *cri de coeur*, but if I had to define the principal theme of this story it might be 'learning to live'. It took me a long time. My most recent book, *Remembering God: Reflections on Islam*, has been described as a 'spiritual autobiography'. This, then, is the other side of the coin: a profane autobiography, and very profane it is.

If we learn anything useful in the course of our brief lives, this is not only from our own experience but also from other human stories, past or present. Dr Johnson told Boswell that 'there has rarely passed a life of which a judicious and faithful narrative would not be useful'. I hope that I have been faithful, if not judicious, in what follows and that it is indeed of use to someone.

PROLOGUE

It was a good plan. It would protect his reputation as a pillar of the legal establishment, an austere Victorian of impeccable morality. At the same time, it would guarantee him a role in the child's upbringing as its guardian. Other eminent men sent their pregnant mistresses abroad but not—surely?—to the 'Colonies', not to Canada?

When Ruth, his lover for ten years past, had broken the terrible news to Francis he had suggested an abortion, all expenses paid, but it is unwise to suggest to a tigress that she should abort her cub. He had to think again, and he thought to good purpose. He believed that he had covered every contingency, and the fact that he was now aged sixty-six meant that his colleagues were unlikely to see him as a potential father.

There were two reasons for choosing Canada. His son Arnold had been killed in 1916, leaving a fruit farm which made annual losses. Who better than his protegée—regarded by some as his adopted daughter—to arrange a sale and, at the same time, revisit the country which had provided her most enduring childhood memories? In 1891 her father, the Old Man, had taken her with him on a visit to Canada. The journey had been full of wonder and redolent of an escape into freedom.

Minor details, such as the name of Ruth's fictitious husband, could be settled later, as could the disease or accident which would polish him off soon after the wedding. All that mattered now was to get her out of the country before the pregnancy began to show. After a decent interval the grieving widow would be able to return to her family, an infant in her arms, no questions asked.

When her ship sailed from Liverpool Francis believed that the crisis was over. He was safe. Ruth, the born rebel who always defied authority just as she defied convention, had been, for once, obedient. Her lover, she believed, was the wisest man she had ever known, and she could only admire the speed with which he had found a solution to their problem. The year was 1920. The Great War, after which there were to be no more wars, had ended two years before. This was the right time for a new beginning, and she was elated at the prospect of having a child who would be all hers, rather than shared with an interfering husband. Whether it was a boy or a girl, the treasure in her womb would be an extension of herself, her *alter ego*, her soul-mate. Meanwhile, as the ship met the Atlantic rollers, the New World beckoned. Engaged upon a great adventure, she had at last, at the age of thirty-nine, found a purpose to her life.

MUDDOCK

The Old Man might come back to haunt me if I did not start with him. The great story-teller must be given his due in his grandson's story, and his autobiography, *Pages from an Adventurous Life*, supplements what he himself told me.

James Edward Jasper Everard Preston Muddock or 'Dick Donovan', the name under which he wrote most of his novels, was born in 1842, the son of an officer in the merchant marine who turned his back on the sea to set up business in Calcutta. Left with his mother and aunts in England, he was sent to a tough school even by the standards of the time. According to his autobiography: 'When the Masters were not thrashing the boys, the boys were thrashing each other . . . The chief thing I did at that Academy was fighting when I was not being caned'. Whenever the fancy took him he was off tramping the countryside, sleeping in fields or woods until his pocket-money ran out; returning to the school he would take his thrashing with a good grace, aware that this treatment was toughening him for the life of adventure and rebellion that he planned. But no one could control him so, at the age of fourteen, he was shipped off to Calcutta, where his father at once set him to learn the use of firearms in preparation for the storm ahead. 'He told me of the unrest that was manifesting itself among the natives and how, with blind fatuity, Lord and Lady Canning refused to believe that anything serious was likely to happen.' This was not the last occasion on which a Viceroy of India would demonstrate 'blind fatuity'.

His father visited Cawnpore, taking the boy with him. They were welcomed by the Ruler, a certain Nana Sahib who, when the Mutiny broke out a few months later, came to be seen as evil incarnate after slaughtering a thousand or more white men, women and children to whom he had given safe conduct out of the city. Young Edward (he can hardly be called 'the Old Man' at this stage) was fascinated by him: 'Very pompous, exceedingly fat, with a suggestion in his walk, his actions and his voice of theatricality'. The future novelist was developing a sharp eye. His firearms training, however, was no help when he finally encountered danger. Armed only with a Malacca cane someone had given him, a cane to which a lead ball 'worked over with fine silver wire' was attached, he hired a boatman to row him across the Hoogley River. The man asked if his two sons could join them and there seemed no objection to this. Half way across, one of the young men produced a long knife. 'Before he could use it, the lead knob of my cane struck him on the arm with the quickness of a cobra. The other fellow made a spring at me, but the business end of the cane caught him full on his shaven pate, and he pitched downwards at the bottom of the boat.' The fifteen-year-old had profited from his tough schooling. But the Mutiny did not affect Calcutta and it was only on a visit to Bombay that he was made aware of its savagery when he witnessed the execution of two rebels, bound to the muzzles of twin canons and blown into very small pieces.

His hopes of a career in India ended with the sudden death of his father. He returned to England, joining his mother in Manchester, but he was restless: 'The call of the wild was a siren song to me, and the love of adventure had become like a fever'. A meeting with the novelist Charles Dickens persuaded him that a literary career was the only one for him, but he had to make a living. He knew of a relative in Australia who was a journalist and printer. This might solve the problem, but how was he to get there? Hearing of a Government agent who was about to travel to Sydney in charge of a group of emigrants and who needed a private secretary, he travelled to London, applied for the job and was accepted. Walking down Holborn a day or two later he was caught up in a vast crowd heading for Newgate to witness the public hanging of Catherine Wilson, the poisoner. He observed that she held in her hand a handkerchief which was carried away by the wind when the trap fell and torn into shreds by the crowd, eager for a trophy.

Arriving in Sydney after the long voyage he started work with his relative, but he was soon restless again. Joined by a friend, he 'humped his swag' (a spare shirt, a toothbrush and a pistol) and set off for the gold diggings to make his fortune. This came to nothing and he set off again, picking up his living as best he could. Lost in the Bush and starving, he was saved by aborigines who showed him how to find edible grubs under the bark of a particular tree. Soon afterwards, at the suggestion of another friend —he seems to have made friends wherever he went—he set off by sailing boat for China. 'Between New Britain and New Guinea we were attacked by natives in a war canoe and had some difficulty in getting rid of them. Probably they would have succeeded in their design of turning us into potted meat but for the fact that we had a little brass cannon on board which we loaded to the muzzle with nails, screws and bits of iron.' He arrived safely in Shanghai at the height of a cholera epidemic and, when he fell ill, was carted off to the French Hospital where he was confined to the Cholera Ward, 'about as grim and ghastly a place as imagination can picture'.

He did not have cholera and was released after two weeks, planning a fresh adventure. There was a rebellion against imperial rule. He had a loathing for tyranny and this sounded like a good cause. Hearing that the rebels were only a few miles from Amoy, he sailed there by junk and set off to find them, only to be captured by a unit of the Imperial Army. He soon talked his way out of this and the officer in charge treated this crazy young Englishman to a tasty meal of stewed puppy washed down with arrack. But he had seen enough of China and sailed back to Australia, passing by way of New Guinea where, he claimed: 'I had the honour of being entertained by Royalty, my host a Cannibal Chief who, at first, was in doubt whether to dine off me or with me'. The gift of a Jack Knife 'so touched his tender royal heart that he fell upon my neck and vowed in pidgin English that I was his friend for ever'.

He returned to England, insisting on being lashed to the mast during a great storm while rounding Cape Horn, but he was as restless as ever. A relative who owned a cotton mill, starved of raw cotton by the American Civil War, commissioned him to sail to New York where he was to contact a blockade runner. In this he was unsuccessful, but he happened to be in Washington when President Lincoln was assassinated. Given his talent for being in the right place at the right time, it is surprising that he was not in Ford's Theatre when Lincoln was shot. He meant to see the body lying in state, but he was not a man to stand in a queue and he 'determined that a dead man, though he had been a president, was not worth all the trouble'.

This was the end of his youthful adventures. He settled in London, published his first novel for which he received a substantial sum, and was taken on by *The Daily Telegraph* as a correspondent. The character of his autobiography changes completely; in effect it becomes a testament of friendship or rather of many friendships with his fellow authors, with artists and with theatre people. Most of his subjects are long forgotten but many were household names in their time. What they had in common was separation from polite society and from the Victorian bourgeoisie. They were 'bohemians', 'savages'. Their ways were different, their morals doubtful and their dress often inappropriate. Some, like Edward Muddock himself, despised 'civilisation' and its restraints, free spirits dedicated to adventure and the arts. That, at least was how they saw themselves, although few if any had truly escaped the mindset and tastes of their period. A group of his friends decided to found a club 'to supply the want which Dr Samuel Johnson and his friends experienced when they founded The Literary Club'. A name had to be found for it and someone suggested The Shakespeare Club, but this seemed too pretentious. 'In frolicsome humour our little society was christened The Savage Club'. It survives to this day but, by all accounts, is no longer either savage, frolicsome or bohemian.

He seems to have had no interest in himself as a person or even in his own success. He probably deplored the fact that his 'Dick Donovan' novels—detective stories and tales of adventure—sold like hot cakes, whereas his serious works, published under his own name, had mixed reviews. Their titles, such as *The Fatal Woman, The Wingless Angel* and *Only a Woman's Heart* suggest that, in our day, they would have appeared under the imprint of Mills & Boon. There were exceptions, particularly when political passions seized him; *For God and the Tsar* is a powerful denunciation of Tsarist oppression in Russia. He might have accumulated a small fortune, but each of his manuscripts was sold for a lump sum rather than earning royalties and the notion of saving money was foreign to his nature. He lived well, however, and in 1880 he rented a splendid villa in Villefranche, the seaside suburb of Nice.

That year he went to Paris on business and was persuaded by a friend to attend a party or perhaps the *salon* of some distinguished hostess. He stopped at the door to survey the assembled guests and his gaze fixed on a young girl leaning against the piano. He stared at her across the room for a while before turning to his companion and announcing, in a voice that must have been audible to everyone present: 'That woman shall be my wife!'

Eleanor Rudd was a Yorkshire girl, visiting her sister Anne who lived in Paris. To judge from a photograph taken at about that time she was no 'English rose' but a dark beauty with marvellous eyes and a gypsy look, in fact it was rumoured that the Rudds were descended from Egyptian refugees who, when their ship was blown off course, had been wrecked on the Cumbrian coast and settled there. The wedding was celebrated a couple of months later. Long afterwards their eldest daughter, Ruth, would ask her mother how she came to marry 'such an impossible man'. Her mother gave the question serious consideration before answering: 'I suppose I was at a loose end at the time'. She was soon to be fully occupied. The couple had ten children, two of whom died in infancy, and, as her husband could never settle in one place for long, she was accustomed to receiving the kind of message that Sir Richard Burton, the explorer, habitually sent to his long-suffering wife: 'Pay, pack and follow'.

Ruth was born the following year in Villefranche and Dorothy ('Dolly') a year later in her grandmother's Yorkshire home in Yarm-on-Tees. Twin girls, Rose and Violet, followed in 1884, born in Geneva where the family were now living. The Old Man, as I may now call him (a true patriarch), was still keeping strange company. There were many Russian refugees in Switzerland at that time, mainly Anarchists and Nihilists. These were people after his own heart and he used the stories they told him as material for his novel, *For God and the Tsar*. From Geneva the family moved to Scotland, then back to France where Ruth passed the formative years of early childhood, speaking French as her first language and retaining a faint French accent up to the end of her life.

The French were still bitter over their defeat in the Franco-Prussian War. They have always been good haters, and she picked up from the maids an ineradicable conviction that the Germans were the most evil people on earth and deserved to be exterminated. She herself soon learned to hate. Wandering in the woods which were part of the estate she found a small bird with a broken wing; she took it in her hands and wept over it. At that moment the gamekeeper came up to her. 'I'll teach it to fly', he said, took the bird from her and dashed it against a tree trunk. For the next month or so she was absent from the house for hours on end, often missing her lunch. In a little hut on the grounds she had found an old rifle and every morning, when the game-keeper passed the hut, she took up the rifle and aimed at him hoping that, one day, it would actually fire when she pressed the trigger. Even eighty years later, recalling the incident, she would consign the gamekeeper to hellfire whenever she recalled the incident. It was as though all the world's cruelty, all the evil that men have done down the ages, had been crystallised in the moment of the bird's death. She would never overcome the anger which took root in her soul.

The four girls were followed by four boys, one of whom died. Children are said to need stability, but these children had none. They were constantly on the move. The Old Man would ignore them for weeks while working on a novel, only to turn on them in titanic anger and impose a rough discipline before disappearing to Russia, where he always kept just ahead of the secret police, or to some other distant country. Moreover money was a constant problem; sometimes he was flush, sometimes broke. He had strong opinions on every subject under the sun and an intense hunger to express them if not to impose them. Since his letters to the press were sometimes ignored, he was determined to have his own newspaper and, when he had received a good sum from the latest novel, his first action was to indulge this fancy, taking as partner a 'Colonial' (Australian or Canadian). On each occasion the family was ordered always to refer to this man as 'Papa's best and dearest friend'. In due course, when the paper was on the brink of failure, the partner would return whence he came taking with him such funds as remained. The first the family ever knew of this would be when one of the children asked: 'Papa,

19

you have not mentioned your best and dearest friend lately'. This would evoke a thunderous response: 'Never let me hear you mention that man's name in my house again'.

Ruth recalled long afterwards an occasion when there was no money at all in the home and the whole family was miserably hungry. The Old Man had gone to London to sell a story to a magazine and he returned in high spirits, having spent the money on two splendid gifts: a Chinese hammock and an ice cream machine. His wife, the Old Lady, sat down on the stairs and began to cry. The children had never before seen their mother cry and joined her, all of them wailing. He was appalled. 'Did any man in the history of the world ever have such an ungrateful family! My first thought was to please you and this is the reward I get'. The theme of ingratitude was a constant one. Years later, when Ruth was seventeen, he burst in upon the family one day to denounce them. 'I gave you life! I begot you, and you show me no gratitude for this precious gift.' Ruth came to her feet and confronted him. 'Papa, do you think us so ignorant as to suppose that you took no pleasure in the act?' He stumped out of the room without another word.

In 1891 he was commissioned to write up the Canadian Pacific Railway, presumably to advertise its tourist potential, and he took Ruth—now ten years old—with him. The journey across Canada made a lasting impression, even if it had its difficult moments. One day he had a mild tummy upset and assuming a dramatic pose (he would have liked to be an actor), announced to his fellow passengers that he was about to die. Ruth always remembered an elderly man, close to tears, patting her on the head and murmuring: 'Poor little orphan! Poor little orphan!' Next day the Old Man was in fine fettle. But this incident was of no account compared with the sight of an 'Indian', a native Canadian, racing the train, his long black hair flowing in the wind parallel with his horse's tail. For Ruth this was an image of freedom, total freedom such as she had never thought possible, an image she would remember to the end of her days. She longed to change places with this man, the wind in her face, the horse between her thighs and the far horizon before her. This was real life, all else was a sham.

They stopped off for a few days in the Rocky Mountains. Walking in the forest one day with the Old Man, something happened that she tried, seventy years later, to describe in a letter. 'My father went ahead and broke down any undergrowth that impeded our way with a thick stick. We came to a clearing in what I suppose was boggy land; it was covered with the thickest, most beautiful moss I ever saw. The moss was covered with little amethyst flowers like stars—the petals seemed to be made of some shining substance. I knelt down to see them more clearly. Then something happened to me. Time ceased to exist, so did my body. I floated away and was part of the little glittering flowers and the moss. I was no longer a human being. I can't describe it otherwise, nor do I know how long it lasted or where I went. I was recalled with a great effort by shouts from my father. He had gone on some way, thinking I was following him. I joined him, dripping mud from my knees down, and I looked at myself with bewilderment'. This experience was never repeated, but at least she knew for the rest of her life that it was possible to escape into freedom from time and from the body, although she often forgot this truth.

They returned to England to find an addition to the family, a girl who had been christened Eleanor after her mother. There was to be one more child, a baby girl who died soon after her birth and who was to have been called Martha. The Old Man had her buried under a different name, remarking that he 'was not going to waste a good name on a dead baby', but if he expected further jewels from his begetting he was to be disappointed. The Old Lady seems, finally, to have gone on strike. From an early age Ruth had felt in some way responsible for her siblings and now, after the Canadian adventure, she felt able to exercise this responsibility Perhaps she realised that an overpowering personality can stunt the growth of small children if they have no defender. Whenever she saw her brothers and sisters bullied or oppressed she made her way to the door of the Old Man's study, often waiting ten minutes until the trembling in her legs was mastered. Then she would give a sharp knock, march into the study, confront her father with a peremptory 'Papa!' and have her say. He might growl and complain of the way his family treated him, but he usually gave in. She was clearly his favourite. He must have seen in this daughter something of his own spirit and, when she fixed her fierce, dark eyes on him he seems to have known he had met his match.

He sent her to a finishing school in Switzerland. The Boer War was raging and the German Kaiser had the impudence to send a telegram to the Boer President, Kruger, congratulating him on a victory over the British. A German girl took the occasion to mock the English girls at the school. The mighty British army had been put to flight by a ragtag troop of farmers. This was more than Ruth could take and she picked up a school bench, bringing it down on the German's head. Immediate expulsion followed. How the Old Man reacted is not on record, but, as a patriot, he probably approved of his daughter's action. None the less, two such strong personalities could not live happily under the same roof. Ruth had an 'admirer', a Scottish engineer who had an interest in what would soon be called aeronautics. He was invited to dinner with the family and the conversation turned to the possibility of flight by heavier-than-air machines (this was two years before the Wright brothers took off from Kittyhawk). The Scotsman suggested that this might be feasible and explained the theory of flight. The Old Man stated with his usual assurance that his guest was talking nonsense. Only balloons could ever rise above the ground. To his utter astonishment the young man dared to contradict him; he was promptly picked up by his collar and the seat of his pants and thrown out into the street.

For a callow youth to argue with the Old Man broke all bounds.

Soon afterwards Ruth left home and, for three shillings a week, rented a small flat in an apartment block in Notting Hill Gate, Mall Chambers, making a bare living teaching the children of friends of her father. She was now a fully fledged 'New Woman', a feminist, an Ibsenite, a Wagnerian and an admirer of the German philosopher Nietzsche whose 'Superman' was now transformed into a Superwoman. But often she wished that she had been born a jungle beast, fierce and free, or perhaps as a great bird soaring high above the little people, the law-abiding people of convention and constraint. She had a bookplate printed for her with the motto *Aquila non caput muscas*, 'The eagle does not catch flies', which showed a magnificent eagle gazing into the far horizon and ignoring the humble flies clustered on the rock beside it. She saw herself as eagle-woman, mistress of the horizon.

She began to make friends among like-minded young women. Of these the foremost was Louise Higgins who, convinced that human beings were only a species of animal and, thinking that most animals were nocturnal in habit, persuaded Ruth that people should sleep by day and live by night. Together they tramped the Sussex Downs by starlight, proud to be awake when the conventional world slept until Louise put her foot down a rabbit hole and sprained her ankle. Other friends were no less sure that contemporary civilisation was unnatural, and they rejected the morals of Edwardian society (Queen Victoria had by now died) preaching 'free love' even when they did not practise it.

Both her parents had been too busy to instruct Ruth in sexual morality and she had two relationships, one of them with a member of the aristocratic Surtees family, and this led to invitations to some of the great houses of the time. On the first such occasion she was kept awake by the creaking of boards outside her room, puzzled until her lover explained that this was due to gentlemen of the party making their way to the bedrooms of ladies who were not their wives. Over breakfast perfect propriety was observed. 'I trust you slept well, Lady Pamela?' 'Indeed I did, Sir John.' 'You were not kept awake by the barking of the dogs?' 'I did not even hear it.' The object, of course, was to avoid leading the servants into sin, and this was not as hypocritical as might appear. If one of these ladies was to have a little accident she could either have an abortion at the hands of a qualified surgeon or she could go abroad for a few months. If such a thing happened to a servant girl her life was ruined or she died during a back-street abortion.

Surtees introduced her to a notorious character of his acquaintance. Major Dick was a womaniser, a moustache-twirler, who had cut a swathe through the Society women of the period. He attempted to seduce Ruth, but she would have none of it. He was fascinated by her. She was unlike any other young woman he had known and he was unwilling to lose her altogether. Could they be friends? It was impossible—against nature—for a man and an attractive woman to be 'pals', so what was to be done? He decided to pretend to himself that Ruth was a young man in need of instruction in the ways of the world. He soon found that she was unshockable and this enabled him to pass on to her a wealth of sexual lore, much of it inaccurate. She was a good learner and sometimes put his theories into practice. He told her that it was easy to discover whether or not a girl was a virgin. It was only necessary to examine her eyes. If they were 'sticky', then she was no virgin. From then on, even into old age, when she met a young woman she would approach to within inches and examine her eyes, a practice which some found disturbing. But what delighted Ruth was an insight into a secret world and the discovery that Edwardian society was neither as upright nor as stuffy as it appeared to be. It was as though these staid figures, so respectable, so self-righteous, had been stripped naked, their raw humanity revealed.

She hoped one day to have a child. Sharing the general belief in Darwinism and in eugenics, her problem was finding a man who could give her a child of exceptional intelligence and perfect physical health. So far as health was concerned, Major Dick told her to examine the teeth of any potential suitor, a sure test of good health, and she took his advice although this too required a close approach. The problem of assessing intelligence was less easily solved but she believed that a sense of humour was often an indication of a good mind. For a brief period she had been a medical student and acquired a skeleton — the real thing, not an imitation — which she hung in the clothes closet in her flat. When a new admirer was honoured with an invitation to dinner she would ask him to hang his coat in the closet, watching his reactions on encountering John (as the skeleton was called). If he was embarrassed or pretended not to have noticed anything untoward the invitation would not be repeated.

She kept in close touch with the family, visiting them almost every week and fighting her siblings' battles for them. Dolly, however, had already made her own way. A close friend of her father, Herbert Greenhough Smith, took a fancy to her and offered an opportunity of escape. She married him when she was seventeen, although he was some thirty years older than herself. Like Major Dick, he was a womaniser, but of a very different type; a man of intelligence and learning, a famous wit whose kindly charm proved irresistible to a variety of young women. In 1891, as a young man, he had gone to George Newnes, the publisher, with an idea for a popular magazine to which his many friends in the literary world, including a certain Dr Arthur Conan Doyle, would be happy to contribute. The magazine, the first of its kind, was called *The Strand* and was an immediate success, not least on account of the 'Sherlock Holmes' stories which were always first published in its pages. He remained Editor for the next forty years.

After marriage he continued with his gentle seductions but Dolly does not seem to have minded. When, on one occasion, he ordered some costly silk underwear for his latest mistress and the store had it delivered at his account address, Dolly thanked him nicely for the gift although she knew quite well that it had not been meant for her. All that mattered was that he was prepared to finance her ambition to become a champion ice skater. She trained day after day under the best instructors and, in due course, became European Figure Skating Champion. Ruth had often said that a woman had to choose between being 'an old man's darling or a young man's slave', and Dolly knew which she preferred. She had little interest in sex. An undemanding and generous husband who was also marvellous company suited her perfectly.

Prince's Skating Club in London was her world and it soon became Ruth's world, for she too loved skating and found congenial company there. The skaters' wives and friends also found it congenial and assembled to gossip rather than take to the ice. One day—this must have been 1910 or thereabouts—a stranger was observed and aroused immediate curiosity. Round and round he went, skating in the old fashioned manner with long, slicing strides, hands clasped behind his back and head in air, but he spoke to no one. Inquiries were made among their friends by the ladies of the Club. His name, they learned, was Francis Errington, an eminent ecclesiastical lawyer married to a 'lady of title', possibly an earl's daughter, with whom he did not get on. He was a small, slim man with a military bearing, perfect features and curly brown hair which he could never quite subdue. Even the most obtuse observer might have been aware of the contradictions in this character. He was stern, aloof, soldierly and yet with a kind of delicacy about him and a pink-and-white complexion that would have graced a young girl. Had they known him better they would have discovered that he had extraordinary charm which he could turn on or off at will and a fastidiousness which made it painful for him even to shake hands with anyone whose vulgarity offended him. It was difficult to guess his age; he might be in his mid-thirties, at most forty. In fact he was fifty-six, but this was one of the many secrets that this very secretive man kept to himself.

Ruth was not only intrigued. She was challenged. It was very unusual for a man not to notice her but this one had never even cast a glance in her direction, and that would not do. Eventually she took up the challenge, skated past him, reversed and put her tongue out. Was this perhaps the moment at which the shield of ice in which he had enclosed himself began to melt? For many years his dignity had been unassailable and intimidating, but it had become a prison from which no escape seemed possible. Intimate human contacts could have no place in his austere life. He had colleagues in Lincoln's Inn but no friends; these colleagues were in awe of him, noting his equanimity under all conditions and doubting whether he was afflicted by any human weakness. He was never angry, but his displeasure could be expressed by a look and they shrank away from his judgement. Some felt awkward in his presence, remembering their minor sins and suspecting that those calm blue eyes saw through them and assessed them in terms of his own high standards. Ruth, however, was in awe of no man, having learned to cope with her father.

They became friends. Quite how this happened is unknown, but the mutual attraction of opposites must have played a part. He was unlike any other man she had known, and she was unlike any woman he had ever met. In trying to understand one another each was exploring a strange world. She was dazzled by his learning. Before going up to Oxford he had spent six months in Dresden learning German and, when he came down from Oxford, he had continued his studies at the University of Lausanne, becoming almost bilingual in French. He had read voraciously, not only in English, French and German, but also in Latin and Greek, yet he carried his learning lightly, never pedantic. He passed the skeleton test with flying colours, hugely amused by this charming eccentricity and teasing Ruth about her 'secret husband'. They were becoming indispensable to each other.

After some months, however, his mood darkened and he fell into long, brooding silences, no longer responding to her teasing.

27

One evening he came to the flat and, having greeted 'John' with sombre courtesy, laid a small revolver on the table. Deeply ashamed, confessing his weakness, he told her that he would commit suicide if she did not become his mistress. It was his air of calm resolution that most impressed Ruth. There was no pleading, only a firm resolve. She knew him well enough now to understand the emptiness of his life. Thwarted by short sight in his ambition to join the Army, following in the footsteps of his father who had retired as a General after a distinguished military career, he had drifted into the practice of Law. Working hard and achieving success, he had always been bored by his profession.

While still very young, dazzled by her rank—he was always something of a snob—he had married his 'lady of title' and, although, to judge from a portrait by Sergeant, she was a beauty, he realised on the honeymoon that he was not in love with her (or so he told Ruth). They had three children, two boys and a girl, but they were soon estranged. For thirty years he had commuted between a boring job and a loveless home, gritting his teeth and doing his duty. He might have gone on to the end with a dry heart, his humanity destroyed, had he not met Ruth. Now, when he had given up all hope—what hope could there be for a man in his fifties?—the possibility of a new life had opened up before him. He could not go back and, unless Ruth became his lover, he could not go forward.

Appalled and confused, she asked him for time to think. Reason was against the proposal. She now knew that he was twenty-seven years older than herself. He might think that she would one day abandon him, but her strongest principle was loyalty and she knew that, once committed, she would be committed until death parted them and there could be no children. Another principle to which she adhered was honesty, openness in opposition to the hypocrisy of the times. He might not enjoy his work but his reputation was of huge importance to him and public disgrace the most bitter humiliation he could imagine. Divorce was out of the question. That would be the end of his career. Equally, if any word about the relationship leaked out, even the faintest rumour, he would be ruined. She would therefore be committed to a life of secrecy and deception, lying to her family and her friends. The thought of a hole-in-the-corner affair revolted her, but this is what she would face. Against these arguments was the simple fact that, in her way, she loved this man, although without passion, and the thought of sending him away, possibly to his death, was unbearable. She could not do it. She sent a note to him in Lincoln's Inn telling him to come to her.

So it began and so it continued for almost a quarter of a century until his wife died and he married Ruth, but even this did not end the life of deception and misinformation. There were still secrets to be preserved and lies to be told, and she became very good at preserving the illusion they had created, but at great cost. It almost destroyed her. Perhaps Francis felt very differently for he loved secrets, he loved hiding his real self from others, and in the presence of colleagues in awe of his impeccable morality he must sometimes have hugged himself and thought: 'You'll never know that I have a beautiful young mistress!' They never did know, at least until after his death when Ruth took her revenge for the life she had been obliged to lead, and by then most of them were dead too.

He continued to live at home—where he was 'Frank', not 'Francis', to his family—although he hardly saw his wife who took her meals in her room, but he and Ruth were able to spend evenings together in the flat and, during the long legal holidays, went abroad, to Switzerland in the winter and to France in the summer, but they could never relax their guard. On one occasion, when they arrived in a Swiss hotel and, having dressed for dinner, started down the staircase Francis seized her by the arm and drew her back. He had seen a colleague or acquaintance in the lobby. They fled to another hotel. Ruth was a very proud woman and the fact that she recounted this incident many times in later years suggests that it marked her deeply.

Despite foreign wars in far-away places—the Crimea, the Sudan, South Africa—Britain had been at peace for ninety-nine years. With a great Empire and a prosperous manufacturing industry her dominance was unchallenged. On the Continent hotel managers and shopkeepers glowed with pleasure when a British visitor came their way, every one of them a *Milord anglais*, his purse heavy with gold sovereigns. For the freeborn Englishman the world was his oyster. The sinking of the *Titanic* was a blow to national pride and there were those who claimed after the event that they had experienced a sense of foreboding as though a cloud had passed over the sun, but it was only a cloud. All was not well, however, in continental Europe with shifting alliances and the decay of the Hapsburg Empire, while the impertinent Germans were building a navy to challenge Britannia's rule over the waves. In 1914 the bubble burst. First Russia came to the aid of little Serbia, about to be crushed by Austria, then Germany to the aid of Austria, France to the aid of Russia and, finally, Britain to the aid of France. Men joined up in haste, convinced that the war would be over by Christmas and afraid of missing the fun.

Francis had at last come into his own. He had been a member of the territorial army since his youth, closely involved in military matters. His father's campaigns, including participation in the conquest of Burma, filled him with pride. Now he was given the rank of Lieutenant Colonel and put in command of the Inns of Court Officer Training Camp in Berkhamsted. He had, of course, falsified his age and no one would have dared question him about it; a person's age was a private matter, and the British valued their privacy. According to the press he trained 11,000 young officers before sending them out to the battlefield. Less than half of them ever came home. Ruth's three brothers joined up as soon as they could, Jasper returning from Burma where he was working and Ted from Canada. After training they were sent to the killing fields, and soon both Jasper and Ted were among the 'fallen' (as the dead were described). In both cases, the Old Lady knew the moment of their deaths and retired to her bedroom, locking the door, to grieve alone before the dreaded telegram was delivered ('We regret to inform you . . .' .)

Horace, Ruth's favourite brother, the person she loved most in the world, contracted appendicitis at the front, was shipped home and died in her arms. This was the most bitter grief she had ever known and although it was not a bullet that ended his life she blamed the Germans for his death and dreamed of row upon row of gibbets upon which they would receive their deserts. When, at the end of the war, the British failed to hang the Kaiser, allowing him to retire to Holland, she condemned her own country in savage terms.

The war over, the survivors traumatised by the experience of the trenches and a vast number of young women whose hearts had been broken beyond mending by the death of the men they had hoped to marry struggling on to make something of their lonely lives, she and Francis resumed their secret life. She was increasingly aware of the contradictions in this strange man between the 'little Colonel' (as the press called him), the robed and bewigged Chancellor of three different Diocese, the scholar, and her sweet-natured lover. She called him a *caprice de la nature*, a 'freak', and gave him a signet ring inscribed with the initials 'C *de la* N'. He was delighted with the gift and, when people glanced at the ring in curiosity, he was convinced that they imagined the initials to be those of an aristocratic French ancestor; another secret to cherish, another deception. Meanwhile, a sexual revolution was taking place with the collapse of pre-war morality. It was partly inspired by the books of Dr Marie Stopes which infuriated a large part of the male population by revealing that women were capable of pleasure in intercourse, requiring husbands therefore to work harder in the act. Respectable married women who had never imagined that they could enjoy their marital duties had become indecently demanding.

Francis had practised the common form of contraception, *coitus interruptus*, which Ruth found frustrating, leaving her unfulfilled while he turned over and went to sleep. From Marie Stopes she discovered the 'safe period' or what is now called the rhythm method. Unfortunately—or fortunately, since their story would never have been told if the technique had worked—she became pregnant in 1920. Since she would not agree to an abortion, Francis faced disaster. For once she could not have cared less for his reputation. He must think and think he did, long and hard, exploring and rejecting a number of solutions. Finally the key proved to be his son Arnold's fruit farm in Canada, in the hands of a local manager since the boy's death in the war. He was much too busy to deal with the matter himself. He had an excuse to send Ruth out to sell the farm, a little holiday for his protegée. While in Canada she would meet and fall in love with a phantom nephew of his to whom she would, of course, have had an introduction. The details could be worked out later.

The first question to be answered on arrival in Montreal was the name of her intended husband since Francis would have to get her a false passport at once. She passed Eaton's department store and Eaton seemed as good a name as any. She needed a photograph—a widow would be expected to have a photograph of her late husband—so she cabled Francis to send her portraits of young officers who had served under him and subsequently been killed. She chose one of the most handsome among them, one who also reminded her of her beloved brother Horace. A personality was being constructed and she began to fall in love with her fiction, aware that few women are so fortunate as to have a perfect husband. She wandered happily around Canada, constantly on the move to avoid any intimate contacts. Francis had warned her to make no friends, particularly women friends. They might become curious about her and they might talk, although the chance that anyone she met would have relatives in England who knew someone he knew cannot have been more than one in a million, but he was taking no risks.

She was in high spirits. There is a photograph of her, displaying her swollen belly in a one-piece bathing suit beside Lake Kilona; she is smiling into the sun, proud of her pregnancy. Sixteen years later she would write to her son at school expressing the joy she had felt. 'It was as though all my dreams of life and beauty and romance had found expression in you. I wandered through the Canadian forests, I watched the humming birds poised before rare flowers. I listened to the catbirds calling and the bullfrogs croaking; not romantic sounds, most people would say, but they belonged to nature and, with you under my heart, they spelled romance. And I had you safely protected in my body and sometimes I wished I might keep you safe all my life . . . And now, when these sullen weeping skies shut out all the light and joy of life, I thirst for the blue skies and blazing sunshine . . . Your life stirred within me, fluttered like a butterfly, and the poetry of forest and mountain stirred within my soul, but I lacked your power of expression.'

One day she would have to surrender her child to the cruel world, but her recurrent fantasy was to escape from it. The child would be moulded out of her own flesh and blood and she had no need of Francis; he had contributed his seed, and that was that. She would set out across the world, breaching the far horizons, the child strapped to her back like an Indian 'papoose'. There must surely be some island in the South Seas where she could live among people close to nature, children of the sun, and raise her offspring uncontaminated by the civilised world's hypocrisy. But now her body made its demands She was seized by intense sexual hunger. She believed that a mother's every thought and every feeling influenced the foetus in her womb. If she had a daughter the girl would not have an easy life, but if it was to be a boy then he might be driven by overmastering desire to

33

contribute his splendid seed—eugenics had raised its head again—to improving the human stock. Moreover her brothers were dead and it was now unlikely that any of her sisters would have children. This son would be the last of the line, the Old Man's sole descendent, duty bound to renew and expand the family. The more women he inseminated the better.

Autumn came and the blue skies were covered over. She was now in her seventh month and quite suddenly she realised that she could not go through with the plan. To give birth so far from home and in total isolation without a single friend to support her was a frightening prospect. She cabled Francis accordingly. He must think again and there was no time to be lost. He made up his mind at once and booked her on the next sailing from Quebec. She was to tell her family that Charles Eaton was a mining engineer and had been offered a wonderful job in northern Italy. Italian doctors were not to be trusted, so she would have her baby in Lausanne, his favourite European city. Francis himself would set off at once for Switzerland to book her into the best clinic he could find. All she had to do was board ship and set sail.

She loved the sea, particularly when it was grand and wild, uncivilised, and she rejoiced in the Atlantic gales which buffeted the ship and whipped up the waves. It never crossed her mind that she might have a miscarriage. She knew that her baby, having overcome so many obstacles, had a will to survive and would not be put out by a storm at sea.

Francis met her at Liverpool docks, bringing with him a wide-brimmed hat with a thick muslin veil attached to it. Suitably disguised she was hurried across England to Dover and, twenty-four hours later, they were safe in Lausanne. The Lake was calm and, despite the season, the sky was blue. On New Year's Eve her pains began.

2

G A I A S A B O Y

The baby did indeed have a will to survive. He was born in the early hours of 1 January, and the obstetrician was astonished to find that he had tied a knot in the umbilical cord without pulling it tight. This was unique in his experience. In every other case known to him the embryo had strangled itself, so he at once bottled the cord in formaldehyde and sent it off to the Medical Museum. It might be said that the infant achieved fame early in life, having shown great good sense in the womb. After a few days Ruth took her miracle baby back to her hotel in Ouchy, the lakeside district of Lausanne. What should she call him. Francis? That was completely out of the question. He must take his supposed father's name, Charles. What else? The chamber maid at the hotel was enchanted by the baby's cheerfulness, exclaiming: '*Comme il est gai, ce petit!*' So why not 'Gai', 'le Gai?' She tried the name out on Francis and he agreed that it had a good ring to it: Charles le Gai.

He thrived, and soon she was able to go away for a couple of weeks with Francis, leaving him with a Swiss woman. They returned to find a very contented baby, drugged up to the eyeballs with a *tisane* which Swiss peasants habitually gave their infants to keep them quiet and happy, sparing the parents sleepless nights. Later he had a proper nanny whose big nose he used as a handle to turn her head when he wanted her to look at something. It was too soon to tell the family of the birth, the date was quite wrong. He was given an official birthday, April 5th. Some years later, when he was old enough to understand, Ruth told him that at the moment of his birth cannons thundered their salutes across the Lake of Geneva and the sky was radiant with fireworks. Since he did not know that he had been born in the early hours of the New Year, he was left to assume that the Swiss nation—perhaps the whole world—had celebrated his birth with appropriate manifestations of joy. Ruth herself may have had some such thought, but this was not an ideal preparation for meeting the real world.

The time had come to finish with Charles Eaton who had served his purpose. He contracted appendicitis—Ruth was still haunted by Horace's death—and died at the hands of those unreliable Italian doctors. She had no need to pretend grief. She grieved. She had come to cherish her perfect husband; letters to her mother and her sisters announcing the tragedy were eloquent with a sense of loss, and they in turn were deeply saddened by the tragedy. But there was a far more serious matter to be considered. Francis realised that, if he were to die within the next few years, his money would have to go to his wife and two surviving children, leaving Ruth and Gai destitute. He decided to hand over the bulk of his capital to Ruth, although this meant that any hopes he might have of retirement must be postponed. He gave her £20,000; in the year 2000 this would be the equivalent of at least £400,000. He had made her completely independent of him, free to do as she chose and to bring up their son as she wished. What he did not know was that the Muddocks, all of them, were totally incompetent when it came to money matters as was the thrice bankrupted Old Man. Initially Francis may have arranged the safe investment of these funds, but after that he never questioned her on this score. The investments ultimately dwindled in value —she would not even have known what the word 'inflation' meant —and, whenever she needed some extra cash for herself or her son, she would say: 'I'll just take a little bit of capital'. By the end of her life there was nothing left.

Francis returned to his Chambers in Lincoln's Inn and Ruth found a pleasant *pension* in the village of Vers-chez-les-Blanc, not far from Lausanne. Taking a risk, she made friends. Following upon the Bolshevik Revolution there were many Russian refugees in the area, and she met three charming princesses, one of them the sister of Prince Yusupov, the murderer of the 'Mad Monk', Rasputin. They were fascinated by the fact that this clever lady was able to bath her baby every day without the aid of even one servant, and every day they came to watch the ceremony and chat about the old days when everyone in Russia, including the peasants, was happy. Fortunately there was no wicked fairy to annul the blessings which these three bestowed on the infant. After Ruth returned to England her sisters would dismiss all this as a fantasy. 'Princesses, indeed. Typical of Ruth!' Many years later confirmation was provided by an elderly man who, as a child, had lived with his mother in the same *pension* and who contacted Gai after hearing him speak on the radio. She and her friends, he said, had been intensely curious about the 'beautiful and mysterious lady with a little baby' who kept to herself but was closeted every day with three aristocratic Russian ladies. Could she be a British agent conspiring to overthrow that beastly Mr Lenin? She did not look English, so perhaps she was a member of a foreign royal family who had made a little mistake and been exiled in Switzerland. An aura of mystery and romance surrounded her.

Ruth's return to London was hastened by a family crisis. The Old Man and the Old Lady were now penniless and dependent on their daughters. A joint decision was made to purchase a family house, each contributing according to her means. Ruth contributed generously, but so did someone who was not a blood relation. Her name was Grace Martin. She had been at school with Eleanor (the youngest) and had formed a passionate attachment to her, a leech-like attachment enforced by attacks of hysterics whenever Eleanor showed interest in a man. For some while they had been living together and she could be regarded by Gai as an honorary aunt, one who in the course of time would influence his life more profoundly than any of his real aunts, saving him from poverty in old age. The Muddocks very probably never noticed that she was better off than them, having been left a number of small houses in South London by her father, a builder and developer. They might however have observed that her friends tended to be wealthy women. In 1923 a house was purchased in Wandsworth Common and Ruth moved in with her son, joining Eleanor and Grace together with the old people. Rose had a flat close by, and Dolly, no longer involved in championships, came at least twice a week, jealous of Ruth as she had been all her life and determined to stake her claim in the family baby. He, soon after his arrival, bestowed baby names on his new mothers; Dolly was Da, Eleanor was Lala and Grace was Goo, although she was the only one who kept this name for the rest of her days. He now enjoyed the care and close attention of six women including his grandmother. Francis never set foot in the house, meeting Ruth only for secret assignations in London and on holiday.

Childhood memories are like still photographs, often mounted in the album in no particular order. Perhaps the earliest picture in Gai's archive was simply a starry sky. At three or four he had his tonsils removed. One of Goo's closest friends, a Miss Morrison, offered to drive him to the hospital and turned up in a huge black car smelling strongly of animal furs, with a uniformed chauffeur. When he stepped out of the car he looked up at the sky and was transfixed. The stars were remembered long after the operation was forgotten. Another night-time image was engraved in his memory. Every summer Ruth and Francis rented a cottage in Brittany or Normandy and, from the time he was four or five, took him with them accompanied by a nursemaid. He looked up at the dark bulk of the cross-Channel ferry, overwhelmed by its size and grandeur and thrilled to be out so late at night. There is also a vivid memory of terror. When he was three he tripped and fell on his face, breaking his nose. Some two years later he had an operation to correct the break. When the pad soaked in chloroform was placed over his nose and mouth he began to suffocate, giving a stifled cry for help. A moment later a drop of liquid fire fell on the back of his throat and he saw a vast sun which grew in size until it exploded into darkness.

Then there was Wandsworth Prison, a grim image. Ruth warned each of a succession of nursemaids that they would be dismissed if they ever mentioned religion to the child. A girl whose ambition it was to be a missionary in Arabia—converting the 'moslem pagans' to the true Faith—broke the rule and, as they passed the prison during a walk, told him: 'There's a red-haired man in the sky who will shut you up there if you're naughty'. This was, in fact, rather naughty of her since she knew that he was afraid of red-haired men but, in any case, he could not imagine a man of any sort living in the sky and he asked Ruth about this phenomenon when he got home. The girl was at once dismissed.

Gai was considered 'delicate', although he was nothing of the sort, and was consigned to his bed at the first sign of a sniffle, a snuffle or a tummy ache, which meant that he spent much of his time in bed. A very early memory is of watching a cleaner perched on the sill of the bedroom window hard at work. It was 11 November, Armistice Day and, when the gun boomed for the two-minute silence, the man came stiffly to attention, then, as though in slow motion and still ramrod straight, he toppled backwards to land in a lilac bush, the very bush in which Gai's imaginary sisters lived (he never had imaginary brothers).

Another picture, although it must have come later, was of barefoot children playing in the snow in some northern slum. He knew that, if he ever got his feet wet, he would die of pneumonia so he was puzzled by the sight until Ruth explained to him that these children's parents could not afford shoes for them. But there was one particular picture which had a profound influence on the child. Ruth had driven with him into London one dark, rainy night and the car stopped beside a bus queue, a long line of people huddled against the cold and the wet in silent misery. Who were these people and what had they done to deserve such punishment? His mother told him they were commuters on their way home after a long day spent in a dreary office under the lash of some petty tyrant, adding that this was what hell was like. He knew nothing about hell but thought it must be a very dreadful place and he took her word for it that these wretches would be better off dead.

In the memory archive there is also the image of a small boy in what seems to be a smock standing at the top of the stairs in the Wandsworth Common house. Ruth put this into context some time later. Gai had gone on hunger strike, stubbornly silent when begged to explain why he would not eat. Three or four doctors followed each other, treating him as an idiot and trying to bully him. Finally one came who had a different tactic. Sitting down beside the bed and smiling amiably, as though nothing important was at stake, he said: 'Let me tell you the facts, young man. If you do not eat you will die, but it's entirely up to you, it's your life'. As soon as the man had gone he went to the head of the stairs, hugging the banister, and shouted: '*Maman*! Fish and potatoes!' His favourite dish was white fish chopped up and mixed with mashed potatoes. Long afterwards—even seventy years later—if a kind friend took him to an expensive restaurant he would give respectful attention to the menu before saying: 'I think the fish would be nice', adding after further thought: 'And perhaps creamed potatoes?' He would always be of a conservative disposition.

He had asserted his will in his own little world, perhaps for the first time, and this was the only world he knew. Whatever existed outside it, including other children, was observed through a window-pane. He saw Francis only on holidays abroad and the Old Man, now in his mid-eighties, had been virtually excluded. Fearing that his temper tantrums at table might damage the child, Eleanor had confined him to his study where he was brought his meals on a tray. Gai sat with him sometimes, fascinated by the stories he told, and went every evening to kiss him goodnight rejoicing in the homely scent of his nicotine-stained beard, a mixture of stale porridge and pipe tobacco. The Old Lady might sometimes give advice but refrained from interfering in a delicate situation, and Goo was a detached observer, always a kindly one and devoted to her smelly old dog. The battle for control was between Ruth, Dolly and Eleanor, each with different ideas on child-rearing, and Gai was in danger of being crushed between the three of them. At one time he considered extreme measures, a children's revolution against the adult world (with himself as Chief Child). Ruth did not count since he was a part of her and she of him, but the aunts would have to be removed, stuffed into the kitchen boiler which glowed red hot day and night. This was a very painful thought. He loved them and had no wish to hurt them, but revolutions require victims and, try as he might, he could see no alternative.

On a more practical level, he could try to play them against each other and this worked occasionally as did an appeal to the Old Lady to overrule her daughters while Lotte, the family cook, was always his ally, but he began to understand what was or was not possible. A very small person cannot compete directly with very big people. He learned never to be competitive, then or thereafter. Equally, a child cannot hope to win an argument with adults, so he learned never to argue and, for the rest of his life, he would avoid argument even when this involved pretending to agree with opinions he abhorred. Tantrums might have had some

effect and he had a temper, but Ruth found a simple way to deal
with this. Whenever he became red faced and raised his voice she
summoned whichever aunts were available, instructing them to
laugh at him. This they did, and he understood from their reaction that anger is ridiculous. In later life he could never be angry
with anyone unless they first became angry with him—making
themselves figures of fun—and only then would he be able to let
loose. His field of action was therefore limited but within these
limits he learned to get his own way.

He noticed that grown-ups were not as constant in purpose as
he was. Told to do something he did not want to do he would
never say, 'No. Shan't!' but would give a non-committal answer
which the other party took for compliance. He would then 'forget' to do what was asked and, very often, this passed unnoticed
or else the aunt in question could not be bothered to insist. His
principle was never to challenge power directly but always to circumvent it if possible, observing the many gradations between
obedience and disobedience. He also paid close attention to what
was said. Up to the age of six he slept with his mother but, as his
restlessness kept her awake, she eventually set up a small bed
for him beside her own. At bedtime, however, he still insisted on
going to her bed and, when she came up, she would lift him still
sleeping into his own. Dolly disapproved of this and decided to
break him of the habit. She knew he lusted after a particular toy,
a blowpipe with feathered arrows, and she promised him he
should have it if he did as she asked. He noted that she did not
say 'for evermore' or anything of the kind. So to his own bed he
went, receiving the blowpipe the following day, and for the next
couple of nights he did the same; then he returned to his old practice. Dolly gave up.

So, under different circumstances, did Eleanor. There were two
small brass bears in the living-room and Gai coveted them. Every
evening he took them up to bed with him, every morning she
replaced them where they belonged. It was weeks before she

accepted defeat. These bears (I have them still) were in fact his defenders. When he was three or four Ruth was unwillingly persuaded by a religious friend to have him baptised. The priest grumbled about his age, grumbling even more when the indignant child told him: 'I'se got bears what eats people what throws water at other people'.

There are fears in every child's mind and imagination, some clear, some inarticulate. His fears were perfectly clear. The first, inevitably, was 'the Hun', the Germans, and this came mainly from Ruth who cherished her hatred of the enemy responsible for her brothers' deaths, but the occasional guests who came to dinner also contributed. When visitors were present he had his dinner on a small side table and listened attentively to what the grown-ups were saying. The women were pre-occupied with servant problems ('silly girls' were going into factories instead of domestic service) but, sooner or later, if the guest was a man, the war came to dominate the conversation, the horror of the trenches and the brutality of the Hun. There was however only one regular visitor, a Dutchman called Charlie Thieme who had worked for some years as an engineer on the Gold Coast (Ghana), and he was haunted, not by the war, but by the experience of nursing two close friends dying of Yellow Fever. Gai became convinced that this would be the death of him, and yet the thought of Africa drew him like a magnet, fascinated him and filled him with an almost erotic excitement. He would go there one day, he was fated to go there. It seemed to be a case of: 'If the Hun doesn't get you the Yellow Jack will'.

Death, however, was not nearly as frightening as a life of penury. Lying in bed beside his mother night after night he had absorbed her anxieties as by osmosis and these related principally to money. When he was seven she took him to Switzerland for a few weeks. Having fallen asleep in his bunk to the puffing of the steam engine he awoke to silence. At the frontier an electric locomotive had taken over. Ruth explained that, in Switzerland, electricity came from the rushing mountain streams and therefore cost nothing. This misleading information filled him with joy. The idea that something so essential came as a free gift of nature in this glorious country, requiring no expenditure, was reassuring.

He had already learned that the great threat hanging over them was socialism. If the socialists ever came to power their money would be seized and the two of them would be consigned to the workhouse to labour ceaselessly, dressed in blue smocks, beaten and humiliated for the rest of their lives. They might even be parted and that would be a thousand times worse than death. When he was five the threat had come very close. The General Strike of 1926 seemed to many people the beginning of a revolution comparable to the Russian Revolution. He sensed a mixture of fear and excitement in the house. Like soldiers going into battle Goo and Eleanor as well as Ruth drove into central London in their respective cars to give lifts to workers unable to get to their offices, helping in a small way to save the country. It all came to nothing and the hero of the moment was a certain Mr Winston Churchill, but Gai had grasped a simple point. There were many more of 'them' than there were of 'us' and, sooner or later, 'they' would become aware of their numerical superiority and seize power. Moreover 'they' were breeding faster than 'us' so the British race would degenerate in the course of time.

He also had worries of a very different kind. Beyond the fence which protected their garden was another garden and another fence, then another and another. He was probably six when he began to wonder what there was after the last of all fences, what there was at the end of the world. There must be something, but what was there after that something? If there was nothing, how could one imagine nothingness? It was unimaginable, but so was endlessness. He talked to Ruth about this and she admitted frankly that she did not know the answer. He lay awake night after night visualising all those fences and wrestling with the problem. He also visualised a steel ladder which ultimately disappeared above the clouds and went on for ever and ever, with platforms at intervals on which the climber could rest, the first only bare boards but the higher ones increasingly comfortable and increasingly beautiful. In this case the problem was how the ladder was supported. However deep its foundations, there must be a point at which it would topple over, so it must be anchored at the top. But did it have a top and, if so, where did it end (if it ever ended)? These metaphysical preoccupations are, I believe, not uncommon in small children, but they are seldom encouraged to think about them nor are they told that these are among the most profound questions which trouble the human mind.

There was little entertainment in the household and the even tenor of life, with its undercurrent of conflict, went on undisturbed, but the family occasionally took in a paying guest from overseas. One was an Egyptian harpist, a little man dwarfed by his instrument, whom Eleanor called 'Mr Hump' from some vague association with camels (Gai slipped behind him to see if he really had a hump), but far more exciting was a pretty Italian girl called Carla, the daughter of a wealthy industrialist, who had been placed under the guardianship of the company's London manager. Guardian and ward fell in love and the girl's parents arrived post haste from Milan. A conference was held in the living-room, and Gai sat on the stairs listening to the proceedings while the father shouted, the mother wept, Carla had hysterics, the young man pleaded, and the Old Lady quietly injected a note of Yorkshire commonsense into the drama. Soon afterwards the couple had a splendid wedding in London.

Central London had only two locations of which Gai was aware. Harrods or more specifically Harrods Zoo, the pet department which housed a variety of exotic creatures, and the Westminster Ice Club, successor to Prince's. It was, of course, Dolly who took him there, happy to be among her own kind, former and current champions, and she put him through his paces working at figures of eight and figures of three. This was boring, but the people were not and one day he fell in love. The cause of his bedazzlement was the reigning Belgian champion, a young woman in a flame-coloured dress. Perhaps it was the dress that caught his attention since he could not see her clearly on the other side of the rink but Dolly soon noticed that he was spellbound and dragged him across the ice, telling the glorious girl: 'My little nephew is in love with you!' For the first time he knew what it was to be painfully embarrassed and, to make it worse, the Champion bent down from her great height and kissed him on the cheek.

There was however only one place where he ever found himself in a crowd and that was in the customs shed on arrival in France for the annual summer holiday. At that time hotels required their guests to dress for dinner and no lady wished to be seen in the same gown two nights running. Everyone travelled with big cabin trunks. Even before the ferry tied up it was invaded by a host of 'bluebottles', porters in blue smocks with brass number-plates shouting and jostling for clients and, when one was secured, the man would run so fast with a trunk bigger than himself on his shoulder that it was difficult to keep up with him and ladies in long skirts were huffing and puffing by the time they reached the shed. Once there, the noise and the chaos were thrilling, but on one occasion the noise abated when the new arrivals heard, above the babble, the sound of a 'common accent', an English working class or lower middle class accent. A murmur went round the shed: 'Profiteer!' The only way such a person could afford to travel abroad was if he had stayed at home making money out of the war, doubtless dishonestly, while 'our boys' were dying at the Front. The British working class never travelled nor, for the most part, did the lower echelons of the strictly hierarchical middle classes for whom 'abroad', inhabited by foreigners who spoke barbarous languages and ate filthy food, was rather terrifying.

Gai's first friend however bridged the class barrier. Every

summer Dolly and her husband, now 'Uncle Bert', rented a house by the river in Weybridge, and, once he was six or seven, he usually spent two or three weeks with them every year. They brought their own cook, Lily, with them and she had a daughter, Frances, a few months older than Gai. She was a child with a pretty face almost completely concealed by a mop of frizzy hair and he took to her at once, although on one occasion she alarmed him when, as they were drying themselves in the boathouse after a swim in the river, she asked if she could please see how little boys were made. Later she set him a puzzle. She was stung by a wasp and, when her mother applied 'blue bags' (used in washing clothes) to the sting, became terrified and began to cry. He had never before seen anyone cry and, to his astonishment, tears came into his own eyes. It was almost as though he felt her pain and fear in himself, but how was this possible? They were two separate individuals and, as he understood such matters, he should simply have been glad that it was she, not he, who had been stung. Now it appeared that one person could feel another's pain and this opened up a new and surprising perspective on what it meant to be human.

There was a double happiness in this riverside paradise. He found a good friend in Uncle Bert who had now retired from his editorship of *The Strand* magazine. Although he did not know it, Gai was a little afraid both of his grandfather and of Francis, formidable men both of them. There was nothing to fear in Bert who had a quality of serenity due, perhaps, to a state of satiety which he owed to his many mistresses. The two of them, occasionally joined by Frances, would sit for hours side-by-side on the river bank fishing for tiddlers in companionable silence, and Bert's dry wit which had enchanted sophisticated society also enchanted the child even when he did not understand the jokes. This handsome, dapper old man with his gold-rimmed monocle, an authentic Edwardian 'literary gent', was funny as well as kind.

But such companionship was no preparation for the encounter

with other children in the raw. Ruth had a close friend, a Miss Frogley, whose fiancé had been killed in the war. She was a Roman Catholic and had found comfort, more than she should have done, in her priest. They fell in love and he was prohibited from performing his priestly offices after taking her to a deserted church and celebrating a 'spiritual marriage' before the altar. They opened a guest house in Rottingdean, a village close to Brighton, and this became a home-from-home for Gai's family when they needed a breath of sea air. At some point—he may have been six or seven—he was staying there with his mother and grandmother when a large party arrived; a fat blonde woman with half-a-dozen children accompanied by a jolly, red-faced 'uncle'. The quiet house was transformed into what seemed to Gai like a zoo and he tended to keep to his room, but one day the 'uncle', presumably taking pity on the lonely boy, invited him to join the family on a walk along the sea wall to Brighton and they set off.

The children shrieked and shouted, they pushed and tussled so that he thought one or other must fall into the sea, they tried to race each other on the narrow wall and nearly knocked Gai over in their play. He was seized with a mixture of emotions—joy and fear, astonishment and wonder—too powerful to be accommodated in his small body and it was his body that reacted. With no deliberate intention he turned round and ran all the way back to Miss Frogley's, finding the Old Lady in the upstairs sitting room and joining her there in peace and quiet. He took up his knitting, which he had put down when summoned to adventure but, within minutes, realising what he had done, he was filled with shame. He had turned his back on an adventure so he would never follow in his grandfather's footsteps. If the phrase had been current in those days he might have said to himself: 'Get a life!' fearing that he never would.

It was only later that he articulated this distress, but there are events in childhood with their accompanying emotions which drill down into the bedrock of memory and remain there, still powerful, for a lifetime, developing with the passage of the years in accordance with the changing personality. Long afterwards if he launched himself into some rash escapade or when he agreed to participate in an enterprise which he would gladly have avoided (preferring to stay at home with a good book), this recollection was always at the back of his mind while, if he gave way to the temptation to stay at home, the old sense of shame returned like an unforgotten pain. It became essential for him to do what he was afraid to do.

It was unlikely that the family was aware of this traumatic incident, but there were many arguments about his education. Finally Eleanor took unilateral action during walks with him on the Common when she urged him again and again to ask his mother to send him to boarding school. She became his first enemy. Ruth had told him repeatedly that one of the nastiest things about the English was their readiness to send their children off to such schools, a symptom of their hatred of children and an abdication of their responsibility, and he had the impression that boarding school was little better than the workhouse. But that was not all. He was sharp enough to detect an unspoken implication in all that Eleanor said, the implication that there was something wrong, even unhealthy, in his relationship with his mother. This was intolerable and yet Eleanor had succeeded in sowing a seed of disquiet in his mind. Could there be something wrong in the fact that he and his mother were a self-sufficient bi-unity rather than separate people? He ejected the thought from his mind and listened to his aunt in stubborn silence.

Eventually, when he was nine, a compromise of sorts was reached and he was sent to a day school on the other side of the Common, finding himself among savages. He had been there a week or so when, as he set off home across the Common, a group of boys gave chase. He ran, and this time there was no sense of shame. He had learned all about cannibals and head-hunters from the Old Man but had been unaware of the fact that they existed even in England. He had no doubt that they meant to kill him and this lent wings to his feet. He ran faster than he had ever done before, frightened but also exhilarated, and took refuge in the flat of a friend of Ruth's, a Mrs Florio whose American husband had spent his large fortune trying to invent a perpetual motion machine, leaving her almost penniless. After taking him home, Ruth drove straight down to the school and threatened to horsewhip the Headmaster who, according to her, had quailed under his desk.

A child who is always with adults picks up an education of sorts —perhaps the most valuable sort—but there was still the question of the 'three Rs'; reading, writing and arithmetic. A teacher was engaged, Laura Hillary, very possibly an educational genius, who had once founded her own school on principles that would be considered modern if not post-modern even today. She taught him more in a few months than he could have learned at any school in a year. He loved her and she would appear later in his life as a friend, but now events took over. The decision was made to give up the house. The old people were still in perfect health and it was agreed that Rose would take the Old Man, now approaching ninety, to live with her in her small flat. Rose was a singularly stupid woman and, being incapable of making a living, had been dependent on her sisters for most of her life, but this was an advantage when dealing with her father; his outbursts were wasted on her. Goo and Eleanor were buying a house and taking the Old Lady with them. Since Ruth had not decided what she would do or where she would settle there seemed to be no alternative to sending Gai to boarding school, however much she disapproved of this in principle. A friend recommended a prep school called Dane Court which was run on very progressive lines. At the age of ten he arrived there.

At least he did not find himself among savages. The school was presided over by the Headmaster's wife, Mrs Pooley, a Danish potter, and she believed in allowing the boys to develop in their own way. She was a big woman and her pots were very big indeed. When parents arrived to take their sons out they were led into the drawing room where a variety of Mrs P's pots were on display, each with its price tag There must in those days have been many attics in the South of England groaning under the weight of these formidable artefacts. For the first few days Gai was miserably homesick and his first letter to his mother (which, of course, she kept) was not a happy one. 'Der *Maman*, plese tak me away. I am so onhapy I thort I wud wak up ded.' If the boys were not savages, they were certainly weird. They took pleasure in a game which he thought was called 'Foot-the-Ball', chasing a large leather ball round a muddy field and fighting each other for it. He had thought that only dogs played with balls and, having no notion of competitiveness, he could not understand why the boy who actually had the ball at his feet refused to give it to whoever else wanted it. Was that not bad manners?

All their habits were strange. He had not been there long when one night, after lights out, three of the older boys crept into the dormitory, seen only by the light from the corridor. The youngest boy in the dormitory, a cherub with fair curly hair, immediately stood up on his bed and dropped his pyjama trousers, whereupon each of the visitors in turn paid tribute to him, treating his diminutive organ as though it was a lollipop. Gai watched this with interest and found it no less peculiar than the practice of chasing balls. There was, however, a far more troubling aspect of school life. After a while he discovered that he was in a nest of traitors. No doubt echoing their parents views, most of the boys preferred the Germans—'more like us'—to the French. He knew from Ruth that to be pro-German and anti-French was treason and a betrayal of the war dead, and he knew that such people should, as she had often told him, be 'put up against a wall and shot'.

In the Spring he became unwell and Ruth attributed this to his swimming in the pool before it was warm enough. She herself had been ill or thought herself ill for several years, running through an average of seven or eight doctors each year, none of them ashamed to take her case seriously and to take her money. Her latest medical adviser was summoned and, with a grave air, announced that Gai was suffering from acidosis. He must be taken away from school at once, and this fitted in well with Ruth's plans. She had just decided to take the water cure in Vichy, a celebrated spa in central France, and had already engaged a professional nurse to accompany her. It made sense to take her invalid son with them, although Dolly, with whom she was staying, insisted that there was nothing wrong with him that could not be cured with a pint every morning of frothing fresh milk straight from the cow. The nurse, a Miss Bean, soon arrived and was treated by Gai with some suspicion when his mother told him that she suffered from phlebitis without explaining what this was, so that he worried that her fleas might jump onto him. In the early summer the three of them travelled to Vichy.

3

F R A N C I S

It was said that the 120-year-old Prime Minister of Morocco owed his remarkable longevity to his annual visits to Vichy. Wealthy French people had great faith in the curative waters which flowed from the town's many springs, to each of which was attributed a specific virtue. The patients, if that is what they were, had to follow a strict regime prescribed by their medical advisers, taking a precise number of cubic centimeters from each of a number of springs. As these were often far apart, the exercise required in walking from one to another probably did them good.

So Ruth and Gai pounded the pavements equipped with little wicker baskets containing several medicine glasses, one for each spring since the waters must not be mixed, returning to their hotel stinking of sulphur to be faced with a platter piled with wild strawberries which was delivered to their room every morning. Neither of them could touch the delicious fruit—bad for whatever it was that ailed Ruth and for Gai's acidosis—but Miss Bean scoffed the lot in spite of her phlebitis. With the coming of full summer and almost tropical heat Francis joined them. He and Gai fished in the River Allier, achieving for the first time a real companionship, and in the evenings his father—whom he always addressed as 'Uncle', ignorant of the truth—read aloud from the comic novels of P. G. Wodehouse. He had a voice of singular beauty and these readings became a source of immense pleasure. Miss Bean, who had nothing to do, was an unobtrusive presence, and the aunts were far away. This was a new life. In late autumn they moved to Switzerland, travelling from Paris to Lausanne on the Orient Express which in those days went all the way to Istanbul and evoked visions of the mysterious East. The wonderful world which awaited the boy was always located somewhere far off, somewhere that he could be a different person among Africans, Arabs or even Eskimos. He wanted to be anything but himself, or rather he wanted to be everyone rolled into one, not just 'a man' but Man as such.

They stayed in a hotel in the mountain village of Villars. A tutor was engaged but soon afterwards he fell backwards on the skating rink and cracked his skull. Gai noticed that Miss Bean locked herself in her room for a while every evening and he gave her no peace until she confessed that she was writing her diary. This came almost as a revelation and put everything in its place. Now he understood that the purpose of life was to have adventures and then write about them as the Old Man had done, but he thought of himself as the passive recipient of experiences. Things would happen to him and he would record every experience that came his way from now until his death.

So he would die one day? He had not thought about this before but determined that it must be an appropriately choreographed end to his story. In some hotel he had seen a reproduction of the famous painting of the Prince Consort's death. He planned something similar. Lying on a great four-poster bed, composing his famous last words, he would be surrounded by three circles: the inner circle would consist of his grief-stricken wives, mistresses and children, next to this his friends attempting to keep a stiff upper lip and, finally, the servants weeping uncontrollably over the loss of their beloved master. He could hardly wait to die. Meanwhile, he began to keep his own diary, although the entries were sparse: 'Skating in the morning. Went shopping with *Maman* in the afternoon. Miss Bean says that too much reading is bad for the eyes'. Although he did not phrase it so, he would be 'God's spy on earth'.

The snow melted and the ski-shop, smelling of the rich grease which was rubbed into leather skiing boots—the smell of Switzerland—closed down. Miss Bean disappeared with the snow, her departure scarcely noticed, taking with her the diary and her fleas, if indeed she had any. Ruth and Gai came down from the mountains to the Lake of Geneva, settling in a hotel in Montreux-Territet where the proprietor, Monsieur Wolfinger, proved a wise counsellor to the boy, and it was here that Gai made his first true friend. Billy was an American boy living in the hotel with his mother. His father, he claimed, was a prominent gangster in Chicago, presumably associated with the even more prominent Mr Al Capone, and he invented wonderful games, the best of which was to fill paper bags with water from a bucket borrowed from the hotel kitchen and drop them from the flat roof onto the heads of passers-by. There was an art in this since it was essential to duck behind the parapet at the moment of impact and peer cautiously over it moments later when the victim was looking down at his wet clothes. Ruth did not approve of Billy, having noticed that when he was bored in the hotel dining-room he amused himself by kicking his mother's shins, forcing her to retreat further and further until she could hardly reach her plate. She, however, was uncomplaining, a pretty golden-haired woman who, according to Ruth, wore expensive jewelley.

Gai had never before in his life been naughty so this new friend added spice to his life, but the friendship did not last for long. Mme Wolfinger, the proprietor's wife, was foolish enough to scold Billy one day for some naughtiness. He went at once to his mother's room, took from her bag the small handgun which she always kept with her, and threatened to shoot the lady. The pair left the hotel an hour later. This scarcely mattered for, soon afterwards, Gai was enrolled in the most wonderful school in the world, the Institute Fischer, and discovered what it was like to be with other children rather than little savages. The school was co-educational and most of the pupils were American so he came to a simple conclusion: Americans nice, English horrid. To his amazement he discovered that he was well liked and that it was easy to have friends, moreover he fell in love with an American girl a year older than himself, Mary Opentock. Monsieur Wolfinger had explained to him that a sensible man should marry at the age of thirty-two, not a year sooner, not a day later, so he foresaw quite clearly that he and Mary would meet again on the banks of a great river in Africa when he was thirty-two. Unfortunately he was late for the appointment, over forty when he stood for the first time beside such a river, and she had not waited for him.

He was totally obsessed with Africa, having read Rider Haggard's novel *She,* a book which attracted the attention of the psychologist Carl Jung who found in it many archetypes, particularly the *Ewig Weibliche,* the 'Eternal Feminine'. This immortal Princess possessed his imagination, as did an Africa that was now magical rather than dark, the home of life, love and ecstatic death. Like his mother he longed to escape from the familiar and this was the distant land where everything was different and black faces replaced white. He raided the Montreux Library and read everything he could find, including two heavy volumes of Stanley's travels, and he pored over maps, fascinated by the French colony of Ubangui-Shari-Chad because it seemed the most remote location he could find. Borrowing a little typewriter from someone in the hotel, he wrote a story called *The Mystery of the Mine*—somewhere along the line he had picked up the arts of reading and writing, though not of spelling—and the only thing that disturbed him about his fellow pupils at the

Institute was their ignorance of African geography. Incredible as it seemed, they had never even heard of Ubangui-Shari-Chad and this was very shocking. Neither then nor later could he understand why other people did not share his own passionate interests.

Nearer home the skies were darkening. The year was 1932 and, just down the road in Geneva, the Disarmament Conference which was to abolish war for ever held its sessions and no one seemed to realise that the League of Nations was in its death throes, soon to be destroyed by the appeasement of Mussolini when he invaded Abyssinia (Ethiopia). Elsewhere—never, of course, in Switzerland—financial markets were in turmoil. One day Francis, who had come for the summer, returned from a visit to the bank ashen-faced. Changing money, he had received only sixteen Swiss francs to the pound instead of twenty and this was the end of civilisation as he knew it. Gai understood this very well, and a new fear now haunted him; its name was devaluation or inflation, and it was as great a threat to any security for which he might hope as was socialism. Ruth had told him that a gentleman could live quite comfortably on a private income of £400 a year, spending some time on the Continent where living was cheap if he ran short. But if money could lose its value, then nothing in the world was certain and he might yet end up standing in one of those bus queues on winter nights. He had no conception of what it meant to work for one's living, never having asked himself what Francis was doing when he was not on holiday and unaware that Eleanor was a physiotherapist and Goo a music teacher. You either had money or you did not and there was very little you could do about it.

But nothing could really spoil the Swiss summer, the Lake which was like home to him, the romance of the Castle of Chillon (close to the hotel), the misty presence of the *Dents du Midi* with its snow-covered 'teeth', or the beauty of Mary Opentock, and he was unworried when Ruth went into a clinic for an operation.

She had fallen into the hands of young Dr Niehans who, years later as the elderly Professor Niehans, would become one of the most famous—or infamous—medical innovators in the world, credited with having prolonged the lives of the German Chancellor, the Duke of Windsor and General de Gaulle as also of Winston Churchill and many others by his cell therapy. Niehans and a colleague had set up a clinic close to the Lake in 1931 and provided luxury treatment for a variety of ailments. Niehans assured Ruth that he could improve her quality of life by grafting a sheep's ovaries into her and she agreed to the operation. She spent some two months in his Clinique and he nearly killed her as well as obliging her to take more than a 'little bit' of her capital. Niehans was a handsome man of great charm and she felt safe in his hands, happy each morning that he cradled her in his powerful arms while the nurses made her bed. At her lowest ebb, when death was very close and she was ready to drift peacefully out of this world, she saw Gai at the end of a long, long tunnel, calling to her, and she struggled back to life. Her main worry before going into the clinic had been who would look after him. Niehans had provided the answer. His little daughter, rejected by her Australian mother whose beautiful figure she had spoilt with stretch marks, was a troubled child. A friend had recommended to him a Mlle Cherpillod—always known simply as Pillod—who could 'work miracles' with difficult children and she had done no less for the little girl. She was engaged to work her miracle with Gai, which she did.

It was impossible to guess her age, a fresh young girl and a wise old woman in one person. Her hair had turned white in her early twenties, and it was now a beautiful snow-white, always immaculate, which set off her gentian blue eyes and perfect complexion. It was those eyes that caught everyone's attention, the eyes of a child, full of wonder, angelic in their innocence. When Ruth got to know her she described her as the only truly innocent person she had ever met and Francis shared her opinion, but innocence did not imply ignorance. Pillod had seen much of the world and gazed upon it without ever judging, let alone condemning. Children loved her sensing that she was in some sense a child herself; she had no need to give orders but was joyfully obeyed. Only once did Gai see her angry and that was when she told him how, while she was living in Paris during the war, she had taken her little Dachshund for a walk and the dog had been kicked to death by some youths because it was a German dog. She shared his intense curiosity about people, speculating with him about someone seen in passing or met briefly. Were they happy or unhappy, what strange secrets did they harbour, what might have been their life experience? There was never a dull moment in her company. She was also a mine of information and he learned from her that one must never describe a Swiss girl or woman as *une Suisesse*. 'When I was little', she said, 'my poor country was so impoverished that peasants, if they had a pretty daughter, would send her to Paris to make money for them through prostitution'. So in Paris *Suisesse* had been a euphemism for prostitute.

Gai would soon be twelve and long afterwards he wondered if Pillod had been a kind of heavenly guide, leading him gently across the divide between childhood and the first glimmerings of adolescence and teaching him, by her example, the way to accept what he could not change and never to judge those whose hearts he could not read. Now it was time to go and in late autumn he returned to England with Ruth, who had by now recovered from Niehans' ministrations. She bought a house in the village of Potters Bar, today a suburb of London, and he was sent to a local day school where he was bullied and had his ear drum punctured by an unkind blow, but this was no less than he would have expected from English boys. Ruth had often explained to him that the English in general were cold, stupid, lacking intellect, lacking culture, and either sexually repressed or perverts. He knew that his great misfortune was not to have been born French or American.

What really mattered was that he now had another friend. Just across the road from his new home lived a dull, very conventional couple called Hands. Their son, known only by his surname, was neither dull nor conventional and Ruth believed that he was the only born leader she had ever come across. He adopted Gai as the first among his followers and appointed him as Second-in-Command of a gang he had formed, a gang of middle-class boys recruited to fight the 'oiks' or village boys—the 'class war' in a teacup. It was their practice to set up a small tent on waste ground as their headquarters and send out their troops to fight the enemy with sticks and stones. Safe in their tent with a bodyguard stationed at the flap, Gai and Hands planned tactics while their gang, nearly always victorious, suffered a few bruises without complaint. Ruth could refuse the Leader nothing. One day he called on her, saluted smartly and announced: 'Mrs Eaton, we intend to hold a pow-pow in your garden on Sunday. We will supply firewood for the bonfire. You will please supply victuals'. She complied without a murmur. A later pow-wow was more sensational. A cousin had told him 'the facts of life' and he summoned a large gathering of the neighbours' children to pass on to them this interesting information. Unfortunately, being completely ignorant of female anatomy, he made a major error in identifying the orifice employed in sexual intercourse, an error which he could have avoided if only he had consulted his Second-in-Command who was better informed. Local parents were apoplectic with rage, but Ruth laughed till tears came into her eyes.

She did not laugh often. She was ill or believed herself ill, and the fact that this illness was almost certainly psychosomatic did not make it any less depressing. For obvious reasons, no doctor was going to tell her the truth, and she never gave up hope that the next one would cure her of what she called 'the bugs in my waterworks'. Having learned nothing from the Niehans experience, she now fell for a Frenchman, a Dr Petavel who had his own clinic just off Harley Street in London. Gai found him rather terrifying, a big man with piercing eyes and a formidable black beard, but Ruth believed his assurance that a course of his special injections requiring a week's stay in his clinic would put her right. After a couple of days she felt really ill and refused any further treatment, reducing the Matron to a state of terror: 'But Madam, Dr Petavel will be very angry. I shall be blamed!' 'Just send him to me!' said Ruth, with a gleam in her eye. He came, and he tried to scold her. Lifting her legs off the bed with some difficulty, she staggered to her feet and grasped the heavy water *carafe* from her bedside table, raising it as high as she could. The big man began to retreat in alarm. She advanced. He hastened down the corridor, and she pursued him. He pulled the front door open and stumbled down the steps into the street. She collapsed on the floor and, as soon as she was sufficiently recovered, telephoned Francis to take her home. She was much better after that. There was so much suppressed anger in her that an opportunity to release it was the best tonic she could have.

And then, in the Spring of 1934, the Hon. Mrs Errington died. Francis had promised Ruth that he would marry her if his wife predeceased him. On her deathbed his wife had extracted from him a promise that he would never marry 'that woman'. At the age of eighty he faced the greatest moral dilemma of his life and he decided to go away to make up his mind. He took Gai with him to a Swiss village high above the Rhone Valley, Montana-Vermala, and asked Pillod to join them in the hotel. His official reason was to give her a free holiday, since she was very poor, and to provide Gai with a companion, but it is possible that he needed her calm presence, needed also the presence of someone innocent of all pretence, all deception. He walked for hours in the forest and wrote almost daily to Ruth, and these are the only letters of his that still exist. They are astonishing. They are passionate love letters of which any young man, in love for the first time, would not be ashamed, and they touched Gai's heart when he read them many years later. 'Do not fear that I will be stern with Gai,' he wrote. 'I want his love too much for that.' He was not stern. He had never before been so gentle. One day Gai climbed a hillside with Pillod and in the evening Francis put a hand on his shoulder—the first time he had ever touched him—and said: 'I am very proud of you, my boy'. This was utterly baffling. Proud because Gai had made an easy climb with a middle-aged woman? It made no sense, but for days afterwards he could feel his father's touch on his shoulder although he had no suspicion that this was his father.

On 5 July he wrote in his diary: '*Maman* is going to marry Uncle. This is the startling news that met me. Uncle is no real relation of ours. He was a great friend of my father. If we were going to live with him ordinarily there would be a great deal of gossip. As it is, when *Maman* marries him everything is alright. Among other things, I will have a step-brother Ralph and a step-sister Barbara both about forty-five and a niece called Rochnara about seventeen.' On 13 July: '*Heil*! My last fatherless day'. They were married in Mayfair the following morning. There was already a shadow over the couple. Francis had feared above all else breaking the news to his daughter Barbara and with good reason. She had listened to him in grim silence, then come to her feet, murmured 'How sad!', and left the room without another word. Ruth told Gai that her new husband—now to be addressed as 'Father' instead of 'Uncle'—had suggested that he might adopt him and change his name to Errington, in which case he would inherit equally with Ralph and Barbara. The diary entry is, in retrospect, sadly ironic: '*Maman* asked me if I would like this. But I think it would be unfair to my dead father, to sever his last link with us. How sad his death must have been! A good-looking young man with a pretty wife and a new baby and everything bright and joyous. Then death and I, his child, remember nothing of him'. In any case Francis soon changed his mind, having decided that this would be too dangerous, likely to arouse suspicion. The deception must, at all costs, be maintained and in this case the cost was high, at least to his unacknowledged son.

Ruth and Gai moved into the Errington home, the Red House, which had been built in the time of Queen Ann and stood on Berkhamsted High Street almost opposite the Parish Church, an unhappy house by any reckoning. In the big garden there was a little chapel built entirely out of sea shells and, although no one was sure of its origin, there was a story that it had been used for satanic rituals. Ruth had the room in which her predecessor had spent some fifteen lonely, bitter years and slept in the bed in which she had died. Waking at night during the first few weeks Ruth sensed the presence of a malignant, vengeful spirit until finally, in the early hours of one morning, she sat up in bed and let out a stream of curses — every curse or four-letter word she knew — surmising correctly that a lady of breeding would soon be put to flight. The 'presence' departed, but something remained, something indefinable which gave her no peace. In another part of the house Ralph (always pronounced 'Rafe') had his own suite of bedroom and sitting-room in which he lived his life, such as it was. He did nothing, which sounds almost impossible. At least he must have had a hobby? He had none. When he was a young man an uncle had left him a sum of money sufficient to provide an adequate income so long as he lived at home, and he was encouraged to do so by his mother's loneliness. She could not do without him. Now, in his late forties, he had his established routine, appearing at meals and drinking a pint of beer at the local pub before lunch; what he did for the rest of his time, apart from reading detective stories, no one knew and no one cared. Ruth referred to him as 'the incubus'.

Soon after this she took to her bed and stayed there, on and off, for the next six years. Francis seemed to take this as natural; for his generation women, after a certain age, were expected to suffer from obscure female ailments. It was no less natural that she should employ a 'lady companion', Miss Foley (a middle-aged

Australian spinster), who acted also as housekeeper. Ruth met Barbara, her step-daughter—the term seems oddly inappropriate—only twice and the Earl's granddaughter succeeded by a great effort in being polite, but she was kind to Gai, determined not to blame the child for the sins of the mother. It was a very cold kindness and he knew that he was being patronised. On the other hand Rochnara (always known as Rochné) was genuinely friendly: 'She has a good figure and looks extremely attractive front face at a short distance off,' he wrote in the diary, 'but side-face she is not so pretty. Her nose is a tiny bit too predominant'. She was, in fact, a beautiful girl (closely resembling the late Princess Diana), but he preferred snub noses. Barbara's husband, Esmé Wingfield-Stratford, was a distinguished and popular historian and he too was kind. But Gai felt like a poor relation in this family, and it marked him. He could hardly have missed the fact that, for them, Ruth was the evil woman who had trapped an honourable man and led him astray. Neither he nor she belonged here.

Gai was sent as a border to a school only a few miles away, Lockers Park, among what would have been called in those days a 'better class of boy' than those in Potters Bar. Lord Louis Mountbatten had been a pupil, as had his father, Prince Louis of Battenberg. While he was there the Old Man died at the age of ninety-two, defiant to the last. He had not seen a doctor for fifty years or more, but Rose had insisted on bringing one to him and explained to him that her father was in the habit of taking baths so hot that no normal person would have been able to put a hand in the water. The doctor warned him that he would have a stroke if he continued to boil himself alive only to provoke a thunderous response. 'I have been taking hot baths for ninety years. How dare you . . .' A few weeks later he did indeed have a stroke in his bath, dying there and then. At the time Gai was in the school sick-room with an attack of flu. Ruth telephoned the Headmaster to say that he was not to be told the news until he had recovered.

Leafing idly through the latest copy of *The Illustrated London News* he was faced with a large photograph of the Old Man: 'J. E. Preston Muddock, the famous author'. It was the most devastating shock he had ever sustained. He was happy, however, at the school and, after a year, passed his entrance examination for Charterhouse.

There were seven or perhaps eight 'great' Public Schools, that is to say private schools, in England—including Charterhouse— slowly changing with the times (less beatings and no more beer for breakfast) but still designed to prepare pupils for their manifest destiny which was to rule a large sector of the globe as well as directing the affairs of their own country. Ruth had always attributed many of the most unpleasant characteristics of the English to these institutions and yet she agreed without a murmur to feed her son into what she regarded as a malignant system, proving, if proof was needed, that rebels never entirely escape the conditioning of their times. Before embarking on his new life he was given a taste of what it meant to be a member of the Establishment. Francis was invited to King George V's Jubilee Service in St Paul's Cathedral. Ruth would not leave her bed, so he took Gai with him and they drove in a grand hire car through streets lined with the humble citizens of London. Impatient for the sight of someone famous, the crowd glimpsed this elderly man superbly robed and with a voluminous wig and they cheered wildly. Gai bowed his head in acknowledgement. In the Cathedral they were seated opposite the King with his chestful of medals and the bejewelled Queen, though at some distance (another image crystallised in memory). It was a magnificent occasion and Gai knew he would never forget it, but there was something missing. What was missing was a sense of reality. Everyone was in fancy dress and everyone was play-acting.

L ater on Gai came to think of these robes and uniforms as masks. They masked the body, obviously, but they also masked the personality, presenting the individual as a 'type' or in terms of a function. But if reality was missing, where, then, was the 'real world' to be found? Certainly not at Charterhouse where he was confined in an enclosed community with its own rules, passions and prejudices, a community which excluded the female of the species and in which adolescent energies boiled as in a cauldron, friendship and enmity equally intensified. This community was not the school as such, with its 700 pupils but his House, 'Robinites', one of a dozen 'houses' among which the boys were distributed, each a little world on its own. Robinites was the furthest from the school and the short walk between the two was the centre of the House's social life. 'Did you see who was walking up with whom this morning? Wonder why X and Y haven't walked up together once all this term?' At first Gai hated his imprisonment among strangers with whom he could find nothing in common. By his third year he was able to write: 'It's possible that I shall never again in my life be so happy'. He was unsure whether the institution had beaten him or he had beaten the institution.

For his first term he was allocated a 'Father', a boy charged with teaching him the customs of the place. The choice of Oswald Farquhar for this task was unfortunate for he was not only intensely conventional but also painfully sensitive and Gai's eccentricity was a torment to him. Gai showed intense interest in all that Faquhar told him but seemed quite incapable of understanding that the rules, so right for everyone else, applied also to himself, rather as an anthropologist might empathise with the customs of the tribe he was studying without wishing to incorporate these customs into his own life. He did, however, object strongly at being obliged to refer to the house Matron, a pleasant young woman, as 'the hag' (a Frenchman would have seen this as an indication of the British attitude to women and a Freudian might have found it significant).

The boys knew how to deal with a flagrant rebel but did not know how to deal with such a slippery customer as this. One of the prefects asked him, more in sorrow than in anger: 'Couldn't you at least try to be more like other people?' The question was absurd. He was who he was. How could he try to be someone else? As had happened with the aunts, mild persistence paid off in the end. Some time later, when Ruth was deeply into Yoga, he took to standing on his head for five or ten minutes in the dormitory. On the first two or three occasions the other boys clustered round him, but after that they accepted that this was the kind of thing 'Leggy' (an apt nickname for long-legged Le Gai) did and ignored him.

His Form Master, an Anglican clergyman, was as baffled as were the boys. He set the class to write an essay on 'Assassination', expecting them all to condemn such wickedness. Gai wrote—and wrote rather well—in defence of the practice and advocated the killing of harmful people including political figures such as Herr Hitler. Ruth, after all, had always been strongly in favour of putting such people against a wall and shooting them. Genuinely shocked his teacher sent for him and tried to explain that killing was wrong. Why? The Bible said: 'Thou shalt not kill'. Gai wanted to know what the Bible, with which he was unfamiliar, had to do with anything. Surely bad men should be killed for the sake of everyone else? The reverend gentleman gave up. He could not reason with this boy.

In his second term everything changed. He needed a hero and he found one in the person of a boy called Quentin Stanham who was the exact opposite to him, an outstanding sportsman, a team player, the perfect Public Schoolboy, and his admiration for Stanham expanded to embrace all the rest. How splendid they were! He was not and never could be a member of this tribe, but now he observed them with admiration. A number of new boys arrived that term, including a trio who always stuck together and became central to Gai's school life. Rodney was a Scot, earnest and hard-working; Ronny was lackadaisical, charming and friendly with everyone, and Bobby was a boy who forced Gai to reconsider his prejudice against the English. Bobby was, as someone remarked of him, 'so damn nice'. Gai, under the influence of Ruth's favourite novelist, D. H. Lawrence, defined him differently in the diary: 'Bobby is unsullied by the withering touch of abstract thought'. This, of course, was high praise from a disciple of D.H.L.

There was a fourth new boy who fitted into no category. Bruce Barker was Jamaican, the son of an Englishman and a Sephardic Jewish mother belonging to a wealthy family who had considerable power in the Island. He was a small, sallow-faced boy, old beyond his years and scornful of the intrigues and passions which surrounded him. He had a wicked tongue and the other boys left him alone while he, for his part, chose only one friend, Gai, with whom he could talk about the things that interested him. Bruce was fascinated by the rise and fall of empires, convinced that Europe's day was over and that the next worldwide empire would be Japanese. One morning, when he opened a letter from his mother at the breakfast table, he passed over a newspaper cutting from a Jamaican paper with a photograph of a magnificent man with a mane of grey hair mounted on a white horse riding up to King's House, the Governor's residence, to challenge the might of the British Empire. This was Alexander Bustamante, leader (with his cousin Norman Manley) of the independence movement. Here, Gai thought, was a man after his own heart, a true hero, and he dreamed that he might one day meet him. If, most improbably, a fortune-teller had joined the boys at breakfast and had predicted that, fifteen years later, he would be working for this man, standing beside him on political platforms and sitting at his bedside reading to him when he was ill, this would have seemed more incredible than any prophesy made by a fairground gypsy.

At fifteen he began to write poetry and, over the next two years, poured out reams of bad verse, in which 'love' was frequently rhythmed with 'dove', leavened by an occasional acceptable though derivative poem such as this sonnet.

> *The shadows, soft and delicate as clouds,*
> *Are chasing o'er the lawn like playful ghosts.*
> *Yet they, these fleeting, thinly woven shrouds,*
> *Follow each movement of their leafy hosts,*
> *While up on high the branches feel the breeze*
> *And, swaying with a soft and rhythmic swish,*
> *Transfer their message from the silent trees*
> *Down to the shadows which obey their wish.*
> *But then the sun goes in. A deathlike sleep*
> *Steals quietly on its way across the ground*
> *As, with a witch's broom, it seems to sweep*
> *The shadows all away without a sound.*
> *Their only strength came from the sun above.*
> *Shadows, how like to Man; the sun to love.*

His worst verses were diatribes inspired by anger. He was a passionate supporter of the King and Mrs Simpson at the time of the Abdication: 'Hypocrites have won the day!' A telegram from Francis praising the wisdom of the British people shocked him. Francis seldom expressed political opinions beyond remarking once on how deeply he had been impressed by Mr Gladstone after attending one of the Grand Old Man's public meetings.

Ruth, who admired the beautiful clarity of Francis' speech, was worried that Gai tended to mumble so she sent him to a local elocution teacher, a Miss Murray-Ainsley. This good lady decided, after reading his poems, that she had at last discovered a young prodigy. In 1937 she took him with her to a Festival of Spoken Poetry in Oxford which was attended by most of the well-known poets of the time and pressed his poems on them. Since she was clearly a respected figure, they were as polite as they could be about these adolescent exercises, but there was one poet whom she did not approach, a tow-haired young man with a pasty face, W. H. Auden. It would be nearly forty years before Auden, by then raddled and prematurely aged, read any of Gai's work.

He himself was reading voraciously. This was facilitated by an odd coincidence. Two Australian sisters, the Misses Armstrong, had a guesthouse opposite the House and they happened to be friends of Miss Foley, Ruth's 'lady companion'. The guesthouse, Oak Braes, soon became his home from home and, except on the two afternoons each week when he was obliged to play football or cricket, he made his way there after lunch with books tucked under his shirt. He could read for hours, breaking off to enjoy the Armstrongs' superb home-made cakes, occasionally inviting a friend—usually Bobby—to have tea with him. When he confessed to the elder of the two sisters that he intended to be a novelist she was deeply shocked. 'I hope', she said sternly, 'that you will not be like those wicked, wicked men Mr Bernard Shaw and Mr H. G. Wells'.

As it happened, he was more concerned at the time with an author whom she would have regarded as far more wicked, unspeakably so. He read a book of essays by Havelock Ellis and was bowled over by the author's exposition of the 'art of living' and the 'dance of life', quite unaware that this old man had once been universally reviled as the author of the seven-volume *Studies in the Psychology of Sex* (the first volume published in 1897), the monster who had kicked aside all the taboos of his time. Even today, more than sixty years after his death, he is described as 'the man who changed western attitudes to sex'. In old age, regarded by many people as a Sage and looking the part, he had become a kind of universal agony aunt before agony aunts were invented and received thousands of letters every year. Gai wrote to him and received a prompt reply. He followed this up by sending the great man a sheaf of his poems, which were well received. No doubt a letter from a fifteen-year-old boy stood out from his other correspondence which was concerned mainly with peoples' sexual problems. Francis, who would have remembered very well the sensational Court case in which the publisher of the *Studies* was prosecuted for gross obscenity or something of the sort, reacted with typical moderation: 'Havelock Ellis? A very interesting man'.

But poetry was not enough. He was beginning to form opinions on every possible subject and he had inherited the Old Man's need to improve the world by giving it the benefit of his views on life and love, religion and politics. When he was fifteen he wrote a book with the title *A Schoolboy Looks out on the World* and Barbara's husband, Esmé, who was one of their clients, sent it to a leading literary agency, Curtis Brown. They asked Gai to come and see them. He was interviewed by two young men who told him that they believed they could find a publisher for the manuscript but that he must think carefully before instructing them to go ahead. It could only be published as a 'stunt'. He was likely to face painful mockery and, if he meant to write seriously in the future (as they hoped he did), the book would hang round his neck like an albatross. The decision was his, but they suggested he should consult someone he respected. He consulted his Housemaster, Aubrey Scott, who persuaded him against publication.

All this should have made him self-confident. It did not, except regarding his capacity to string words together. This is a common mystery. There are people in whom self-doubt is so ingrained that they are never cured by success which suggests that some forgotten incident in early childhood may determine, for each individual, the degree of self-confidence with which he or she will be equipped for a lifetime. One day the Scottish boy, Rodney, remarked to him: 'You'll have to be a gentleman of leisure, won't you? I'm sure you could never make your living'. This confirmed his own fixed conviction, and it terrified him for he was already obsessed with the question of money. If he could not be a successful novelist he would starve.

Rodney reinforced another of his obsessive doubts when he asked him: 'Leggy, what sort of girl do you think would ever like you?' If this had been said maliciously he might have taken it less seriously, but it was said with genuine concern. He looked at himself in the mirror, over six foot tall and weighing less than eight stone. Of course Rodney was right. What sort of girl would want to take this bag of bones into her bed? The fear of rejection was so deep seated that, in later years, he could never make even a cautious approach to a woman unless he had received quite unmistakable signals of invitation. After reading a good deal of Freudian psychology he thought he detected a possible reason for this. Ruth had been determined to breastfeed him but her breasts were dry. She had persevered none the less while the baby, scarlet faced, screamed with frustration and tore at her body in fury. Could this, he wondered, have left him with a permanent expectation of rejection?

Happy enough and yet full of anxieties, one matter to which he gave no thought was his parentage and the fantasy figure of

'Charles Eaton' was forgotten, but when he was fifteen Ruth at last told him the truth. By then the diary was running to considerable length, every trivial incident and every passing emotion faithfully recorded, but there is no mention of this revelation although the actual scene was engraved on his memory. He was in bed at the Red House, recovering from some minor illness, and Ruth sat at his bedside in her dressing gown. Having told him all that there was to tell, she made him promise never to let his father suspect that he knew, to tell no one else and not to mention it in his diary. The secret must remain a secret for ever and he must lie when necessary to protect it.

How he reacted is uncertain since nothing is recorded in the diary. Perhaps he did not react at all since he had the capacity to become completely numb in the face of any shock, but he was now involved in the great deception and was obliged to keep a strict guard on his tongue. On April 5th each year he received a birthday gift from his father, both of them knowing that this was not his birthday, and each year in the Christmas holidays his father took him to a Swiss resort to skate and ski so that they were constantly together. Still his lips were sealed and not a word escaped him to betray the fact that he knew that 'Father' was indeed his father. It was not until many years later, when Ruth and Francis were long dead, that he began to have a recurrent dream in which he told her that she must confess to Francis that she had betrayed their secret to their son or else he would do so himself.

One big secret at the root of the tree should suffice for any family. There was however another, a secret shrouded in mystery, but it would be almost seventy years before Gai discovered that his grandfather, the Old Man, had also been a deceiver. This was revealed through an invention unimaginable in the 1930s, the Internet. Quite unknown to his family, Ruth and the aunts, the Old Man had been twice married before he met Eleanor Rudd in 1880. At the age of seventeen he had married an American 'theatrical' (whatever that might mean) of

73

the same age. Soon afterwards he had sailed to Australia and there was no record of what happened to the girl although there is evidence that he had fathered a child (mother unknown) in the mid-1860s. He had married again in the 1870s and there was at least one child, a girl called Evangeline, a great beauty who became a famous violinist, the mistress of the artist Edvard Munch (painter of a sinister modern 'icon', *The Scream*) and a model for Matisse. This unknown aunt, who did not die until 1952, would fascinate Gai in old age, not least because he would realise that Ruth, who had so little in common with her full sisters, might have found a true soul-sister in this remarkable woman. To judge from a poem she wrote and from her letters to Munch, she had been so like his mother. But how had the Old Man—referred to by his biographer as 'the Old Goat'—kept his past hidden? There was no evidence of a divorce so it is possible that he was a bigamist, Ruth and her sisters illegitimate.

Was life possible without deception and secrecy? Perhaps the act of living required it. But Gai became obsessed with the need to discover Truth as such, the ultimate Truth, and this was comparable to physical hunger. How could anyone live their lives in an impenetrable fog of unknowing? This thirst is, of course, an aspect of what makes us human. No one can think or act without a metaphysical basis for thought and action. In most young people it is, however, either assuaged or stifled by the gratuitous assumptions of the time, supposed to be self-evident. Only the doubters who are out of tune with the spirit of their times remain unconvinced and continue to seek answers to the basic, perennial questions.

He began to read philosophy, guided by C. E. M. Joad, a populariser and radio personality who made it all seem easy. He read or tried to read Descartes, Kant, Hume, Spinoza, Schopenhauer and Bertrand Russell. He became increasingly depressed by their mental gymnastics, their arid speculations and their unfounded faith in logic and reason. These were not sages. He might as well have been eating sand as seeking nourishment from this quarter. They knew nothing and were simply spinning ideas out of their own poor heads. Even a schoolboy could do that. He was seeking men who could see far beyond the horizon which limited his own vision, men who knew. Western culture treated these 'philosophers' as great men and students in universities studied their works with respect, but what was that to him? Ruth had instructed him to pay no attention to what others thought or believed.

He took it for granted that he could not discuss this with any of his friends. His dread of rejection operated here and he feared nothing as much as being a bore. Then and later he needed a clear invitation before he could speak of ideas that were important to him, but by the time he was sixteen he had at last found common ground with the other boys. He shared with them an intense interest in people and their secrets and he discovered that he was a good listener. So he listened with inexhaustible patience becoming, in effect, the House agony aunt. Particularly once he had a study of his own, boys came to him, confessing their 'pashes' and asking if he thought the objects of this passionate love reciprocated their feelings. He had at last found his role in the House and he relished it. Often he passed on these precious secrets and was reproached for doing so. He had a simple answer: 'Say to me the magic words "Secret Compartment" and I won't whisper a word of what you've told me'. Oddly enough, none of his interlocutors availed themselves of this facility. It was almost as though they wanted him to betray their confidences.

It did not occur to him that the Housemaster, Aubrey Scott, knew what was going on until later when he read the letter Scott wrote to Ruth after he had left school: 'Gai won through to a position of his own as the confidant of people of quite different types without in any way sinking his individuality in the herd . . . A lot of people will miss him, including myself'. Scott was deeply in love with one of the boys, a handsome, athletic Dane called Ulf, and one day in Gai's final year invited him round to his quarters for a sherry as he had done occasionally in the past. After some desultory conversation he said: 'Tell me quite honestly, what do you think about me and Ulf?' Intensely embarrassed, Gai thought that he was being asked for a personal opinion, whereas the real question was obviously: 'What does the House think?' He could only mumble a vague reply. In fact the House could not have cared less, except that some boys were jealous of the frequency with which Ulf was taken to the cinema by his House-master.

Scott was a homosexual of a type that is probably rare today. There were many of that generation who were brought up with the idea that sexual activity was impure, even filthy, and most of them probably overcame this. Those who did not had two alter-natives. Either they married 'pure' wives whom they 'defiled' only for the purpose of procreation, turning to prostitutes when nec-essary, or else they formed intense but chaste attachments to handsome young men and, if they were sometimes assailed by naughty thoughts, promptly suppressed them. Scott would have been incapable of seducing a pupil and when—early in the war —Ulf was killed by a bomb while dancing at the Café de Paris in London he was a broken man. He died not long afterwards.

'Pashes' were a different matter, natural enough in adolescent boys deprived of all contact with the opposite sex. It was even claimed that the Headmaster had said they were 'a good thing' as long as they did not lead to sexual activity. Gai gradually developed a 'pash' for Bobby, a quiet and happy love since all his erotic fantasies were centred on film stars; much of his time on holiday was passed in cutting out pictures of his favourites from movie magazines and sticking them into scrap books. This was a serious business. He believed that life would be worthless unless he could one day hold Merle Oberon, a Eurasian beauty, in his arms, but even then he could not be happy unless he also possessed Vivien Leigh. He was faithful to neither of them. The young Ingrid Bergman's sweet vulnerability melted his heart and brought tears to his eyes, and a dozen others set his pulse racing. It was agony because he knew that his fantasies had no substance. These 'stars' were as far out of reach as the stars in the firmament and Hollywood was as inaccessible as heaven itself.

On a school visit to the National Gallery he bought reproductions of two paintings to hang in his study, quite unaware of the significance of his spontaneous choice. Seventy years later they would hang on either side of his bed, recognised as representing the two poles of the life he had lived. The first was *St Jerome in a Rocky Landscape* by Patinir, an image of austerity. The hermit saint sits by his fire, quite alone, far from a little farmhouse nestling in the mountains. These mountains are bare, jagged rocks, white and without a trace of vegetation. The whole feeling is one of remoteness and separation from the busy human world. On the other side is *La Bohemienne* by Franz Hals, one of the most sensual and implicitly erotic pictures in the gallery. This is no sumptuous nude but the portrait of a rosy-faced gypsy girl, her plump breasts bursting out of her ragged bodice. Her sly smile is shamelessly inviting. No one could doubt the purpose for which she was created and the reason she was painted in the moment of her brief flowering.

Meanwhile real life consisted of friendships, including a real friendship with his Housemaster. In his final year, when he was in the History section of the Sixth Form, he formed a close bond with another of the masters. Major Ives owed his position more to a distinguished war record than to his qualifications but he was a teacher of genius. He could imbue his pupils with his own enthusiasm. He also possessed the qualities of serenity and gentleness which one found sometimes in men who had experienced, in the trenches, the worst that human wickedness could throw at them and, at the same time, witnessed a heroism and stoicism almost beyond imagining.

Ives had a consuming passion for Shakespeare. The characters in the plays were real people to him and he analysed them in depth, applying to each the techniques of psychoanalysis. A time came when they were doing *King Lear* and he devoted a whole session to Edmond, 'The Bastard', attributing his malignity to the circumstances of his birth. A bastard, Ives explained, was inevitably an outcast from society, owing no debt and no duty to it. Such a man sought revenge for an injury that was not his fault and, since he was the product of an act of immorality, had only contempt for moral principles; he was a loner, every man's hand against him and his hand against every man. Little wonder, then, that 'bastard' was a term of insult. Gai listened carefully and examined himself. Was this true of him? He thought it might be. He cared nothing for society or morality and, like Edmond, he was an arch-deceiver.

He wondered whether his inability to believe anything that other people took for granted was an aspect of his exclusion from society. It probably had more to do with Ruth's insistence that he must never borrow his beliefs from others, and the fact that most people took something as self-evident was, both then and later, enough to make him doubt it. Ives, who had described Shakespeare as a 'universal sceptic', paid him a curious compliment when he said to him in a tone of wonder, even of respect: 'You are the only truly universal sceptic I have ever known!' He was not referring specifically to religion. He meant scepticism in the widest possible sense. He realised that his rather weird pupil wanted to know why it should be assumed that our rational powers, so well adapted to finding food, shelter and a mate had any application beyond that. How could anyone prove that 'real life' was indeed real? Long afterwards he would come across a story of the Taoist sage, Chuang Tzu who, having dreamed one night that he was a butterfly, awoke to wonder whether he was in fact the man Chuang Tzu who had dreamed that he was a butterfly, or a butterfly dreaming that it was a human sage.

At seventeen, now approaching eighteen, Gai felt that he had passed a whole lifetime at Charterhouse. He had arrived there still a child, he would soon be leaving as an adult. But in the Red House time had stood still. Francis still took the train to London five days a week, convinced that if he stopped work he would die, although what he actually did in his Chambers was a mystery. Ralph's routine never varied, and Ruth spent most of her time in bed attended by the faithful and devoted Miss Foley. Sometimes she felt a little better, but these brief spells were always followed by a relapse. During the school holidays, except when he was in Switzerland with his father, Gai's hopes were regularly raised and then dashed, as were Miss Foley's, and the two of them, both a little tearful, took long walks on the Common every time a relapse had cast them into despair. 'She seemed so much better last week', Miss Foley would say, her voice breaking, 'and now — well, you've seen for yourself, Gai!' Yet another doctor had proposed a course of injections which, he guaranteed, would put Ruth on her feet again. When his bill arrived — a bill for nearly £2,000 at present-day values — she wrote him one of her 'stinkers', as she called them, begging him to sue her so that she could be carried into Court on a stretcher to demonstrate the effects of his treatment. The bill was not repeated.

Her principal enemy was the British climate, which she cursed day in and day out. Early in 1937 she set off with Miss Foley for the South of France and, for the next twelve months, took up residence in a hotel in Menton on the Italian frontier where Gai and Francis joined her for each holiday break. As soon as Gai arrived for the first time she sent him out to search the local bookshops for a dictionary of French slang. All he could find was a dictionary of prostitutes' *argot* and this delighted her. It was full of juicy insults which she could use whenever she encountered some officious petty functionary. She had somehow to release her anger and she could never target her family, but men who had been given a little authority over their fellow citizens and used it arrogantly were her chosen victims. In full flow she was so formidable that she even put to flight an Italian frontier guard who had tried to stop them when Gai and Francis were pushing her along the seafront in her wheelchair ('Please Sirs, take her, take her wherever she wants, but take her away!') In the hotel, however, she was all sweetness and light. The maids came to her room regularly to pour out their troubles and, when one or other had been dumped by her boyfriend, to cry on her shoulder.

Gai wandered the coast, slipped, although he was under age, into the Casino in Monte Carlo, and he learned to drive on the mountain roads with an instructor who confined himself to shouting: 'Quick, quick, double de-clutch!' on every possible occasion. This was the start of a lifelong love affair with the car, which came to represent freedom to such an extent that, when deprived of it, he felt a kind of claustrophobia. Francis thought he should learn to travel on his own and treated him to a trip to Corsica in the Easter holidays. In the summer he suggested a visit to Florence, but Gai had other ideas. Algeria was tantalisingly close, just across the Mediterranean, and the combination of a gangster film set in the *Casbah* of Algiers with his favourite novel, P. C. Wren's *Beau Geste*, filled him with longing. There was only one place he wanted to go.

French officialdom tried to stop him. The seaplane from Marseilles to Algiers landed to refuel in Minorca and a young man who wanted to join the civil war in Spain might use this as an opportunity to reach Spanish territory illegally. He managed to persuade the authorities that he was not a potential warrior and set off. Everything, every moment, was more thrilling than anything he had previously experienced. Even the night in Marseilles, most of it spent wandering the streets and taking coffee with a group of Algerian sailors, was an adventure. The flight in a seaplane was an even greater adventure and his first evening in a hotel in a suburb of Algiers was spent kneeling in the road, collecting sand from the gutters—real Sahara sand—

and feeding it into little bottles which he would keep 'for ever'. He wandered in the *Casbah*, took photographs in the 'Street of Prostitutes', provoking screams of rage and then pursuit by women much too fat to catch him, and he ventured into a small nightclub where he ordered a lemonade. There was a dancer, a girl who could not have been more than sixteen, clad only in a diaphanous robe which half veiled, half revealed the details of her young body. He was so overcome that, when he left the club, he forgot to pay for his lemonade. Flying back to France he had only one worry. Was it possible that anything more wonderful could ever happen to him?

He returned to Charterhouse for his final term and regaled his friends with slightly embroidered accounts of Algiers, telling them how he had been chased through the narrow alleys of the *Casbah* by a troop of beautiful prostitutes and fallen in love with a naked dancer in a nightclub. They were delightfully envious. But by now they were living under the shadow of war. On 29 September the Munich agreement was signed. Rodney asked him: 'Don't you think Mr Chamberlain is the greatest Englishman who ever lived?' Gai wrote in his diary: 'Chamberlain has brought peace without honour' and, the following Sunday, Robert Birley (the Headmaster) denounced appeasement from the pulpit in Chapel, a brave action for the youngest Public School headmaster in England but one that may have contributed to his post-war eminence as Sir Robert.

By this time Gai had been accepted for King's College, Cambridge, in October the following year. Realising that he was unlikely to pass the general entrance examination, since he was incapable of working at any subject that did not interest him, Major Ives had suggested he take the History scholarship exam. Even if he did not qualify for a scholarship, this would get him into the college, particularly as Esmé was a Fellow of King's and prepared to put in a good word for him. Ruth or Francis had decided that he should leave Charterhouse early so that he could spend a few months in Paris polishing up his French before going on to university, so 19 December 1938 was the end of that particular lifetime.

That evening he did his rounds, saying goodbye to some fifty boys and running out of things to say. After 'lights out' he retired to his cubicle to write up his diary and lit a candle. He confessed to dreading his return to the Red House: 'It's the sort of house in which one ought to hold a weekly orgy, just to remind it that humanity exists'. He was interrupted by Ronny coming for a farewell chat, but eventually he was alone as he wanted to be. 'I'm too old to cry . . . It's after midnight and I'm cold and tired and sad, scribbling this by candlelight. What I feel is a very ordinary sense of grief, not worth describing, but it's heavy. I'm not sad because it's ended but because I shall change, forget, grow into another being out of sympathy with this "me". I want to shout "Stop!" . . . Listen to the wind in the trees, scattering the snow, and listen to the ticking of the clock. It seems to me that I have been granted an intimate glimpse of Time naked, something that it is not good for man to see. We must all hide the weak, timid creature that is in all of us, only allow it out by candlelight when the snow is falling.'

Strange times! As 1938 drew to a close it was impossible to doubt that war was coming, a matter of 'when' rather than 'if', but most people put this out of their minds in the way that people refuse to think about death although they know that, sooner or later, they must die. Britain and France might have been compared to rabbits caught in the glare of a car's headlights and unable to move. The driver was Adolf Hitler and it was no longer possible for the rabbits to negotiate with him. They awaited his good pleasure: life or death. Visitors from outside Europe had already fled. Miss Foley had returned to Australia and, earlier in the year, Bruce Barker's parents had ordered him to take the next sailing back to Jamaica.

Francis had left early for the Swiss resort of Mürren while Gai stayed over Christmas at Ruth's bedside. He joined his father on 28 December, finding him in uncommonly high spirits. He was now eighty-five but still a keen skater and, while drifting around the rink, had taken to offering advice to ladies struggling with their figures of eight. That morning he had been helpful to an American woman who, mistaking him for an official Instructor, tipped him, an indication that he still looked twenty years younger than his age. Moreover he had made friends, first with a German Baroness who denounced Hitler as 'a common little man', then with a distinguished international banker, Swedish with an Irish wife. He kept the best news till last: this couple had three daughters. He named them: Erin, who was probably eighteen; Birget or Bridget whom he supposed, mistakenly, to be sixteen, and the youngest, Moira, who was probably ten or eleven.

Next morning, on the skating rink, Francis introduced him to the middle girl of the trio whom he called 'Bridgy': 'A delicious smile,' Gai noted, 'and the most beautiful dark brown hair, a perfect mouth and friendly eyes. Never before have I been so struck by a first impression'. It was incredible that such a creature should exist on earth, even more incredible that he should actually meet her, never before having met a real, live girl (unless one counted Rochné, his half-niece). His film stars—even Merle —were blown away in a gale of emotion. He was, none the less, obliged to insert a tone of adolescent cynicism into the diary; after all, he was 'grown up' now and a man of the world. 'I was instantly attracted, and that was enough. I put my imagination onto the job and, within the hour, I was in love with her, although I can no longer visualise her face. I begin to build my plans, what I will say to her when we next meet.' Planning was all very well, but he never did say the things he meant to say.

Later the same day he met her parents and was hugely impressed by their acquaintance with leading statesmen of the time (at the end of the war her father would become the first President of The World Bank). Next morning she was on the rink again. 'She kept skating to the edge and flopping into the bank of soft snow so that she was half-buried, then—full of laughter— wriggling to a sitting position, clothed in sparkling snow crystals'. But he was not her only admirer. Two other boys came up to vie for her attention. He would have liked to shoot them and, later, a terrible thought possessed him. 'Damn! Damn! Damn! It has occurred to me that the family may be leaving soon. Over dinner I asked Father if he knew when they were going. "At the end of the week, I think," he said. The Fates have given me a wonderful piece of luck and then snatched it away.' That evening was 'the most wonderful evening of my life'. When he arrived at the ballroom of the Palace Hotel she was on the dance floor with an American boy. 'I thought—No, she's too beautiful for me! She's dancing with that good-looking American. She won't be interested in me.' She detached herself from her partner and came over to greet him. He was speechless. Her mother told him that she wanted to be a writer, and she herself had mentioned that she had written poetry for a year but 'got fed up with petty versifying'. This proved—surely?—that 'the Fates have something in store for us'.

The following evening was New Year's Eve. He and Francis were with the family. He did his duty and danced first with the youngest, Moira, 'the most precocious child imaginable'. It was an 'Excuse Me' dance and, as soon as they came level with her sister, who was dancing with an English boy, the marvellous child calmly took possession of him, much to his annoyance, leaving Bridgy to Gai. They were still dancing when midnight struck: 1939, his eighteenth birthday, though he could tell no one. Could he kiss her, might he kiss her if only on the cheek? He leaned towards her and thought she leaned towards him, but then he became aware of the eyes fixed on them, his father's and those of her parents. There was no kiss, and this went down in his private annals as another failure of courage, a repetition of the flight on the Brighton sea wall long ago. Her parents invited him to have supper with them: 'lobster mayonnaise and a delicious Swiss wine called Yvorne'. There were streamers and little cotton wool balls to throw. 'I had a huge bundle of streamers and didn't know what to do with them, so I put them in Bridgy's lap and she laughingly tossed them back at me.' He walked back to his own hotel crunching crisp snow. Now he was well and truly gone, somewhere over the moon, somewhere above the clouds.

He found her standing forlornly beside the rink next morning. She had chilblains on her toes and could not skate. 'The pity of it', he wrote. 'If only I could take her foot in my hands and kiss it, warming it with my breath. Everything to do with her calls up an agony of feeling, all telescoped into these few days. When she walks I am afraid that she may fall. A thousand dangers crowd over her head . . .' She was framed against the backdrop of his favourite mountain, appropriately named the *Jungfrau*, 'the Virgin'. The landscape itself was transformed. It is something easily achieved in movies, less so in real life, for the sun to become a little brighter, the sky a deeper shade of blue, the snow of a crystalline purity under the brighter sun. He registered in memory a small, clear picture like a Persian miniature or a holy icon, and this was how he would remember her.

The following morning, when he met the family, he was told that they were leaving the following day, three days earlier than planned. Francis guessed, correctly, that they were cutting their holiday short because they felt that Bridgy was receiving more attention than was good for her; understandable in view of her age, though it was nearly sixty years later that he discovered she was not sixteen at the time but fourteen. The fact that she was very tall for her age and unusually mature had deceived every-one including Francis. Still—and always—obsessed with the passage of time, the impossibility of fixing the elusive moment, Gai wrote in the diary: 'I am going out of the light into pain and darkness, yet I must be grateful . . . That one should forget, that is the vile, miserable thing. She and I are dying here and now. If our future selves meet it will be as strangers'.

January 4th was the final day. He gave her an absurd gift to give someone who lived in Switzerland, a little model of a Swiss chalet such as tourists buy. 'Would it bore you terribly if I wrote to you?' he asked. She gave him her address in Basle. He and Francis saw the family off in the little mountain train, and he began to compose his first letter to her. Back at the hotel tears stained the diary page. 'There was a girl, young and fresh and very beautiful who looked me in the eyes when we first met and who, in spite of her friendliness, remained shrouded in her Scandinavian mists, always a little aloof. I shall never quite forget her.' Nor did he and, in years to come, he drank her health each New Year's Eve; she had indeed become an icon. The coincidence of first love with his eighteenth birthday was a powerful combination, but there was to be another factor which sealed the episode in time. A curtain was soon to come down on the world he knew, the world in which he had grown up. War was coming and, by the time it ended, everything would have changed and the pre-war period would be a closed book. He left his wooden skis in the hotel for use the following winter. He never skied again.

The transition from the waters of a mountain stream, such as the one that rushes through the valley below Mürren, to the dead water of a stagnant pond should be gradual. Gai wished he could have travelled by stage-coach, allowing the changing landscape to abate his fever. On the Oberland Express he had a two-berth compartment to himself and pretended that Bridgy was in the upper berth. In the taxi crossing Paris she was beside him but, when he reached Berkhamsted and entered the Red House, she fled. He had written to Ruth daily while he was in Switzerland and Francis had told her that 'this girl was an excellent first love for Gai', so his mother was ready to embrace him in sympathy, joy and sorrow. He spent hours drafting his first love letter and addressed it, not to Bridgy's home, but to her school, The Cheltenham Ladies' College, although Ruth warned him that the school was likely to intercept it. They did so, forwarding it to her mother who replied telling him that he could, if he wished, write to her from time to time 'for news of the girls'. He had no interest in 'the girls', but wrote none the less and, two months later, received a friendly reply: '[Bridgy's] letters are always gay and she is in the lacrosse team. She is 5ft 9¼ inches now. I do hope she will stop growing—she's not weak—and thank God she can carry herself well'. He wished Bridgy would write him just such 'gay letters'; then he could congratulate her on that extra quarter-inch.

Francis knew no one in Berkhamsted and Ruth's acquaintance extended no further than two old ladies. Gai could have gone out and found friends—found girls—for himself, but he was completely lacking in initiative. Ruth had always done everything for him and he expected her to wave a magic wand and present him with a host of people his own age. She constantly apologised for failing to do so and he was reduced to standing for hours at the window of his room watching the passers-by, dreaming of Bridgy and going almost every afternoon to the local cinema where he could lose himself in fantasies. He had, however, one friend. Peter Heyworth had been in a different House at school and they had not known each other well, but now circumstances and loneliness drew them together. Peter lived on the other side of London, but they met regularly for dinner in Town, talking without respite of life, death, love and the unknown delights of sex. This was a friendship that would endure until Peter's death more than forty years later.

Gai was not entirely idle. In his last six months at Charterhouse he had been working on a novel of school life with the title *Curtain Raiser* and Scot had even offered the use of his private study so that he could write in peace and quiet. Now he had to finish it. 'Sometimes I think it's a work of genius; more often I feel that it's amateurish drivel.' As hero of the novel he split himself into two. On the one hand there was the schoolboy, Marcel Lawrence, 'Marcel' standing for Proust, an author (much admired by Francis) whom he found both boring and fascinating, and 'Lawrence' for D. H. Lawrence; on the other was the Housemaster, the man he thought he might be in his forties—wise, witty, compassionate, a little cynical. He finished it just before leaving for Paris on 1 May and sent it off to Curtis Brown, the literary agents. His hand was shaking when he stuck stamps on the parcel. His whole future depended on the book being published and he had decided that, if he was not a successful novelist by the time he was thirty, he would commit suicide. What alternative did he have? He could never hope to earn a living in any other way nor did he want to.

For an eighteen-year-old, Paris in the Spring should have been very heaven. It was nothing of the kind. He would look back on this period as the most frustrating of his life. He was like a hungry man invited to a splendid banquet but unable to reach out to any of the goodies, paralysed by his own shyness and by his sense of inadequacy amongst people who seemed so sure of themselves. He was, he decided, 'no good at living'. He was to stay for three months as a paying guest with an elderly French couple, the Marquis de Lostanges and his wife, who had rather a grand apartment on the Avenue Bosquet. 'She is a delightful old thing, very talkative. Her husband breaks into the flow to make a joke or a pun, whereupon she exclaims, *"Ravisant! Ravisant!"*' The Marquis himself was exactly Gai's idea of a traditional French aristocrat; wise, charming and kind. He also seemed to embody history. He could remember, as a child, knowing a great-uncle who had a misshapen little finger on one hand acquired when, as a small boy, he was playing on the floor of Marie Antoinette's *boudoir* and the Queen had suddenly moved the little table at which she was writing, crushing his finger.

There was a second paying guest staying in the flat, a Latin American from Bogotá, Luis Saenz. Luis, a student, adored his professor, Jean-Paul Sartre by name, and talked of him constantly. He wanted to introduce Gai to his hero and showed him a photograph of an ugly little man in a grubby raincoat. 'I'm not interested in professors,' he wrote in the diary. 'I'm interested in girls.' Sartre had by then written two or three novels, and Madame warned him not to read them; they were obscene. Seeing the look of doubt on his face, she hurried up to her bedroom and returned with one of the novels in which she had thoughtfully turned down the pages on which the worst obscenities occurred. The offending passages seemed grubby—like the man himself—rather than erotic. Later, of course, Sartre gained cult status as a 'philosopher', having made the remarkable discovery that we exist. Was this an advance on his seventeenth-century predecessor, Descartes, who had discovered that we think?

The intention had been that Gai would attend a course at the Sorbonne on 'French Civilisation' designed for foreigners who might not be aware that France and civilisation were synonymous, while other countries were more or less barbaric. There was a group of beautiful, long-legged American girls in the lecture hall, and Gai waited hungrily for one or other of them to speak to him. It was impossible for him to risk a rebuff by introducing himself to them so he remained hungry. He told Madame about them. 'You would have been in danger,' she said, 'with your dreamy and romantic soul'. After a month he gave up attending the course, not least because Francis had warned Ruth not to give him enough money for him to get into trouble and he needed the 250 francs monthly fee for other purposes.

Luis soon became fond of his shy, introverted fellow lodger and decided to do something to bring him out of himself. He arranged for the two of them to go to a fair with a couple of very young girls he had picked up somewhere. Gai's girl was a bouncy brunette who clung to him on the Big Dipper and asked: *'T'es vicieux, toi?'* Was he vicious? What did she mean and what did one say to that? He had no idea. Luis tried again, deciding that a more intellectual type might suit. Sartre had a habit of seducing his female students, so he persuaded one of the grubby philosopher's discarded mistresses to invite Gai to tea. It was a disaster. Gai did not know why he was there or what was expected of him and the girl was clearly baffled as to why this hopelessly shy Englishman had been landed on her. What did Luis expect her to do with him? Rape him?

All human life was here in Paris, open to exploration, but he spent his time reading voraciously, mainly American novels—

Caldwell, Dos Passos, Faulkner—as well as Proust and going to films, and he developed a mother-son relationship with Madame de Lostanges. 'Madame understands me as I thought only *Maman* did.' He could never have too many mothers, any more than he could have too many girls. He and Ruth wrote to each other at least three times a week, as they had done when he was at school, and the theme now was how much alike—or unalike —they were. She had often quoted to him the saying: 'Life is a comedy to those who think, a tragedy to those who feel'. There could be no doubt as to her, but to which category did he belong? A sentimental thinker, perhaps? A romantic intellectual?

'The difference between us,' she wrote, 'is that I act without thinking, and you think without acting. When a nature like mine comes up against one like yours, the unconscious instinct of A is to dominate B. I saw quite early that a nature like mine could quite easily have a paralysing effect on one like yours'. This was the most perceptive comment she had ever made on their relationship. He would be plagued throughout his life by what he thought of as pathological laziness. But this might have been more accurately defined as paralyses in the face of any need for action, whether it was a matter of seizing an opportunity or of making a simple phone call to fix a meeting with a friend.

A few days later she wrote: 'You are growing remarkably like me. I used to think you had a completely different type of mind to mine. It's a much better one, but just the same type'. This, also, in a way, had some truth in it. Like her, he was intuitive rather than rational. But then she reverted to her image of herself as the primordial mother. 'I seem to be very primitive in my feelings. [When you were small] I would have protected you with my life. I gave all my time and strength; I fed you, licked you and cuffed you. Now I feel you should scratch for yourself and find your own worms. I think that now my affection is for what I believe you to be and for the sympathy that is between us, not for the fact that I bore you.'

Corresponding with Ruth, talking—mainly about himself—with Madame, analysing each day in his diary and reading, time passed pleasantly enough, but he had only to open a door to be in the midst of the glorious city. He stayed at home, effectively paralysed just as Ruth had feared he might be. It never occurred to him to go out in the evenings to bars or clubs (if he could afford them) and meet people. Then, in mid-May, an English girl, the daughter of friends of someone Ruth knew, arrived to stay in Paris with a family and learn French. Her name was Ann and, like him, she was eighteen but years ahead of him in maturity or in the appearance of maturity. They exchanged notes and arranged to meet.

'She's pretty,' he wrote, 'or perhaps more attractive than pretty; intelligent and friendly, nice eyes'. He might have added that she was a very down-to-earth person. She was soon promising to 'cure him of his romanticism', a hopeless task, but now, at last, he had a real girlfriend, not in the present-day sense of the term but simply a friend who was also a girl. From then on they met three or four times a week, sight-seeing, going to films or just talking together in her room or his, none of this conducive to improving their French. 'Strange,' he wrote, 'how being with Ann makes me happy. I don't imagine I'm in love with her, but she is just what I needed. There's something so open and frank and unpretentious about her'. She might be all these things, but to him she was a mystery.

She teased him, and he had never before been teased. 'I'm going to be extremely rude to you,' she would say, 'It's good for you!' He did not know how to take this. He had a photograph he had taken of her enlarged and, when he gave it to her, decided to say something very daring. 'I'm going to kiss it every night before going to bed', he told her, expecting one of two possible reactions. Either there would be a maidenly blush, or else she might say: 'Why not kiss the original?' or something of the sort. Her response floored him. 'In that case it will soon be disgustingly sticky!' He never knew what to expect from her, but he began to suspect that she knew him very well, particularly after she had read the manuscript of his novel *Curtain Raiser*. One evening they passed a loving couple embracing in a doorway. 'If I catch you doing that,' she said, 'I'll stick a pin in you or, if I'm not there, you'll come running to tell me: "It's happened at last!"' That was exactly what he would have done but it was disconcerting to find that she knew.

One sultry afternoon they sat side-by-side on his bed, two virgins wondering what 'it' was really like but not yet ready to find out. The tension was almost tangible and Gai fell silent. She began to laugh. 'What are you laughing at?' he asked. 'Us,' she said. What did she mean by that? Later she asked what he was thinking about. In a strangled voice he said: 'I was thinking I would like to kiss you. Would I get a slap in the face?' 'Of course you would.' Absurdly, he thought she meant it. The relationship trembled on the verge of something more, each waiting on the other and neither of them making a move. On 8 July she returned to England. It would be nearly five years before they met again.

The de Lostanges family moved to their summer home in Saint-Germain-en-Laye, a little town overlooking Paris and in the midst of a magnificent forest. The house and garden were a delight, but it was here that he felt the most bitter sense of isolation. The de Lostanges' daughter, a tough, sophisticated businesswoman, joined them with her husband. Her friends were frequent visitors, and he was aware that these people disliked him, though he did not know why. Trying to be helpful, Madame kept reproaching him for what she called his 'glacial air', but the more he felt himself disliked, the more dislikable he became; distant, aloof, tongue-tied and, no doubt, with an appearance of arrogance. His hosts' grandchild, eight-year-old Marie-Lou, told him: '*Maman* and *Papa* don't like you, but I love you', and she asked her grandmother: 'Do you think, when I'm big, there will be husbands like Gai? I would like to have a husband just so'. He had to take what comfort he could from a child's love, telling himself that children were more perceptive than adults, but this was humiliating.

Curtis Brown chose this moment to return the manuscript of *Curtain Raiser* to him. They thought it better than Alec Waugh's *The Loom of Youth*, the classic school novel written by a schoolboy, but—that 'but' was like a bullet fired into the heart— publishers were taking no risks with war on the horizon. The foundation stone of his future life as a novelist had gone. He must persevere or go to the wall so he planned a new novel, a story of young love. A beautiful, utterly lovable Canadian heiress had come to stay for a few days and allowed him to hold her hand. The hideous young man with her was—according to Madame— set on marrying her for her money. Was there no one to shoot him dead? Here, heaven-sent, was a theme for the novel. 'Gai must be tired', Luis told Madame. 'He gave birth to a young girl during the night'. 'How is that?' she asked. 'Is Gai the new Adam?'

Ruth and Francis were on holiday in the Swiss resort of Caux and the plan had been for him to join them for their final week. He had hardly seen a newspaper for a couple of months and he had no radio, so he was astonished on 20 August to receive a telegram warning him: 'Do not come'. On the 24th General Mobilisation of the French army was announced. He had gone into Paris for the day and thought he detected an atmosphere of despair. 'I believe there will be war and we'll be defeated', he wrote. That evening there was another telegram from his father: 'Be ready to leave for England, Saturday the 26th'. After hasty farewells he met his parents on their way through Paris and they went on together to Calais. There was chaos on the docks and there were no porters. He and Francis between them dragged two cabin trunks up the gangway onto the crowded deck and sat on them. Exhausted, they arrived at the Lord Warden Hotel in Folkestone and Ruth ordered tea. 'I am sorry, Madam', said the pompous waiter, 'but we do not serve teas after five o'clock'. Gai could guess the expression in Ruth's eyes as she rose to her feet. The waiter retreated, then ran through the baize doors into the kitchen with Ruth in pursuit. She returned to announce that he had taken refuge in the oven, a big oven for baking bread. Tea was served within minutes.

He drove into London from Berkhamsted on 1 September and was confronted with a newspaper placard: Germany Invades Poland. He went at once to Lincoln's Inn and Francis, normally a benign but distant presence, took command as though reinvigorated by the prospect of war. The eagerness of fathers of that generation to offer up their beloved sons as sacrifices to the war god (as in the famous case of Rudyard Kipling) must seem strange nowadays, but within thirty minutes they were in the Inns of Court OTC (Officers Training Corps) recruiting office facing the Colonel in command, who treated Francis with such respect that Gai, who felt like a lamb led to the slaughter, realised for the first time how important his father was in these circles. The Colonel was anxious to please. Of course he would be only too happy to accept Colonel Errington's step-son in the OTC. He was sent for a medical examination and failed on the grounds of his short sight. They returned to Berkhamsted and this curious incident was never mentioned again nor did Ruth hear of it. Forty-eight hours later Britain declared war on Germany. 'I listened to the King's speech on the wireless, a lot of fine words.' Soon afterwards, he wrote: 'A disgusting speech by President Roosevelt, the coward has turned coat; America neutral'. Within a few hours everyone in the streets was carrying a gas mask slung over their shoulders and the police were in tin helmets, expecting an air raid which might destroy London that same night.

Nothing happened, but there was a panic evacuation of children from the East End of London, where the docks were an obvious target. Ruth and Francis were told to expect the imminent arrival of eight children, but they never arrived. Gai drove over to Bedford, where Goo and Eleanor now lived. They had been ordered at short notice to take in two families; two slovenly women with four 'brats' between them, dirty and undisciplined. They were however as displeased with their hosts as their hosts were with them and returned home after a few days, preferring to face bombs rather than live in such an alien household. But who was going to live and who was going to die? For the moment the dying was far away in Poland and, at the time, no one really cared about the Poles. Before the advent of television, wars in distant places did not seem real.

Francis was showing the first signs of age. It was as though he was visibly drying up. One night when Gai was saying goodnight to Ruth she told him: 'In Caux one evening when I walked with Father to a seat overlooking the Lake and watched the sun setting over the water I had a premonition that this was the last time we would ever watch the sunset together, and I began to cry. He started to talk about the servant problem if war came'. Francis had always been careful with money, to say the least, turning down the offer of a judgeship with a knighthood attached to it since this would involve a reduction in his earnings or, so he told Ruth, 'because Swiss hotel managers would put up their prices on sight of me'. Although she professed not to care, Ruth might have enjoyed being Lady Errington. Now he was obsessed with the fear of poverty, although — in terms of present-day values — he was a millionaire. When the cost of the evening newspaper rose from one penny to a penny-halfpenny he stopped delivery.

On 9 October Gai arrived in Cambridge to read history. He had two years ahead of him before being called up, assuming that the war had not ended by then. In peacetime he would have had three years in which to obtain his BA, and it was often said that the third year was the best, but everything was in disorder now and the future was hidden in dark clouds. Unaware that the process of 'growing up' takes a lifetime, however long one may live, he was impatient to reach that constantly receding point at which one can say: 'I've arrived!' He decided that he did not like being eighteen. 'This is a lousy age to be; too old to be unconscious, too young to be wise. Callow — that's the term so often applied to it. Superficial judgement, since there is seldom a firm foundation upon which to build a personality at this age. A chrysalis stage, but the unfortunate pupa is wide awake.' What kind of insect would eventually emerge into the daylight, a butterfly or a wasp; or perhaps some strange hybrid, neither one thing nor the other?

GAI AT CAMBRIDGE

Under normal circumstances the University would have provided a memorable and a formative experience, but this was wartime and, so far as Gai was concerned, these two years were overshadowed by what was to come. His sharpest memory of Cambridge would be of nights spent firewatching in a little room at the top of one of the spires of King's Chapel, exchanging news with other watchers in other high places, their voices carrying over the sleeping town in which no chink of light was visible. The darkness—every window 'blacked out'—took him back to an earlier age before electricity came to dim the stars.

He had made a mistake in deciding to read history. He was passionately interested in stories, in drama, in personalities and, ultimately, in heroes. That was what he had thought history was about, but this view was out of fashion, indeed it was despised by the historians of the time as 'schoolboy history'. If the brilliant young dons who would normally have taught him had stayed on there they might, conceivably, have aroused his interest in social and economic history, but they were whisked away after the first few months to make their contribution to the war effort. Jack

Plumb, who had interviewed him for entry to King's and who would later be recognised as an outstanding historian, went to Bletchley Park to decipher German codes and others disappeared into thin air. They were replaced by several distinguished old gentlemen. He was taught economics by Clapham and Pigou. These two had been eminent figures in the early years of the century, always opposed to each other, but in 1918 they had been cast into the shadows by John Maynard Keynes, the dominant figure in this field for many years to come. Now they had returned from the grave. In alternate tutorials, Clapham explained to Gai why he should take no notice of anything Pigou told him, and Pigou warned him not to take Clapham seriously. Economics remained a closed book to him.

He was condemned to study English constitutional history in the eighteenth century, the manorial system in twelfth-century England, European social history in the late Middle Ages and kindred subjects. He could not decide which was the more boring, particularly now when life, love and death were the only realities, and he felt a sense of outrage at being expected to waste precious time on such trivial studies. Where were the great men, the kings and queens who had lived their dramas on a Shakespearean scale, the mighty battles which had decided the fate of the world? The crisis came one afternoon when he had been at Cambridge for three months. He had in front of him a heavy volume on constitutional history and had read a few pages when he realised that that he had not taken in a single word. The book might as well have been written in Chinese. He re-read the page before him three, four, five times, and still it was meaningless. He closed the book and that was the end of it. He never opened another book on his set course, but he did attend lectures fairly regularly and squirrelled away in his memory any facts which aroused a minimum of interest and set him thinking. He knew that his chances of getting through the Tripos examinations depended upon his being able to speculate interestingly on the basis of the few facts he knew. But did it matter, since his life might soon be cut short?

He made friends or rather close acquaintances, including four young men who were expected to become major figures in the world. Francis Noel Baker cleared the Cambridge Labour Club of Communists by sheer political skill and was bound to become Prime Minister one day. After the 1945 election he was the youngest MP in the House of Commons, but nothing came of it. Donald Bain was sure to be an outstanding writer, but was never heard of again. Alain John, who fed Gai on calcium tablets to make him more lively, was a sculptor of great talent but was killed in the war. Charles Shute, one of the most brilliant minds he would ever meet and a social lion, went on to become a distinguished scientist. There were six or seven others who were pleasant company, including an Indian, Majumdar, who frequently brought his friends to Gai's room insisting that he read the poems of T. S. Eliot to them. Eventually he knew *The Waste Land* almost by heart. And then there was Vivad, a Siamese from a wealthy family. His idea of cheering Gai up when he was feeling so ill with flu that he would not have noticed had Helen of Troy walked naked into the room was to bring him a pile of French pornographic magazines. But his only real friend was still Peter Heyworth, who came to stay at the Red House on several occasions and visited him at King's whenever he could. In his second year the Charterhouse trio—Rodney, Ronny and Bobby— came up to Cambridge and were immediately more important to him than any of his new acquaintances. Remembering the agonies he had gone through at school trying to think of things to say to Bobby, he was amazed to find how easy it was now; Life (always with a capital 'L'), their hopes and fears for the future and, of course, sex were interests they shared.

Gai joined the Union, the Political Club and the ADC (Amateur Dramatic Club), having distinguished himself at Charterhouse playing the Abbot in Auden and Isherwood's *Ascent of F6*. He also joined the Cambridge Liberal Club simply because he was asked to do so by the young woman in charge and could think of no reason to decline. He was promptly made Treasurer, supposedly managing the paltry funds raised each year by a dance at the Dorothy Café and deposited with him in an old toffee tin by a shy girl who simply said: 'This is for you,' so that he imagined he had a secret admirer until, one day, he fancied a toffee and opened the tin to find £125 in cash. In March of 1940 an international Students' Congress was held in Leeds and he attended as the Cambridge Liberal Club delegate. The proceedings were dominated by H. G. Wells, by now old and sick but restored to bouncing virility by the presence of so many adoring (and adorable) young girls.

This was the period of the 'phoney war'. The Soviet Union had a non-aggression pact with Germany, so the Communists, who dominated the Congress, were opposed to the 'imperialist war': 'They sit in a *bloc*', Gai wrote, 'they clap as a *bloc*, they feed as a *bloc* and speak as a *bloc*, all saying the same thing, one after another. Do they sleep and dream as a *bloc*?' When they sang the *Internationale* the Conservatives, for some mysterious reason, responded by singing *Deutschland über Alles*. After five days of argument and serious frivolity, the Congress voted to end the war at once. The British press took this up as evidence of the degeneracy of the younger generation, and 'Lord Haw-Haw', the Irish Nazi propagandist, crowed in triumph on the radio. At that moment it was difficult to see what purpose was served by continuing the war. Poland was lost, swallowed up by Germany and the Soviets. On the Western front there was stalemate. The persecution of the Jews in Germany was public knowledge, but few people cared.

In retrospect, the interesting question is whether the vote would have been different had the extermination camps been foreseen. Probably not. At that time a belief in eugenics was widespread, regarded as the logical conclusion of Darwinism. If evolution was to continue, inferior breeds must be eliminated.

H. G. Wells himself (a 'scientific socialist') had written in an early book that, in the ideal society, scientists would have to exterminate unwanted people, 'the weak and silly and pointless types', because the scientists 'will have an ideal that will make the killing worth the while', leaving only those 'capable of living fully and beautifully'. Hitler could not have said it better. Wells had also been in favour of eliminating the 'swarms of black, brown, dirty white and yellow people'. Genocide was the practical application of Darwinism. If the ruling principle of life was the survival of the fittest, then who could doubt that the white race was the fittest to survive? Had they not conquered the world?

Was Gai fit to survive? Someone had given him an introduction to a well-known screen writer, Ian Dalrymple, to whom he had sent the manuscript of *Curtain Raiser*. A letter awaited him when he returned to Cambridge, a letter which destroyed what little confidence he had in his future as a novelist. Dalrymple came straight to the point. 'Your work is rather boring, but young intellectuals tend to be boring. You must not overestimate its significance or yours. Your excuse for wanting it published is either insincere bumptiousness or an illusion. You may, with any luck, emerge from the morbid and somewhat nauseating pre-occupation with yourself. You'll have done, I hope, a decent job by then and been cured of your introspection. I'm saying things that will either wound you or else bounce off your conceit'. The letter continued on the same lines but ended on an unexpected note: 'I'm every bit as egotistical as yourself, and it does us no harm to realise the truth about ourselves'. Stunned as he was, Gai wondered if Dalrymple had been motivated by subjective factors, but the wound would never completely heal.

The 'phoney war' continued for another six weeks. It ended with a bang. On 10 May Germany invaded Holland and Belgium, making the French defences—the Maginot line—irrelevant. Churchill replaced Chamberlain as Prime Minister and, on the 14th, made his famous 'Blood, sweat and tears' speech. 'I've always admired Churchill, even if he is an old scallywag. He's the nearest thing we've got to the romantic conception of a Great Man.' On the 15th Gai wrote in his diary: 'Slept badly. At 7 a.m. I heard from the radio across the road that Holland has capitulated. I lay for an hour thinking of the war, of getting a bullet in my belly (or below), of being crushed under a tank'. But life went on. This was followed by another entry: 'Punting on the river with Jo Wiseman and Peggy; pleasant, though the girl really is rather repulsive'.

On 18 May General Gamelin, the French Commander, issued an Order of the Day. 'The fate of our country and that of our Allies, the destinies of the world, depend on the battle now in progress. Any soldier who cannot advance should allow himself to be killed rather than abandon that part of our national soil which has been entrusted to him.' A few days later Gamelin was replaced. At the end of the month it was announced that the University was to 'go down', in other words to close, so that the students could make their small contribution to the defence of their country, and on June 1st the British army and some French units were evacuated from Dunkirk but without their armament. Then, on the 14th, with dreadful inevitability, Paris surrendered to the enemy. Ruth and Gai wept in each other's arms, feeling the shock as surely as if they had been physically abused. 'We thought of the pollution of our beloved city', he wrote. 'Think of the *Bosche* leaving their filthy excrement on French soil!' A few days later the aged Marshall Petain took over the government of France and, on the 21st announced in words that sent a chill down the spine: 'I have been in touch with the enemy during the night . . .' In horror movies the real horrors always happen at night. France had surrendered. Ruth's friend, a certain Madame Rollet, came to see her, red-eyed and almost hysterical. An Englishwoman she knew had told her that this was a judgement on the French for neglecting the Sabbath.

It was not only France that had been defeated. So had Britain.

It was impossible to deny this. The Island was virtually unarmed and the enemy was less than thirty miles away, needing only a few weeks to prepare for invasion. It was said that Churchill, after his 'No surrender' speech, had put his hand over the microphone, adding: 'and hit them over the head with beer bottles as that's all we have'. This was gallant but crazy. The Soviet Union was out of the picture and there was not one chance in a hundred that the United States would enter the war. Even the material aid they were providing, at an extortionate price, was a foolish waste according to Joe Kennedy, the American Ambassador in London; the country, he reported, 'did not have a hope in hell' of surviving. On the other hand Hitler was prepared to make peace on very favourable terms, or so it was said, allowing Britain to keep her Empire, and that was the crucial point. What was Britain without her Empire? Nothing. A small, overcrowded offshore island with a foul climate, fit only to sink beneath the waves over which she had once ruled. With it, she was still a Great Power. Reason dictated that this opportunity should be grasped with both hands and there were reasonable men in the Government. Lord Halifax, who had missed becoming Prime Minister by a whisker, was all for peace. Churchill, almost single-handedly, kicked common-sense aside, but so did many people in the country. Comparisons have sometimes been made between Britain and Japan, two isolated island peoples, warrior peoples, who prefer death to dishonour. The country was in a *Kamikaze* mood.

Ashridge Hospital, close to Berkhamsted, was filled with the wounded from Dunkirk, including French soldiers. Ruth and Gai visited the hospital and she talked at length with the French, holding back her tears. She promised one of them, who was clearly in very great pain, that she would return with fruit for him. 'You must not inconvenience yourself, Madame (*Ne faut pas vous deranger*)', he whispered. Travelling on the underground, a workman in overalls grasped Gai's arm: 'That 'Itler! 'Oo does 'ee think 'ee is? Went through the last war, I did. Think that scum is going to rule us? Me, I'll fight to the finish'. Gai joined the Home Guard. It has been caricatured as 'Dad's Army', but in fact every able-bodied man who was not in the forces or otherwise engaged joined to learn how to repel the invaders, and nobody joked about it. They were shown how to fill beer bottles with petrol, stuffing a rag into the mouth of the bottle, prepared to climb on top of tanks and drop these improvised bombs through the hatch. They planted telegraph poles in open fields in the hope of wrecking German transport planes as they tried to land. It was good for morale. At least they were doing something.

He had not only joined the Home Guard, he had also fallen in love again. Next door to Goo and Eleanor in Bedford lived a couple with three daughters, the middle one an eighteen-year-old called Brenda. Gai must have seen her sometimes as a child, but it was only in July 1940 that he became aware of her existence when her father invited him to come round to play ping-pong. He was struck immediately by her likeness to Bridgy, 'tall with long, curly brown hair, rippling hair, a lovely voice such as one rarely finds in an English girl, and tremendously lively'. She had a joyous vitality that delighted him and he was bursting with happiness. 'Do you never do anything but laugh?' she asked him. He noted: 'I came back to Goo and Eleanor's tired with laughing, feeling fully alive for the first time in months'. Her father's family had come originally from Portugal—they were Sephardic Jews—and her mother was an Englishwoman. Goo and Eleanor saw one side of her: a typical healthy, cheerful English girl, just the right cure for Gai's peculiar nature. In his eyes she had a touch of the exotic, as though a spark of the warm South had enlivened her English clay.

The following evening they went to the movies together. 'I put a cautious arm round her, so cautious that, afraid to move, it got pins and needles.' She insisted that she was going to pay and slipped a half-crown into his pocket, then fled. He chased her, grabbed her and forced the money back on her. This game continued for a while, chasing each other, both of them laughing and shouting. Hearing them go past, her father, failing to recognise his daughter's voice, said to his wife: 'Listen to those disgusting soldiers chasing girls down the street!' Gai returned to Bedford —he was always welcome to stay with Goo and Eleanor—three weeks later and took Brenda out again. Returning, they stopped at her gate to say goodnight. 'I kissed her—O Boy, O Boy!—I kissed her not five minutes ago, and twice!' The diary was always up to date. 'How surprised she'd be to know she is the first girl I've kissed properly, but that's something I shall keep to myself, at least until it no longer matters.' Now he had another icon to add to Bridgy in the snow, although this time the background was an ordinary street in an ordinary English town, framing a girl with laughing eyes under a street lamp. This was the first time a boy had kissed a girl since the creation of the world. If he had been foolish enough to say this to anyone he might have responded to their mockery by telling them: 'Be patient! In fifty years' time all will be revealed'. He would often remind people, when he was in his seventies, how personal his books were, but they would never know just how personal, how the sentiments of youth had been transformed and incorporated into the philosophy which he somehow fitted into an Islamic framework.

Crudely summarised, the argument would have gone something like this. The basic principle of Islam is *Tawhíd*, the absolute Oneness of God, and this is reflected in the uniqueness of each human creature, each a potential 'Viceroy of God on earth'. It follows that the experience of the individual is also unique; nothing that happens to him or her has ever happened before. Moreover, the ultimate Creator of events is God Himself, for how could any event, however seemingly trivial, be independent of the One Reality as though isolated in the midst of nothingness and fading into nothingness? Since God is, by definition, infinite as well as absolute, He never repeats Himself.

Even if there were millions of worlds in which He chose to express what is within His 'treasury', no moment of time or beyond time as we know it could be a repetition of the previous moment. In other words, everything is new, freshly minted, and the notion we have of the 'commonplace' only demonstrates our unawareness. So the young man's feeling that this kiss was without precedent would ultimately be validated.

There were to be more kisses and better still—more exciting and more intimate—there were wrestling matches on the carpet of Goo and Eleanor's living-room, watched with approval by the two women ('So nice to see Gai relax!') One evening Brenda succeeded in grabbing the diary, having first asked if she might read it and been refused. She was quite as strong as Gai and it took him several minutes to wrest the precious volume from her, after which they lay side-by-side on the floor, gasping for breath and laughing. The scent of her body was on him. He could not remember when, if ever, he had been so happy, and the world beyond that room, the world at war, did not exist. But it was still there. The *Blitz* was by now under way, a savage competition between the destroyers, the *Luftwaffe*, and the destroyers of the destroyers, the R.A.F. People followed the daily count of German planes shot down just as, later, they would follow the football results.

Hitler had abandoned the idea of a sea invasion and the attempt to wipe out British airfields had not destroyed the country's air power, such as it was. He had now turned his attention to the cities, particularly London, in the hope of bombing the people into submission. Berkhamsted was thirty miles from London and safe from the *Blitz*, but it was unthinkable for Gai to miss such an historic event. He made frequent trips into Town, often staying overnight in Mall Chambers, the little flat Ruth had first rented at the beginning of the century. 'I find the bombs stimulating', he wrote, 'until I remember how much suffering they cause'. At first the mass of people sleeping in the Underground stations were a strange sight, but very soon this seemed the most natural thing in the world and he noticed them no more than one notices people in the street. Stepping over sprawled legs on his way back by Underground either to the flat or to catch the last train home, his thoughts were of Brenda.

On 7 September, after a good dinner, he looked up and noticed that the sky to the east was a peculiar shade of red, matching the last glimmer of sunset. This meant that a wide area must be on fire, so he set off in that direction as a '*Blitz* tourist'. He took a bus as far as he could and then began to walk. 'The sirens went and people started to run in the opposite direction to me. By then I had lost my way and, in any case, the atmosphere of panic aroused all my cussedness. I carried on as fast as I could, and soon I was alone in deserted streets, the glow in the sky brightening as darkness fell. I came to an interminable street winding between huge warehouses. A few screaming bombs fell not far away, but by now there was nothing I could do except carry on and the desire to see the flames became an obsession. At one point I was turned back by the police so headed down-river, passing along the only street that was not blocked. The smoke began to tickle my nostrils and light spray from the fire hoses fell on me. Then I came into sight of the fire itself; great liquid-seeming flames curling up into the smoke. I looked up at Mars, shining perfectly red through the smoke. Down another street my way was blocked by hoses till a man at the door of a warehouse told me: "Better come in 'ere mate. It's private, but you'd better come in". So in I went and, a moment later, a small high explosive bomb exploded in the street, rocking the building and knocking the man flat. Having lit up the docks with incendiaries in the afternoon, the bombers had returned.

'I asked where I was and was told I was on Wapping Wall, and I had no choice but to stay there. This turned out to be a large pepper warehouse and with me were some fifteen people who had been rescued by water from their burning homes. One of them, a woman, was weeping not because she had lost her home but because her pet monkey, terrified by the fire, had bitten her for the first time in its life. Everyone friendly and rather amused that I had chosen to come to a place from which they only wished to escape. "Them docks is a bleeding mess all the way down", they told me, and the barges on Greenwich Reach were all aflame. Firemen took it in turn to come in for five minutes' rest and a drink to moisten their parched throats. I went to the door from time to time, determined to miss nothing of this adventure, and saw two incendiaries fall on the warehouse opposite, then the next building to us was hit, and by now it was as light as day in the white radiance of the incendiaries. Finally I settled down uncomfortably on the sacks of peppercorn, wishing I had Brenda there to cuddle, while bombs shook the building in a dull, muffled way.'

When Gai returned to the Red House next day, Ruth admitted that, in his place, she would have done just what he had done. Meanwhile the house had come to resemble a tomb. Francis still went to his Chambers every day. The trains to and from London often took two hours on the journey, stopping and starting as the bombs fell and, by the time he sat down to dinner with Gai and Ralph—Ruth was again bedridden—he was in such a state of exhaustion that it was difficult to understand how he could carry on. He would push a tiny piece of meat and a boiled potato round his plate, but he seemed to have given up eating and was too tired to speak. Ralph, of course, had nothing to say, and the young maid who served them, her face as white as the little cap she wore, spoke only in a whisper as though in Church. Gai wrapped himself in daydreams, always of a tropical beach and a beautiful tropical girl, but the need to escape became almost overwhelming.

On 29 December he dined with Peter Heyworth in an underground restaurant, the Trocadero, and the bottle of wine they shared had its effect. The building shook under the impact of the bombing and it was obvious that a major raid was in progress.

Gai had a kind of premonition that this was the Big Night, not to be missed, and, when they came out into the street, muzzy with wine, he persuaded an unwilling Peter to accompany him in the direction of the red sky. They came to the fires, such fires as had not been seen in London for three hundred years. This time it was not the docks that were burning but the City, the financial centre of the world. People stood staring at the flames as though transfixed. 'We observed their flame-lit faces, completely impassive. All the fury of chaos might be hurled against the human race and you would still see these faces—watching! What power can gods or devils have against such stubborn flesh?' He and Peter walked on, along an avenue of fire, and came to St Paul's, settling on a bench against the towering wall of the Cathedral. The most enduring photograph of the *Blitz*, still regularly reproduced in the press, was of St Paul's that night—untouched as though eternal—against the background of flame and smoke. Had it shown the base of the Cathedral, it would have included two tiny human figures watching history in the making. This was the last Great Fire. Hitler had done his worst, and the spirit of the people had not been broken.

The diary waxed fat. Long afterwards, taking up the 1940 volume which he had not looked at for half a century, he was appalled to find that it ran to more than 300,000 words, equivalent to two substantial books. Every meeting with a fellow creature was recorded and analysed but in old age he could not fault this, having come to believe that every meeting is predestined, therefore significant. Brenda and the *Blitz* ranked as equally important, though perhaps Brenda had the edge. 'I suppose it's a vanity', he wrote, 'though I must be allowed one vanity, this feeling that I immortalise those with whom I come into contact. God knows, if I were Keeper of the Gates of Heaven, there would be a crowd flooding in. Some pious person, in a position to do so, should recommend me for the post!' He could never take himself entirely seriously despite all the solemn self-analysis. Like everyone else he was a figure of fun. Death, he thought at the time, makes fools of us all and of all our pretensions, and one day the diary itself would be consumed by fire. That fire had a name: Time. There must, he knew, be something permanent, something beyond time, but he still had no idea what this might be.

The University was again open for business, and Gai returned to King's on 7 October. An entry in the diary prefigures a belief which he formulated long afterwards but which dated back to his childhood. 'We are the writing on a slate and cannot influence the hand that writes. We are the silent observers of our own lives. Consciousness comes to watch the unfolding of an individual life, then departs again when the performance is over. It is as passive as a film audience. Behind all this there must be a cause for joy.' And soon afterwards there was indeed cause for joy, an eight-page letter from Brenda, most of it copied word-for-word into the diary. 'Now a lecture for you. I don't know how to say it, but it goes something like this. If you want more fun out of life when you're with your own set—Let yourself go! Don't be so perfect! One may admire good manners and gallant attentions, but there's an art in being untidy, unconventional and rude, and still being a gentleman. You aren't natural!' Gai took the point and absorbed the lecture, so much more important than any lecture the University offered, but he was now involved in a more weighty correspondence.

Quite exceptionally, *The Times Literary Supplement* devoted a whole page to a review by the poet Edwin Muir of a novel by L. H. Myers, *The Root and the Flower*. The author was described as the only truly philosophical novelist writing in English. Gai got the novel at once and was more deeply impressed than he had ever been before by any book he had read. It almost seemed as though the author was his *alter ego*, himself writ large, but this man must have come to terms with himself and achieved a state of unshakeable peace. The story was set in India at the time of the emperor Akbar, but the characters were not Indians; they were modern Europeans thinly disguised, their characters both magnified and clarified by the exotic setting. This was an opportunity for acute and devastating social comment, specifically on the British upper classes amongst whom Myers had spent most of his life. Gai wrote at once to the author and received a prompt reply. Within a few weeks they were corresponding regularly and it became clear that Leo Myers, at the age of sixty-three, also felt that he had met his *alter ego* in this nineteen-year-old.

The letters were not as Gai had expected. There was no peace in them, on the contrary he detected a note of inner torment, almost of desperation. His letter had, in fact, reached Myers at a critical moment. At sixty-two he had turned savagely on the society to which his wealth and charm had given him easy access, writing to his old friends telling them, with cruel brevity, that he wished to have nothing more to do with them. He would, he had decided, live the life of a recluse, devoting his remaining years to caring for his sick wife to whom he had been constantly unfaithful for forty years. As he might have foreseen, the result of this sacrifice was bitter loneliness, and it was at this point that Gai's letter came to hand, demonstrating—so it seemed to Myers—an extraordinary intuitive understanding of his nature and of his deepest feelings. It was not long before Gai felt able to say to him: 'It seems to me, if I may judge from your letters, that you have put all the serenity you possess into your books, leaving none for yourself'. He might have added, 'and all your wisdom too'. Leo Myers replied: 'I think your comment was shrewd and probably true'. The correspondence would continue until Myers' death.

Early in the new year Brenda dropped him. It was some while before Gai understood that she had put him to a kind of test and he had failed it. She was interested in another boy and brought the two of them together. Instead of trying to hold his ground he had withdrawn into himself, still haunted by Rodney's question when they were at school: 'What sort of girl do you think would like you?' How could he compete? Anyway, it would be undignified to do so. His fragile self-confidence was not helped by contact with some very sophisticated people in the university. Today they might have been described as the Cambridge *glitterati*. He himself would have liked nothing better than to glitter, but he was convinced that he had a very dull sheen. The fact that, under the smooth veneer, they might suffer from their own insecurities never crossed his mind. Charles Shute introduced him to John Lehman, the editor of New Writing in which the cream of *avant garde* stories and essays were published, but Gai never dared offer to contribute. He played the 'Demon King' in the Christmas Pantomime — *The Sleeping Cutie* — produced by Dadie Rylands, probably the best-known figure in Cambridge at that time, an aesthete on the grand scale who knew 'everyone', but he had no idea how to profit from the contact. He felt inept in the presence of such people and tormented himself on account of this ineptitude. 'What a useless idiot I am!'

Even with less intimidating people — apart from the Charterhouse trio — he could not be open about his hopes and ambitions. They might be ridiculous, but they were his. One day, queuing up for a movie with a very serious-minded friend, John Robson, he was asked what these hopes and ambitions were. When he hesitated, Robson tried to help him out. 'For example, do you want to read certain particular books in your lifetime?' The question appalled him. Read books? He wanted to live Life (with the usual capital 'L'). If he had felt able to answer honestly he would have had to say something like this: 'Apart from being a successful novelist, I want to start by bumming my way round America, hopping freight cars just as the poet W. E. Davies did or like the characters in Dos Passos' novels, loving many women, suffering joy and torment at their hands. I want to live for a while in a brothel in New Orleans and become the friend and confidant of the girls (as well as being the lover of the most choice among them). From there, provided I am famous by then, I might go to

Hollywood and sample its delights before travelling on to a South Sea Island, preferably Raratonga, where the girls must surely be children of nature such as Ruth always admired. Then it will be time to find holy men in the Himalayas and join them in meditation before proceeding to China in search of a true Taoist Master. Fulfilled, I will retire with my beautiful wife to my home in the Swiss mountains to write all about it'. This would have been a fairly accurate summary of what he asked of life.

He was living on four levels, which kept him busy and left no time for course-work: the war, girls, his philosophical correspondence with Leo Myers in which he appeared mature beyond his years, and plans for what he called *The Voyage* (the title of a novel by Charles Morgan). Hours were spent poring over maps of the world, tracing his route, amending it, refining it. Travel to distant places meant, he thought, being able to change colour like a chameleon and enter into different personalities. That was freedom, true freedom. To be trapped within the person he was seemed like a kind of imprisonment. But between the present and the day he could set off on his voyage stood the huge, dark bulk of military service. Very soon he would be absorbed into the army, and he could not guess how long it would be before he could emerge from it into the daylight (if he ever did emerge).

Meanwhile, he needed to be in love again. There was a pretty girl called Kathy who taught ballroom dancing to undergraduates and had a flat in King's Parade which she shared with a friend, Mary. This pair had been integrated into university life, and Gai found a warm refuge in their flat. He knew he was not really in love with her. If the term had been current at the time he might have said that he 'fancied' her. She, for her part, liked him and understood him, but that was all. His kisses were tolerated rather than welcomed. Like Brenda, Kathy told him about himself, his favourite subject. 'You're someone who will always be spoiled', she said. That was a sound prediction. A time would come when he wondered why this was so and concluded that it was a case of God 'tempering the wind to the shorn lamb'. His apparent helplessness persuaded the most unexpected people to protect him and fight his battles for him. The diary also records a particular conversation. He had told Kathy, who was a kind girl, that she need not concern herself with the fact that he loved her. That, he said, was his business and need not concern her. 'But I can't keep taking and not giving in return', she said. 'I'm the best judge of what I get out of it!' 'You're an odd person, Gai.' 'Am I excused on that score?' he asked. 'One always has to excuse you,' she said, ' that's the whole trouble'. This too amounted to a prediction. Years later Peter told him: 'You have an extraordinary capacity for getting away with murder!' In any case, he had decided that unrequited love was the most intense kind of love. The troubadour asked nothing of his Lady except the right to worship her.

Such preoccupations seem, in retrospect, preferable to the more dangerous obsessions of the politically aware. The Left had considerable influence among the undergraduates and many of their ideas percolated down through society over the next thirty years, emerging as the theories of what became known as the 'loony Left'. Gai toyed briefly with socialism, but found that the university socialists could be divided into two groups. On the one hand were those whose love for 'the people' precluded any concern for individuals, on the other were the authoritarians who believed in social engineering. Both groups had only contempt for anyone who did not share their faith, and both tended to be unkind to their friends and rude to servants (on the grounds that servants should not exist in a just society). Neither of them trusted 'the people', real people, and both were convinced that they knew best.

The Tripos examinations came and went, and Gai scraped through with a Third Class Honours degree, sometimes known as a 'Gentleman's Third'. When he said his farewells he was close to tears and believed he was taking leave of good and enduring friends, but few of them were remembered for more than a year or two. 'Goodbye, I expect we'll meet as refugees in Canada', said one of them. There were many who dreamed of escaping German occupation by fleeing across the Atlantic, even if that involved rowing the whole way in a small boat.

Gai returned home and the Red House closed in on him. 'Father is breaking up,' he wrote, 'too worn out to do anything but sit in the Library staring straight ahead of him. He should have died before now'. Ruth described old age as 'that most loathsome of all diseases'. Why did the body cling to life when it should have the sense, the decency, to give itself gratefully back to the earth? She had always been in favour of euthanasia for the aged, whether they wanted it or not, and she planned her own suicide when the time was right.

Thinking about the future Gai, like everyone else, tended in practice to discount the war. Nothing was achieved by expecting death in battle, anticipating a German invasion or assuming that the war would go on for years and years. That would reduce every plan to the level of idle fantasy. Meanwhile nubile girls were like sparks of light in a world that was dark and full of menace. In a few months' time Gai would be a soldier. He had imagined himself in many roles, many identities, but this was not one of them. What concerned him and filled him with horror was less the prospect of fighting than the loss of liberty. He would be under orders, his days and even his nights controlled by others. Freedom, his deepest ambition, was as distant as ever, and so was his voyage. Life, real life, had not yet begun and would not begin until he was free.

7

M I L I T A R Y

It was a bright summer. That, at least, was how he would always remember it. In the course of his travels he would hump his diaries (much as the Old Man had 'humped his swag') from Jamaica to Egypt, to India, to Africa and to Trinidad; some were humble notebooks covering a few months, others fat volumes taking in at least a couple of years. It was surprising that only two were lost (together with a sheaf of Conan Doyle's letters to Uncle Bert), but one of these covered the period July 1941 to December of the same year. Recollection must briefly replace the archive.

He spent three months in Berkhamsted before his call-up. Petrol rationing prevented him seeking freedom in the car, but there was something better. A family at the back of the Common had stables with three horses for hire. While he was a schoolboy Francis had tried to encourage him to take up various sports and paid for his lessons in fencing, golf, tennis and, when they were on holiday together in Northumberland, fly-fishing. None of these really seized him, but, from childhood, he had liked horses and one Easter holiday they had stayed in a riding school where a retired Cavalry officer put him through his paces. Now he had Honey at his disposal, a gentle, rather meditative mare, with whom he rode out to Ivanhoe Beacon from where he and his mount could survey three counties and try not to visualise German troops marching across the peaceful countryside. Honey was a good companion and left him free to pursue his own thoughts.

When possible he met Peter in London. He also met Bobby, who had acquired a girlfriend named Margaret; a big, friendly 'home counties' girl who was little concerned with sexual rules. She had a more or less steady boyfriend, a bald Jewish Trotskyite who was not in the least troubled when she found relief from his political preaching with other, younger men. Gai met her with Bobby and, when they parted amicably, started to take her out in Town. One evening, returning her to her lodgings after a movie, he was kneeling on the back seat of the taxi kissing her when she touched him where he could never have imagined a girl would touch a man, at least in a cab. He followed her up the stairs to her room and they went to bed. They played happily through the night, finding mutual pleasure, but stopped short of proceeding to the final step.

Ruth had impressed upon him the idea that 'Nature' would use him to compensate for an infertile family. Perhaps he had a premonition that she was right and, in old age, he would wonder if he had been attracted to particularly fertile girls. Bridgy and Brenda, when they married, would produce eight or nine children apiece. Ruth had also warned him constantly of the threat of the 'perambulator in the hall' which spelt the end of any hopes a young man might have of freedom and adventure. The sexual drive can take many forms or rather — to stand Freud on his head—it happens that many human needs which are not, in essence, sexual seek an outlet through eroticism. Gai had no interest in conquest or in competing for a woman, nor was he primarily concerned with sensual pleasure. It would always be the discovery of a woman's body, his 'new found land', that satisfied his deepest longings. This precious territory was the real world, his real world, and the intimacy of this discovery was an escape from his personal isolation. Years later a young woman remarked that he only came fully alive when he was making love.

In the morning he hurried home to tell Ruth what had happened and to receive her congratulations. He wrote to Aubrey Scott with the news and received, in response, a gentle lecture. Such experiences would, said his former Housemaster, 'coarsen' him. Gai thought that a little coarsening might do him no harm; it might even be a way, belatedly, of joining the human race. But it was his beautiful half-niece Rochné's reaction that he would always remember. 'Really, Gai', she said. 'How can you be so interested in sex? The lower classes do it!' He kicked himself afterwards for not having thought to ask her how and by what strange procedure the upper classes reproduced themselves, or were their babies conceived through spontaneous combustion?

That same week Peter Heyworth was seduced by a sailor in an Underground station, discovering that he was undeniably 'queer'. Ruth said she had always known this on account of his broad, potentially child-bearing hips. To Gai this was an offence against the Goddess, and it seemed incredible that any man living in a world full of beautiful women should prefer his own sex. Who would dine off slops when a banquet was laid out before him? But their friendship was not affected and, as time went by, Gai gained an insight into the secret homosexual underworld, necessary for someone possessed as he was by a hunger to understand strangers and to discover their hidden identities. To look around in the street or in a theatre was to see so many packages of secrets, people whose outwardness was no more than a mask concealing their real identity. The novelist he still hoped to be must tear the masks off.

But now the time had come to discover war and to discard the last vestiges of a prolonged childhood. In 1941 it was still the practice to send graduates from Oxford or Cambridge direct to the Royal Military College at Sandhurst on the basis that they would already have had rudimentary training (known as 'Corps') both at their Public School and at university, but the course was reduced under wartime exigencies to six months after which, unless they were found lacking, they would emerge as subalterns ready to lead their men into battle. However unmilitary they might be, they were assumed to have been born into the officer class and most could be whipped into shape. Old traditions were maintained. All the officers at Sandhurst were from the Brigade of Guards, the cream of the British army, and such customs as passing the Port after dinner continued. This was luxury compared with conditions in ordinary OTCs (Officer Training Camps).

At the beginning of October Gai entered the College. He had expected to be lost among uncongenial military types but found himself among his own kind. The intake was, with one or two exceptions, entirely from Oxford or Cambridge so that he might have thought himself back at the university for a third year, but there was a big difference. The majority of the cadets were uneasy at finding themselves in uniform and there was a comradeship— a sense of being in the same boat—that he had not found at Cambridge. He was among friends or potential friends, and with one friend in particular. The cadets slept two to a cubicle and Gai was paired with someone who became, in due course, the nearest thing to a brother he could ever have hoped to have. This was Chris Ewert-Biggs, an only child like him and, like him, the object of his mother's passionate love. They had so much in common that it seemed sometimes as though they could read each other's thoughts. They differed only in one respect. Chris had a profound hatred of violence whereas Gai found violence exciting.

'Last night Chris and I talked till all hours. He cannot, as I do, blind himself to the fact that what we're learning here, day by day, is to be professional killers. He has an almost physical horror of causing pain—his early daydreams were of saving foxes from the huntsman. A few years ago he tore some pages from his parents' copy of Hemmingway's bullfighting novel *Death in the Afternoon* and burned them. He says that, if he didn't have such a sceptical mind, doubting his own motives, he would have been a conscientious objector. He belongs, it seems, to the future. The pity is that the present must drag him down and force him to develop the fangs that the times require. I think that this horror of violence will be a characteristic of the men of the future.'

As far as possible they did everything together, patrolling the grounds on bitter winter nights on guard duty and passing the time palm-beaching, as they called it. This was a kind of joint daydream in which they found themselves on a tropical beach, each with his girl. They would walk in silence for a while, then ask each other: 'How far have you got now? What are you doing, what's she doing?' But their attempts to ease their way were not always successful. On one occasion, facing the prospect of a twenty-mile route march, they went separately to the Medical Officer complaining of chilblains on their toes and expecting to be released from the march. The doctor was sympathetic and told them they could, exceptionally, accompany the marchers walking along the verge of the road. This, of course, was much more painful than marching in step with the main body. But, on a different occasion: 'Followed Christopher's example and reported sick with a sore heel. Excused drill, P.T. etc. for three days. The two of us watched Battalion Parade from a landing window, gloating'. Square bashing was still an important part of their training, subjected to choice insults from the drill sergeants, insults which always ended with 'Suh!' out of respect for cadets who would soon be officers. 'You miserable, crawling little toad, Mr Smith. You're a disgrace to the College—Sir!'

The dominant figure in their lives was the Company Commander, Captain Oakshot ('of Bagshot', as they always added). He was living proof of the fact that human beings can be bred for a specific purpose. Even in rags, he would have been immediately recognisable as an officer of the Brigade of Guards.

Everything about him—his carriage, his profile, his voice and his manner—betrayed this and he must have come from a long line of men cut in this mould. He inspired, if not terror, then certainly trepidation in all the cadets, with one exception. Tony Lambton— Lord Lambton, heir to the Earl of Durham—seemed unaffected, and this led Gai to theorise about the role of the aristocracy as 'windows' in an otherwise enclosed prison. Or perhaps they might be compared to boulders in the stream which carries the mass of people down the deep descent which ends in the human anthill. They were, to a limited extent, free spirits exempt from the fear of authority which oppressed others even if this went with a certain disdain for the commonality. If one could not be free oneself, then the next best thing was the presence, in society, of a few privileged individuals who let in some light and air. There was nothing he resented more in the English than their mean-spirited hatred of privilege and their constant parrot cry that 'no one is above the law'. Submission to the fetters of the law— however necessary for the good of society—was also a form of imprisonment. The Old Man would certainly have agreed.

Much depended on being favourably noticed by Captain Oakshot or, failing that, not being noticed at all. There was a delightful and well-liked cadet, John G., who might have stepped straight out of *Brideshead Revisited*, a young man whose great pleasure had been to accompany his mother to exhibitions of ancient lace. One black night of pouring rain he was walking up the long drive that led to the RMC (Royal Military College) when a passing car stopped and the door was thrown open. With a joyful cry of, 'You sweet angel, how absolutely divine of you!' he jumped into the car. The driver was Captain Oakshot. Within days John was transferred to the Army Medical Corps, probably as a stretcher bearer. Gai was more fortunate. There was a night exercise. His platoon headquarters, to which he had to take a message, was sited on the bank of a rushing stream. Excited by a sense of adventure, he dived through a wood, untroubled by the whiplash branches, and plunged through the stream to deliver his message to the platoon commander, dripping water but so pleased with himself that, if he had possessed a tail, he would have wagged it. He had not noticed a tall figure in the darkness and was taken by surprise when the familiar, terrifying voice barked: 'Good show! Jolly keen!' He was made.

It was probably because he had come to the Captain's attention that, a few days later, he was appointed Chairman of a debate on the proposition that 'The only good German is a dead German'. For the first time in their association he saw Chris profoundly angry. Gai knew that he must, at all costs, prevent him from speaking in the debate. Whatever he said, it was likely to be something that would get him thrown out of Sandhurst. The cadets assembled with the officers and Gai took the Chair, refusing to notice Chris's repeatedly raised hand. Finally Chris ignored him and came to his feet, looking around for a few moments before speaking. A junior member of the Royal Family had just died and all the officers wore black armbands. 'I find this proposal astonishing,' he said, 'considering that all the officers present are in mourning for a dead German'. He sat down. Captain Oakshot jumped to his feet, incoherent with rage, but all that could be heard was something about 'bloody bad taste'. Summoning what little courage he possessed, Gai said: 'Excuse me, Sir, but I did not call you'. To his amazement the Captain collapsed in his seat, so disciplined that he obeyed even such brief authority.

There were no immediate repercussions but, in the long run, Chris had sealed his fate. He and Gai had agreed that they would like to spend the war together. When they had to fill out forms indicating their preferences they both put down the I Corps (Intelligence Corps) as first choice and Chris's local regiment, the Royal West Kents, second. It was Chris who went to the West Kents. Long afterwards — more than thirty years later — Gai would trace out in bitter sadness the line which led, from those few words spoken in the debate, to the death of this gentlest of men when, taking up his first appointment as British Ambassador to the Irish Republic, he was blown up by the IRA while driving from the airport into Dublin. Incredibly—at least to Gai—the pusillanimous British authorities, instead of hunting down and killing every known member of the organisation, took no revenge.

Meanwhile their rigorous training was transforming the cadets into—at the least—half-baked soldiers and, to his own surprise, Gai was happy. 'An eighteen-hour Scheme today. Morning and afternoon spent in advance and attack. A late lunch cooked over fires we built for ourselves and then, towards dusk, a 'pincer' river crossing followed by a three-mile march and a couple of hours' rest in an old barn, lying around on the floor, singing and talking. Finally we set off home by sections, ordered to cover the six miles back to the RMC without moving along any roads (they were patrolled by officers). I was with Chris and two others and we were back at the College soon after midnight—along roads most of the way, diving into ditches whenever a car approached. I enjoyed myself.'

Happiness was other people, appreciated all the more on account of his solitary childhood, and happiness was fostered by small acts of kindness. The only cadet who had not come direct from Oxbridge was a Chinese, Kung, the nephew of Chiang Kai-Shek, the ruler of China—what was left of China, largely occupied by the Japanese—and a real soldier, tough as they come. One morning, long before dawn when Gai, with a streaming cold, was queuing for hot water to shave and wash, Kung, who had been at the head of the queue, stopped as he passed with his steaming can. He surveyed this woebegone figure for a moment, then gently took the empty can from him, replaced it with his full one and took Gai's place in the queue. When, long afterwards, Gai wrote of the place occupied by 'small acts of kindness' in the scheme of things (particularly in Islam), it was always Kung's gesture that he had in mind. Chris, of course, was kindness itself, but Tony Lambton also contributed to his sense of being among friends. New Year's Day, 1942, was Gai's 21st Birthday, a major occasion in anyone's calendar, but he passed it on the longest route march ever. Returning after seven hours on the road, he headed for the canteen, cold, exhausted and famished. Tony, who was sitting with his usual sycophantic entourage, jumped up, pushed his way to the counter and bought him a double helping of sausages and mash. He thought it the best meal he had ever had.

At the end of February the tight-knit community of Sandhurst began to unravel as the cadets turned their attention to the choice of a tailor. One officer's uniform, complete with Sam Brown belt and with a single pip on the shoulder (signifying the lowly rank of Second Lieutenant), might look just like another, but there was a subtle distinction between a Savile Row uniform and one of humbler origin, at least in the mind of the wearer. When the fittings had been completed and the finished article was delivered, all available mirrors were in use and each fledgling officer marvelled to discover how handsome he looked. The Passing Out Parade, attended by proud parents, was a grand occasion in the traditional manner. The fact that the war was going badly—in the Far East, at sea and in Egypt—could not dim the occasion or spoil the triumph, nor was the shadow of death perceptible, though many would die before the end.

Next day they went their separate ways to their regiments or services of choice. Unlike Chris, Gai had been accepted into the I Corps. He set off for Oxford, where the Corps had its headquarters, and settled into rooms in Pembroke College. Within a few days the Commandant sent for him and complained that he did not appear to be qualified for any of the jobs available to members of the Corps. How did he come to be there? The answer, in fact, was that he was good at interviews because they stimulated him and brought out the theatrical facet of his nature, but he could hardly say this. The same question would be raised many years later when his superiors questioned how someone so unsuitable to be a government servant had arrived in the Diplomatic Service and the answer would have been the same. An Interview Board was a captive audience which stimulated him to win their liking. If he could send them home saying to each other, 'What a nice chap', his lack of qualifications might be overlooked.

Gai's friends usually chose him rather than vice versa and they were often strong characters whose protective instincts he aroused. Perhaps this was an aspect of the 'spoiling' Kathy had predicted. In his first week at the depot it was Michael who appointed himself his protector, advisor and tutor in the ways of the world, and Michael, who was astonishingly handsome—a truly Byronic figure—was a successful womaniser. What Gai soon discovered to his horror was that this paragon of maleness had nothing but contempt for women, dismissing every girl who fell for his charm as a 'tart' and referring to sexual intercourse in terms of appalling crudity. A committed Roman Catholic, his problem, he admitted, was that, if he ever married, his wife would inevitably come into the 'tart' category. He might just be able to respect her provided she did not welcome the act of intercourse. Chris had once defined Gai's religion as 'erotic mysticism' with a Wagnerian touch to it. Michael was consigned to the category of blasphemers against the Goddess, the lowest of the low, but he had an entry to Keble and that was worth its weight in gold.

The Government had taken over part of Keble College to house forty or more young women who worked for MI5, the Security Service. They had been selected by an elderly full Colonel who clearly had two criteria, breeding and beauty. He must have had the eye of a true connoisseur. These girls, all from 'good families' and therefore assumed to be trustworthy, would have put any beauty parade to shame. Since they were too grand to go out with callow undergraduates, the young I Corps officers were, of necessity, their escorts. No doubt there are people who do not enjoy an erotic thrill at the mention of MI5, but no one who was in the

Intelligence Corps during the war could feel anything but delicious nostalgia, lingering over the M, the I and the 5, the secret code for paradise. Many of the girls went on to splendid marriages; one of them, older than the rest, married the future Prime minister, Anthony Eden, and another (one of Gai's favourites) married a Duke. Their work, however, was mundane to say the least. Most of them had the job of reading intercepted letters sent home by serving soldiers to identify any subversive or defeatist sentiments in the text. Britain was, of course, something of a police state during the war.

One evening Michael announced: 'I've found the right tart for you. She's barely eighteen, but she's a beauty'. He took Gai to a room in Keble and presented him to a girl who could only be a dream come true, the product of a fevered imagination. With jet black hair and a round face Louise—'Lou'—could have been a young Merle Oberon. She was Gai's type brought to life in flesh and blood, created specially for him. Michael asked her: 'Do you want me to bring you some more men, or will Gai do?' then left them alone together, and they talked for an hour or more as though they had known each other for years. A few days later Michael slapped him on the back: 'You gorgeous thing, you! I ran into Lou last night. She likes you very much'. 'How do you know?' Gai asked. '*Elle me la dit!*' said Michael; 'She told me so'. Had he known then how to thank God his thanks would have overflowed.

He took to going round to Keble almost every evening if he could get away and, within a week, he and Lou thought they were in love or perhaps they really were. He wrote in the diary: 'I put one of Chopin's *Nocturnes* on her gramophone and we slipped into each other's arms. "Do you like me at all, darling?" she asked, "because I like you terribly". "I think I'm beginning to love you", I said'. The diary continues: 'Towards midnight I slipped out of the college. I could have stayed there, so warm and happy, everlastingly, for that is the only true repose, a repose so vast that one floats on the surface of a river that has no source and no end, but flows and flows and flows'. It was the first time his feelings had been reciprocated and, at last, Rodney's haunting question—'What sort of girl . . . ?'—was banished. Sometimes they went out for drinks with her girlfriends, but most evenings they stayed in her room with music on the gramophone, loving each other as much as was possible with the other girls dropping in and out, attracted perhaps by the happiness in that room. He knew what the others thought of him. They told each other he was 'very sweet', not exactly the epithet he would have chosen, but far better than being thought horrid, and his cup was filled to the brim (and Rodney consigned to perdition) when the most beautiful, the most sought after of them all—the future Duchess —said to Lou: 'When you've finished with Gai, you can pass him on to me'.

The days were taken up with lectures, TEWTS (Tactical Exercises without Troops), pistol practice and motorcycle rough riding, which provided thrills as well as spills. All this training must be useful for something but Gai was not sure what this something might be and, when he was told that he would be sent on attachment to an infantry regiment in Scotland at the end of the course, he began to feel like one of those 'eternal students' who pursue one course after another until their hair turns grey. Chris was already on his way into action. 'I've been given fourteen days' embarkation leave', he wrote, 'and the worst thing is that friendships will be torn apart, leaving me with my excessive cowardice and the company of my suburban and aggressive fellow officers. *Morituri te salutamus*! Gai, now that I'm being sent to build sandcastles in Libya, I feel a parasitical need to cling to our friendship. I expect you understand.'

The person Gai clung to parasitically as the course ended was Lou. He had known her for less than four weeks, but in wartime relationships ripened fast and he thought of her in the way that a soldier thinks of his wife when torn from her arms to embark upon a fearful future. He had a week's leave when the course

ended and he took a room at the Randolf Hotel for three nights before returning to the Red House. On the first night, when he took
her to his room, it required some argument to persuade her to discard her clothes and he promised 'not to go all the way', which
suited him well enough since it saved him from fear of possible
consequences which, with a girl of eighteen, would have been a
nightmare. He told her that he loved her. 'But you're only a very
little in love with me' she complained. 'Then at least,' he said
rather grandly, 'my very little is as much as most people's all'. The
body, said the Sufi poet Rumi, is 'the shadow of the shadow of the
shadow of the heart', referring to the layers or masks—the
'envelopes', according to the Hindus—which conceal and, at the
same time, express the essence of the human creature, and he
thought that this girl's body shone in every part with an innate
beauty. He was awed and intoxicated. If this was romanticism, so
be it. He was already learning that we are able to impose our
vision of the outward world and of its people upon the world as
such, and no one can find fault with us since no one can say what
objective reality is in itself. He might have quoted Nietzsche:
'There is no such thing as facts, there are only interpretations'.

Returning to the hotel by moonlight in the early hours, having
escorted her back to Keble after they had torn themselves apart
for the last time, he recited over and over again the lines from
Othello:

> *If it were now to die,*
> *'Twere now to be most happy, for I fear*
> *My soul hath her content so absolute,*
> *That not another comfort like to this*
> *Succeeds in unknown fate.*

Early in May his orders came. He was to join 151st Division in
the north of Scotland on attachment. After a week in a Brigade
HQ of the Royal Scots Regiment he was sent to Cruden Bay on
the coast of Aberdeenshire, a peacetime centre for golfers but now

taken over by a battalion of the Royal Scots. Loneliness assailed him and Scotland seemed like a foreign land. The first of several passionate love letters from Lou, though a source of joy, stabbed him with pain. She was so far away. 'It hurts physically, like warming frozen fingers before a blazing fire', he wrote. Friends had taken her to the Randolf Hotel to cheer her up and she had cried so much that they had to take her back to Keble, where she had sniffled for the rest of the evening in front of his photograph. She swore that she would drive Brenda and Kathy from his mind, but in that she could not succeed. His loves were cumulative, one did not replace another but was added to it in a personal history, even a personal mythology. His Goddess was many-faced.

When he arrived in Scotland he had no idea what an 'attachment' meant. In fact it could as well have been called a 'detachment'. He was there to observe and learn, specifically to learn how an army functions from Command to platoon level. For the most part all that was asked of him was not to get under people's feet, not to get in the way, so he had time on his hands and, as he had no friends in the Mess, the long evenings were spent writing letters. Ruth expected and received a couple of letters every week, his correspondence with Peter would have filled a book, and the meditations that he sent Leo Myers always received a prompt response, but there was someone else now to whom he could spill out his soul. On his last day in Oxford he had sought comfort in his favourite teashop, Fuller's. These teashops, always offering delicious cakes, were a feature of English life and he would see their disappearance after the war as a symptom of a declining civilisation.

He had found himself sharing a table with a woman on her own, an elderly woman—he thought—at least forty if not forty-five, but pleasant. They began to talk and they went on talking for two hours. As soon as she mentioned the fact that she had published two novels and that she had lived in Africa he was hooked, and she drew him out skilfully until he had told her all that there was to tell about himself and had poured out his distress over parting from Lou. Her comments struck him as both kind and perceptive. Her name was Mary, but he soon invented his own name for her simply by combining her initials. She was MEO, and so she would remain for years to come. When they parted she had asked if she could write to him and he had welcomed this.

Now he could bounce his ideas off four people, the four points of his compass, sure of receiving applause and encouragement from three of them, Ruth, Leo Myers and MEO. Peter, now an officer in an artillery regiment, tended to be critical, urging him to face up to 'real life'. As, day after day, he walked the granite cliffs—he supposed they were granite—over a raging sea, the screaming of seagulls in his ears, his mind and imagination were in high gear, racing beyond his comprehension. Somewhere out there, just beyond his reach, was the truth, and he was as hungry for it as he had been as a schoolboy fumbling with philosophy. What mattered was that now he could be sure that it existed; ultimate, absolute truth existed. It was for him to turn himself into an instrument for apprehending it through sharpening and purifying the inward eye of intuition.

While still at Charterhouse he had discovered a book that set him on his course; *The Primordial Ocean* by an Egyptologist, Professor Perry. The author had a theory that the ancient Egyptians had voyaged to every part of the world in their papyrus boats spreading their mythology and symbolism far and wide. To prove his case he had spent a lifetime researching the myths of the ancients and of so-called 'primitive' peoples of his own time. What he revealed was an astonishing unanimity of belief, however different the images in which that belief was expressed. He had not proved his theory about the Egyptians, but he had proved something quite different and far more important.

Behind the tapestry of forms there were certain universal truths regarding the nature of reality, the creation of the world and of mankind, and the meaning of human experience; truths that were as much a part of us as our blood and our bones. From this Gai had moved on to mysticism, Christian mysticism in the first place, then Hindu Vedanta, and here again he had detected a profound, half-concealed unanimity despite the differences in spiritual terminology and interpretation. These people had gone beyond dogma and belief. They had achieved direct vision, real knowledge of the Real. His agnosticism had been based on the simple fact that there were different religions, seemingly irreconcilable. They could not all be true, so all must be false. Others might have substituted 'scientific truth' for religious 'myths'. He could not, since science was founded upon unproven assumptions regarding the infallibility of reason and the objectivity of sense-experience. Here, however, was a perspective that made sense.

He had come to Scotland with a selection of the *Upanishads*, several books on Vedanta and one on Taoism, and the more he read the more he was seized by the conviction that the truth was hereabouts. Wandering the cliffs, alone except for the seagulls, he let what he had read sink into his mind and, perhaps, sink deeper still, waiting patiently to see what would finally emerge when the process of digestion was complete. He soon realised that he must, as he put it, 'ride loose in the saddle', avoiding rigidity. Faced with contradictions, he could not let them trouble him. The sterile exercise of mental argumentation served no purpose. If the mind was a kind of eye, his eye was still closed so he must walk as a blind man feeling his way in the hope that searching hands would find, here or there, an undeniably solid object, and now he felt that he was close to doing that. He knew, at last, that there was a Reality beyond this world and that everything else was *Maya*; not 'illusion' but a lesser, relative reality. He supposed that he had always known this, as had everyone in their heart of hearts, for in Eckhart's words, 'the Truth is native to man', or, in Islamic terms, Revelation comes only to confirm a knowledge that has always been within us. Solitude supported his reflections.

'Free for an hour or so this morning I walked out to the headland and a passer-by, if there had ever been one, might have been astonished to see a British officer seated cross-legged on a rock, gazing out to sea and circled by seagulls.'

From Cruden Bay he was sent to another unit in the Division in a different part of Aberdeenshire, then to several others, sometimes involved in their activities and sometimes ignored. He felt like a tourist. On one occasion he was sent to umpire a three-day divisional exercise but, when he arrived on his motorbike at the headquarters, he found that it was another officer of the same name who was listed. The opportunity to enjoy a taste of freedom was irresistible so he set off, a happy truant, riding the empty roads in bright sunshine to the fishing village of Peterhead where he booked into a hotel for the night. Lying on his bed he read the *Bhagavadgita*, seeing clearly before him two diverging paths. One was the spiritual path of asceticism, self-denial and detachment with its vast reward; the other was the way of the world, the enjoyment of sex, of people, participation in the flow of life and the blind plunge into adventure. It seemed to him that the choice had already been made for him irrevocably. He was committed to the richness of human life and, addressing the *Gita*, he quoted some lines which the poet Yeats had addressed to a celebrated Catholic theologian: 'So go in peace, Von Hügel, though with blessings on your head'. But it was not a final choice. Secretly he intended to 'have his cake and eat it'. He meant to surround his adventures with the glow of a light from elsewhere, integrating them into a spiritual path, piercing the worldly dimension with the sword of transcendence. He meant to have it all.

He was back at Brigade Headquarters in a Mess sprinkled with kilted *Lairds* when a letter came from Ruth to say that Francis, now in his eighty-eighth year, had been diagnosed with prostate cancer and was dying. It was a letter of such intense grief and passion as he had never imagined she would write. Two days later there was a telegram to say that he had been misdiagnosed.

133

There was no cancer, but he was dying none the less, as much from exhaustion as anything. Daily reports followed. Some days Francis lay half-comatose, holding her hand for hours on end, yet the next morning he was sitting up in bed 'working', whatever that meant, convinced that he need only find the right doctors to put him back on his feet. What else were doctors for? He had scarcely had a day's illness in his life and claimed that, when he was a boy, the local doctor, when summoned to attend a member of the family, had been expected to use the tradesman's entrance. Now he had driven himself to the limit and there was no more lifeforce in him. Gai wrote in the diary: 'Just as, when I'm in love, I see the whole world illuminated, so now sadness and deep pity expand so that they embrace all that exists. Tonight I sit in my room listening to the piano in the room below; its nostalgia is heart-breaking. Even this cheap music speaks of sadness, the passage of time, the end of love. Every phrase whispers "Never-more."'

On 3 July 1942, Ruth reported: 'During the night Father opened his eyes wide and looked at me, then gave a sweet smile, took my hand and said, "I think I'm dying. How many years!" then re-lapsed into a semi-coma'. He died in Ruth's arms four days later, murmuring: 'There are waves and waves and waves . . .', then asking her: 'Is there a happy place?' Given compassionate leave, Gai took the train south the same evening and arrived at the Red House next morning. Coming into the bedroom where Francis was laid out on the bed in which he had slept for the past thirty years, he kissed the cold forehead, never having kissed his father in life and never having been acknowledged by him as his true son. After cremation the 'Little Colonel's' ashes were scattered around the Inns of Court War Memorial on Berkhamsted Com-mon so that he could join the young men he had trained and sent out to die nearly thirty years before.

Gai slipped away to Oxford, seeking the source of life, and spent the night with Lou, telling himself: 'Seize the moment as it flies'.

Lou would grow old and die and so would he. The radiance that was cast on youth from elsewhere would fade and be extinguished, but the embrace of their naked bodies must—surely?—partake of eternity. Death and love, the Latin *mors* and *amor,* were indissolubly linked, as he had learned when he was twelve and Ruth had taken him to a performance of Wagner's *Tristan and Isolde* at Covent Garden. The story of the opera had haunted him ever since, as had the music of the *Liebestodt*, the 'Love-Death', and he remembered being told that the Spaniards called the sex act 'the little death'. It was the ultimate escape from banality.

Soon there was another death, the death of Ruth's love for Francis. It was Ralph, afraid to face her, who told Gai the contents of the Will. She was to receive the income from £7,000 and he would get the sum of £1,000; everything else would go to Ralph and Barbara, including the Red House As neither of them understood money matters and they had no idea of the value of the Estate, this did not at first provoke any reaction. It was only when Ruth spoke to the lawyers that she began to grasp the enormity of this 'pay off'. It seemed to her that she had been treated like a faithful housekeeper who is lucky to be left a bequest. Although she was given the right to live in the Red House for as long as she wished this would, in effect, be as Ralph's lodger. That was the worst humiliation.

She had always seen the world in black and white; there were no grey areas. Love turned, almost overnight, into hatred. She concluded that Francis had never, for a moment, loved her. He had used her, and she had wasted her life in faithful devotion to a man who cared only for his reputation. The motives behind the drafting of the Will were debated for years afterwards, but there could be no agreed explanation. Gai wondered if his father, with the example of Ralph in mind, had believed that possession of a private income might destroy him. On the other hand, was it possible that, like other men in his position, he had, at the end of his life, turned against the woman whose sexuality had led him to abandon the values he was supposed to exemplify? Long afterwards, remembering what his form master, Ives, had said about bastards, he wondered if Francis had wanted, at all costs, to keep the knowledge of his illegitimacy from him. Why else had he insisted that Ruth destroy any letters which might reveal the truth? His son was the only person likely to read them in the future. Had he been trying to protect him, had he been motivated by guilt, or was he the cold, ruthless man Ruth now believed him to have been?

The most curious aspect of the whole business was Gai's reaction. He felt no disappointment. He might reasonably have expected to inherit a substantial sum, but he had never really expected this. Perhaps he had never thought of himself as a member of the Errington family. He had been the poor relation, tolerated but not fully accepted. Theirs was another world to which he did not belong.

Ruth determined upon revenge. She had always believed in revenge as a moral principle and would have regarded the common saying that 'two blacks do not make a white' with contempt. Revenge evened the score, restored the balance when an injustice had disturbed it. She recalled with grim relish something Francis had once said to her: 'You're a formidable woman, Ruthie. I would not like to make an enemy of you'. By contesting the Will, exposing the whole story of his hypocrisy in open Court, she could destroy his reputation, the only thing he valued, and in this she found a ready ally. One of her oldest friends was an eminent solicitor, Colclough by name, who had very probably been in love with her forty years before and whom she might have married if Francis had not appeared on the scene. Colclough, when she told him the whole story, was not only profoundly shocked but fiercely angry. He took up the case with passionate dedication as though engaged upon a crusade.

The aunts urged Gai to dissuade her, if only for his own sake, but he knew she had to go through with this if she was to retain her sanity. His own feelings for his father were unaltered. He drew what seemed to him an obvious conclusion from the fact that nothing we do today can change what we did yesterday: nothing therefore that happens in the momentary present can spoil what happened in the past. The years of affection, tenderness and companionship that Ruth and Francis had shared were inscribed on tablets of stone. Eventually his conviction would be fitted into the Islamic framework. The past is ever present in the divine Knowledge and becomes present again for us at the Last Judgement. One day he would be able to say *Amín* to his parents' story—So be it!

R U T H   A T   5 0

It was the summer of 1942 and Gai was at the Red House on extended leave. Ruth, now sixty-two was rejuvenated, with the light of battle in her eyes. If she could expose one 'whited sepulchre' to public shame she would, she believed, have struck a blow for truth. Colclough, her solicitor, advised caution. This was, he said, the most extraordinary and complicated case he had ever dealt with; Gai, he added, should take it as the theme for a novel. But Ruth was sure she would win. The real enemy was not Francis as an individual or the family who had rejected her and her son, but hypocrisy as such and all the evils she had encountered in her life. The Old Man's spirit burned bright in her. Gai shared her feelings — as he always did — and, at the same time, felt a warm affection for his father. He was accustomed to accommodating within himself quite contradictory feelings, just as he was always able to hold simultaneously what appeared to be irreconcilable beliefs, somehow bringing together both 'Yes' and 'No'. Long afterwards he would learn that, in the Islamic context, God approves the 'reconciler of opposites'.

Ruth told him that if, by pressing a button, she could extermi-nate the whole of humanity except for the two of them, she would do it. She had said the same thing some years previously and, on that occasion, he had asked her sarcastically what, in that case, they would do for servants. This time he begged her to remember the sense of unity with all living things of which she had often spoken. How could she exclude the human creature? She admitted that she might make an exception of uncivilised peoples who were as yet unspoiled. 'Man,' he told her rather pompously, 'is not the cruel, greedy creature you imagine. He is dominated by one thing, fear. He's like some poor rat in a corner, snapping at all comers. Fear of giving himself, fear of having his individuality invaded, fear of insecurity. Eliminate those fears and he is transformed'.

Later, when he was away on another course, she wrote: 'Not to fight would be a sort of death to me, an acknowledgement that at last I was beaten by life, a kind of moral suicide. My fighting spirit, which I had thought was snuffed out, has uncurled and raised its head. *Kundalini*, is that it? For thirty years I was dominated by this man. Now I am free. You don't know what that means to me — to be a free spirit at last'. Gai might have commented that we are all defeated in the end by time, old age and death, but did not. Soon afterwards there was another letter: 'For thirty years Father worked gently, persistently to change me. My frankness had to go, my freedom went, of that I was conscious; of my fearlessness I cannot tell. I became too weary and muddled to think about anything. The last few years my spirit began to die. Then, just in time, I was released, and now I feel like a lark. I have an irresistible impulse to rise and sing, in fact sometimes I get up and dance, and then think how foolish I must look. I can be myself again. I'm free!' Gai remembered the letters she had written, only a few weeks before; letters so full of love, so sorrowful as she watched her beloved dying. So this was the end of love, gone as though it had never been? Since understanding was his business, he tried to understand.

He had been sent to Matlock in the Peak District for a course, living in a grand Spa hotel to which elderly people had once come for their health, no doubt a quiet hotel from which noise was excluded. Now, while the different sections planned tactics in an imaginary battle, motorcycles raced up and down the corridors, scattering deafening thunder flashes as they went, together with tear gas canisters, to simulate noise and chaos of battle. Almost all the other officers were Canadians, a particularly friendly group. They were appalled, shocked and delighted by the promiscuity of English girls. 'It's incredible!' his roommate told him. 'Seems like it means no more to them than a handshake', but he used a more earthy term than 'it'. Ruth could have explained to them that, in wartime, Nature compensates for the loss of life and war is the great aphrodisiac.

He returned to Oxford while the Army — or someone in the bowels of the War Office — considered what to do with him. Time had passed and he had cooled on Lou. In any case, her love was now focused elsewhere and she had become engaged, but the diary is peppered with the names of those marvellous Keble girls: Angela, Philippa, Tina, Ruby, Joan, Ann, Janet, Dereka (whom the Adjutant described as 'the Come-Hither-Don't-You-Dare girl'). After a few weeks a new posting arrived, together with a second pip, promoting him from Second Lieutenant to Lieutenant. He was to proceed at once to Aldershot where he would join a special unit composed of young officers whose job, he gathered, was to take messages on their motorbikes from one headquarters to another when normal means of communication failed. At the time he did not even notice that it was described as an 'Interpreter Section'.

Someone somewhere had got it wrong. It was soon discovered that he had only one foreign language, French, and that was not of a standard to qualify him as an official interpreter. The unit was soon going overseas. Their destination, they were told in great secrecy, was a province of France, and that must surely mean that the 'second front' would be launched any day. They had forgotten, if they had ever known, that Algeria was a province of France, but soon afterwards there was a rumour that they were bound for West Africa. 'I give up! It's impossible to predict anything. In a month's time I may be dancing in Paris, dying of Yellow Fever in Senegal, still rotting here in this horrible town or making love to one of the Keble girls.' He noticed from an invoice that fourteen gross (2016) of condoms had been supplied for the unit and remembered Chris telling him that, during the First World War, his father had been required to fill a similar order when he was serving in Turkey. The girl at the counter, wide-eyed, had exclaimed '*Quel homme!*' — 'What a man!'

He was in the doctor's waiting room about to have his injections when a telegram was brought to him as temporary head of the section: Lieutenant Eaton is being replaced and should be instructed to proceed at once to the depot in Oxford. He was back where he started, but not for long. The I Corps finally accepted that they had no place for him and he was to be transferred to the Royal West Kents, Chris's regiment. In a week's time he would proceed to Blackburn, a northern mill town, to join a battalion stationed there.

While Gai was waiting for his transfer, Leo Myers invited him to stay for the weekend. This would be their first meeting face-to-face, and he feared disillusionment. Could this man live up to the image he had of him? He did. 'Writing this in my beautiful room in Tilecoats. Leo more than lives up to my expectations. He is, I think, the kindest and wisest person I have ever known. We talked till late last night, drinking whiskey, and he never dominated the conversation but led me on, asked my opinions, letting his calm, shrewd friendliness envelope me.' Leo talked of his many love affairs, 'both sublime and sordid', and described his weird childhood as the son of F. W. H. Myers, the founder of the Society for Psychical Research, in a house always filled with 'psychics' of the most dubious kind. The only jarring note was political. He was moving from anarchism, learned from his friend Herbert Read, to the position of an 'armchair Communist', convinced that Britain under Churchill — whom he had known and whom he hated — was on the way to becoming a fascist country. This wealthy, urbane man enclosed in his luxurious home made a very unlikely Communist, wilfully blind to the brutality of the Stalinist regime. He had joined the ranks of those whom Lenin had described as 'useful idiots', but there were at that time a number of rich people who, feeling guilty on account of their good fortune, adopted a utopian theory which exempted them from making any personal effort to help others. Ideology substituted for charity.

Gai was being sent out into the cold but his 'support team' was in place. Ruth shared every moment of his life. Leo Myers had written to her after his visit to say that Gai was the son he would have wished to have, praising him to the skies. MEO was always there for him, and Peter wrote him an astonishing letter: 'Interesting that such diverse characters find an understanding in you, that they look to you almost as a pillar of stability, a rock, which in fact you are. Right or wrong, you've taken a line, and it's those who take a line who influence others and form history'. If that is so, he reflected, I must be a trembling rock. From Chris, who had lost an eye at the battle of al-Alamein and was convalescing in Palestine, there was a brief but touching letter: 'I have an awful feeling of having lost myself . . . It will be necessary to start living again after this blank in my life, and you are part of the foundation for doing so. That's why I don't want to lose you. Do you understand?' Kathy wrote, apologising for having been 'cruel' to him in Cambridge and seeking his advice on a personal problem. There was an affectionate letter from Margaret, explaining that, when she liked someone, she wanted to know 'all of them' and making love 'brings you closer', at the same time he was bombarded with love letters from a Czech refugee girl he had met in Matlock. What more did he want?

He was insatiable for praise, comfort and support. The self-confidence he needed to keep his head above water depended upon it, and yet a hundred words of praise could be wiped out by one word of blame or reproach. When he looked within himself he could not find the qualities which others, some others, found in him and could only conclude that they were deceived. Equally, he could find nothing in himself to love. Such people — men and women — are dangerous. If they cannot really believe that they are loved, then they have no sense of obligation towards those who love them and can act callously within troubling their conscience. He wondered also if he had any strength in himself, the strength upon which his future would depend, although he knew that he was stubborn by nature. Surveying himself, he saw just how many-layered people are, strong at one level, weak at another, simultaneously arrogant and humble, and one day he would apply this to the mystery of religious faith. The believer who lived for his religion might, none the less, be an unbeliever at the same time. By the same token, there might be the light of faith in the unbeliever's heart, unperceived but, eventually, decisive. God alone could sort out these tangled webs. It was beyond human power to do so and, therefore, to judge.

He arrived in Blackburn, a grim product of the industrial revolution, in February 1943. The Commanding Officer was on leave and, since the whole tone of any military unit is determined by the CO, he sought out a company clerk, likely to be a useful source of gossip and, after buttering him up, inquired casually about the 'old man'. The reply was intriguing: 'Well, Sir, he's kind of sexual like, always saying he loves things of beauty'. This association of beauty with sexuality and therefore with the 'dirty' side of life was indicative of a certain British puritan tradition which distrusted beauty in all its forms, not least in places of worship; a dour, joyless tradition. When the CO returned, Gai was welcomed with surprising warmth. This lover of beautiful things had deplored the fact that there were no 'Oxbridge' men among his officers; now he had one and, moreover, this was a Kingsman. In the diary Gai tried to reproduce the man's manner of speech: 'Won emerges from King's Chapel abso-lootly dronk with bee-oo-teh'. Within days, though brown-eyed, he was the Commanding Officer's 'blue-eyed boy', the official favourite who could do no wrong.

He was not much given to feelings of shame but now he felt ashamed, mired in hypocrisy as never before. This man represented everything of which he disapproved, yet he relished his privileged position. When the CO remarked: 'You and I know that the country is being rotted by filthy socialism', or, 'I know you agree with me that the Russians aren't fit to lick an Englishman's boots', he nodded agreement. When the CO confided to him his post-war ambition to be a prison governor he understood quite well what lay behind this but smiled his approval, and references to the men — the ordinary soldiers in the battalion — as 'scum' aroused no objection. Gai enjoyed the man's gentle teasing. The junior officers had been on a cross-country run in pouring rain one day and, in the Mess that evening, the CO asked: 'Now tell me, Eaton, did you enjoy this afternoon's run?' 'Very much, Sir, it was fun.' The response was accompanied by a deep chuckle: 'You little liar, you shocking little liar. Don't you know that lying to your Commanding Officer is a capital offence?'

He soon had an opportunity to tell some real lies. The CO asked him to give a series of lectures to the men on the British Empire and to invite them afterwards to express their views. The intention was obviously that he should note any subversive opinions among the 'scum' and report them. To his surprise, subversive opinions were precisely what he did find, including criticism of Churchill, and he took a secret pleasure in reporting that the men were full of patriotic zeal, filled with admiration for Mr Churchill and proud of their regiment, all this with his usual air of deep sincerity. But he was seething inwardly. With every day that passed he was becoming more anti-authoritarian and a particular incident provoked a fury of indignation such as he had never before experienced. A new draft had just arrived and the men, travel-weary and soaking wet after marching from the station, were assembled in the mill which was the headquarters of one of the Companies. They waited an hour or more for the Company Commander to welcome them. When he finally arrived he spoke briefly and to the point. 'Now that you're here, you'd better damn well understand one thing. You'll mesh in or we'll break you. Let me repeat. Every one of you will mesh in. We'll break anyone who doesn't!' Gai's anger simmered for a quarter of a century until it found expression in a book he wrote in the late 1960s with the title: *King of the Castle: Choice and Responsibility in the Modern World.*

Today it might be thought that any sacrifice of freedom and dignity was justified in the crusade against the evil of Nazism. At the time the war was seen rather differently. One evening in the Officers' Mess a young subaltern remarked that the German Generals ought to rise up and get rid of Hitler. There was a shocked silence until the Adjutant spoke up. 'If I had been born a German', he announced solemnly, 'I hope I should have been totally loyal to Herr Hitler'. The Commanding Officer nodded his approval. So this war was just a repetition of the old game of rivalry between nation states, football with the added spice of blood-letting?

Given time Gai might have boiled over with disastrous consequences, but at this point he was told that he would be accompanying the next overseas draft. He was going into battle, and he was torn between fear and excitement. At one moment he imagined himself running across open country under a hail of bullets, at the next he was being decorated for gallantry under fire. At least this would be a kind of freedom, a chance to find out what he was made of and so resolve the contradictions in his own character. Officers who were going overseas were given a routine medical checkup. The Medical Officer weighed him. Eight stone (112 pounds), and he was over six foot. 'There's no way I'm certifying you fit for active service', said the MO. 'You'd be blown over by the first breeze.' One evening the CO told him sadly:

'You're being snatched from us. A pity'. On 25 March he was sent to an Infantry Training Centre in Maidstone, a small town in Kent. This centre was the first stop for new conscripts where they received their initial five weeks' military training. It was also a last refuge for officers who, for reasons of age, health or whatever, could not be placed elsewhere.

They had nothing to do except pretend to be useful. There were three Companies, each commanded by a Major who was free to play golf as much as he wished and to spend his weekends in London. The junior officers filled in forms and supposedly supervised training exercises, but there was no need for supervision. The training was done by middle-aged, battle-hardened sergeants who could have done the job blindfold and dead drunk since the same routine was performed every five weeks. The only occasion on which the subalterns had a function was during hand grenade practice. If a nervous recruit dropped his grenade in the trench after pulling the pin it was the officer's privilege to pick it up and throw it as far as possible, or, if a grenade failed to explode after being thrown, he was obliged to crawl out to it on his belly, stuff gun cotton under it, light a fuse and crawl back to the trench.

He could, of course, learn more about people as one draft succeeded another. He learned a great deal from a contingent of ex-policemen, all in their thirties. During exercises in the countryside, the men and the sergeants picnicked together while the supervising officer was expected to eat his sandwiches in solitary splendour. Seated behind a convenient bush, Gai listened avidly to the gossip that went on. The ex-policemen compared notes on the 'villains' they had framed. There was no shame about this since they only framed men who were, they believed, guilty, and they were therefore giving justice a helping hand. A constant theme was the almost incredible gullibility of judges and magistrates who would believe any tall story told by a police witness. They were respectful of their betters and yet a little scornful of these 'toffs' who had no experience of real life, and they had sometimes been tempted to extend their lies to see just how far they could go without being doubted. The British policeman was, of course, beyond reproach.

A question Gai asked himself constantly was whether it was really necessary for officers and men to be segregated as though they belonged to different species, a situation in which it was essential for the officer to wear a mask on all occasions. Surely, if he was worth his salt, he could afford to be himself and still command respect? The principal theme of Leo Myers' great novel had been the process of masking which transforms people into 'types' — soldiers, judges, aristocrats or whatever — rather than persons. Leo believed that the adoption of a social mask led, eventually, to the destruction of the person in his uniqueness, his breadth and his depth, and only persons could truly communicate with one another, only persons were open to the spiritual dimension. Gai watched with horrified fascination this actual process at work when a young man newly commissioned arrived at the camp.

This youth was determined to conform to what he thought was the officer type. It seemed likely that, on rising each morning, he practised the appropriate facial expressions before the mirror. He changed his tone of voice to give it a harsh, peremptory tone when speaking to the men, and he strutted rather than walked. When his turn came to inspect the night guard on the gate for the first time, Gai was told to supervise him. The usual procedure was to count the bodies on bunks in the guardhouse and sign the register, 'all present and correct'. The young man, however, decided to do it by the book and ordered the men to line up for inspection. Walking down the line with the air of a General inspecting his troops, he found fault with each soldier, a button undone here, a loose shoelace there, or a slovenly posture. Having made a nuisance of himself he marched back into the guardhouse, picked up the leaky pen provided and signed his name with a splendid flourish. A moment later he turned to Gai. His face had crumpled. He looked like an unhappy child on the verge of tears. 'Oh', he said, 'I've made a blot!' It was a moment to relish.

Gai was reading voraciously, chiefly on religion and mysticism, and, in addition to Rilke's poems and the writings of the Taoist sage, Chuang Tzu, this included two books recommended by Leo Myers: *I and Thou* by Martin Buber, the Jewish mystical writer (whom he would meet some years later), and *The Right to Live* by a close friend of Leo's, the pacifist Max Plowman. Particularly with the example of Nazism close at hand, they reinforced his conviction that blind obedience to authority was the source of warfare and the foundation of tyranny. If human beings did not have this inherent readiness to obey orders there could be no armies, and, if senior civil servants were not prepared to carry out their master's orders meticulously, there would be no tyrants, no dictators. If that meant the end of civilisation, so be it. A time would come when he would assert, rather questionably, that Islam did not approve obedience to secular authority. Despite the confusion in his mind, he was beginning to be certain of something, but of what he did not know.

Almost any book that seemed to offer keys to what lay beyond the visible world was grist to his mill. 'I'm re-reading Berdyaev's *Solitude and Society*. Very, very good. Ah—the consolations of philosophy! Life would be intolerable without such glimpses of spiritual freedom. Even so, I feel myself shrivelling. And this camp! I do believe I might be happier in a concentration camp— at least there would be comradeship in the midst of misery. This place is utterly soul-destroying, deadening, and I may be here for years.' There was a sour atmosphere in the camp. While the Majors were happy enough playing golf, all the junior officers were trying to get away, pulling strings, if they had any to pull, to obtain a transfer. They felt useless, they were useless, effectively out of the war. They might tremble before the prospect of active service but, at least, in the presence of death there would be a sense of living, living on the edge.

Gai had only one friend and he was a Company Clerk, on the wrong side of the dividing line between officers and the rest. John Davidson who had, in fact, refused a commission, was a writer who had published a number of stories, a friend of Auden and Isherwood. He was also a homosexual. Until the war he had enjoyed an idyllic life, half the year on his tea plantation in Ceylon, the other half in his house in Salzburg writing articles and stories. Gai met him for drinks in a local pub fairly frequently and was quite unaware of the fact that these meetings were likely to be observed and reported. Even if he had realised the danger in which he was placing himself, it would have made no difference. John was someone with whom he could talk happily for hours and who might, when the time came, be able to provide contacts in the literary world. That would more than compensate for any false conclusions that might be drawn from their meetings.

In any case, he now had a girl, and he was seen with her more often than with John. There were regular dances in the Town Hall, dances at which forty or fifty girls sat on chairs against the wall waiting to be selected by a man. Officers, of course, were never rejected. Gai took some time to make a definitive choice but, when made, it was a good one. Betty was a pretty nineteen-year-old who worked for the local council, cheerful and affection-ate, just the tonic he needed. After dancing or going to a movie, they would return to her home—her parents, whom he never met, having tactfully retired upstairs—to kiss and cuddle on the living room carpet.

He had sensed from the start that his Company Commander, Major S. (a bank manager in real life), disliked him, and he had the same impression with the Commanding Officer, an elderly man whose health and temper had been spoiled by long service in India; a sour, leathery man. This was in painful contrast to his privileged position in Blackburn. As long as he had John and

Betty he could put up with it, but a time came when the Major's hostility turned into something much more deadly, something suggestive of hatred and contempt. He found fault with everything that Gai did and, on one occasion, reported him to the CO for 'slackness'. For the first time the possibility of receiving what was called an Adverse Report, which would deprive him of his commission and send him to the ranks, occurred to him. He knew that the sergeants liked and respected him, as did the men, but that would be no help in such an situation.

At the end of May he arranged a meeting between Ruth and Leo Myers. He was to go up to London, meet Leo at Paddington station and take him to the hotel in which Ruth was staying. This should not present any problems. As he was not on duty the chosen weekend, it would be a matter of routine to get permission from Major S. But, when the time came, the Major was not to be found and, if he waited any longer he would miss his train. He went anyway, and damn the consequences. The meeting went well, and he had the satisfaction of seeing a dawning friendship between his mother and the man who meant so much to him. On returning to Maidstone he was immediately summoned to the Major's office and faced a terrifying onslaught in which one particular phrase stood out: 'So you rushed up to Town without permission to meet your boyfriend'. He was baffled. Boyfriend? Did the wretched man take him for a homosexual? Was this the reason for his contempt and hostility? There could be no other explanation. For the moment, preoccupied with Betty, he had forgotten John Davidson. The diatribe continued: 'I find you contemptible, and so does everyone else. My son is in the army, and if he was ordered to serve under you I would tell him to disobey the order. I wouldn't let him near you'. The closed, stubborn expression on Gai's face further provoked him. 'Think yourself superior to everyone else, don't you? Well, let me tell you you're inferior. If you analyse yourself you'll know that! I've spoken to the CO. You're up before him this afternoon.' Having said nothing up to this point, Gai exclaimed: 'Good!' The CO put him on a month's probation. If he did not 'pull his socks up' he would get an Adverse Report and be reduced to the ranks.

Shattered, humiliated and yet defiant, Gai began to plan his escape. He realised that the onslaught had been directed not at the person he was but at a supposed 'queer' or 'pansy', but he could not altogether overcome the thought that he might indeed be contemptible. The Major's words had penetrated his defences and touched him where it hurt. The following evening, however, he was invited to a party given by one of the sergeants for a platoon that was passing out after training. Half-afraid to face people, he made his way to the pub where the function was being held. Afterwards he wrote: 'Ye Gods! What an evening! I joined them soon after nine and, for the first time in my life, was greeted with Three Cheers. It's years since I've blushed, but I believe I did then. I could only gasp "Thank you!" Then one member of the platoon took me aside to explain why they had all liked me so much, the implication being that I was the only one of the officers who was "human" and who treated them decently. They all bought me drinks, and I was soon fairly drunk—no, very drunk and very happy. I danced with the ATS girls in turn and, at the end, they queued up for a kiss. As a point of honour, I kissed each of them properly—or do I mean improperly?'

For someone who always assessed himself in the mirror of other peoples' eyes, this was profoundly confusing. He no longer knew whether he was despicable or admirable, but he realised that there was a kind of war going on between the officers and the other ranks, and he had instinctively aligned himself with the other ranks. That, apart from the imputation of homosexuality, might even account for the hostility of his superiors; he had let the officer caste down and that was unforgivable. He was now ordered, as a special humiliation, to join a *Cadre* for 'potential NCOs' and do P.T. every morning with the men. He began to plan what he called his 'gesture' of defiance. He would ask for an interview with the CO and would do something that might either bring him before a Court Martial or get him out of the army. He worked out the details, not only in the diary but also in letters to his support group. Ruth replied at once with a telegram saying that she was with him whatever he decided to do. Leo was similarly supportive, and MEO wrote him a letter of passionate friendship. Peter, however, recommended caution: 'Do, please, think of the consequences'. But his most effective encouragement came from unexpected quarters. The sergeant in charge of P.T. took him aside after his first session and told him: 'I shouldn't be saying this, Sir, but if I were in your position I wouldn't put up with it'. And then John Davidson, when they met to discuss the situation, told him something even more encouraging. The Regimental Sergeant-Major had said in his hearing that this was an 'indignity such as he had never heard of in twenty years' service'. So the Army itself was on his side.

While the CO was out and his door unlocked he inspected the office in which his gesture would be made, noticing a pile of papers on the desk. They could, perhaps, be swept to the floor? If he was going to shout a few choice insults, just what insults would be appropriate? Should he strike the desk with his swagger stick? He would have to play it by ear, depending upon the inspiration of the moment. But, whatever he might plan, this must appear as a spontaneous loss of control so he posted his diary home in case they searched his room after the event. He ended the last entry in high spirits. 'I feel a match for anyone. *Bonne chance*, Gai! Come out into the sunlight! You know what's good and what's delightful, don't submit to the grey folk. Yippee!'

He thought he was in revolt against an individual or perhaps against the army machine, but in fact he was challenging authority as such, power as such, and even—though he would never have guessed this—his own father, with whom he had never once dared to disagree. Indeed, he had never challenged his aunts when he was a child or, for that matter, his mother. He had never dared to challenge anyone, and now a pressure that had been building up for years demanded release. He made an appointment to see the CO on the afternoon of July 5th.

He waited on the veranda outside the office. He could almost feel the adrenaline pumping into his system. He was made to wait for almost an hour after the appointed time and the adrenaline turned sour in his body, his courage sank into his boots and he began to tremble. Finally he was marched in and, after saluting, stood to attention facing his foe who looked smaller than he remembered him, smaller and greyer. The one thing he had not planned was his opening gambit. What was he to say? It hardly mattered since he had no intention of entering into an argument which he would inevitably lose. He began by complaining rather lamely of the intolerable and totally unjustified humiliation to which he was being subjected, coming finally to the point. He was not prepared to continue with the *Cadre*. Instead of being furious, the CO was almost paternal. 'Now, my boy, you must take your punishment like a man . . .' At this rate he would not be able to do anything and a sense of total failure overcame him. If the Colonel did not lose his temper, he could not let loose as he meant to do. Then the swagger stick fell from under his right arm, hitting the edge of the desk as it fell, and at last the CO's tone changed and took on that note of authority which Gai needed to provoke him: 'Pick it up!' He did so, but did not come back to attention, and this resulted in an angry command: 'Stand to attention!' repeated even more angrily when he failed to comply.

Exactly what happened next is uncertain. Gai did not have the diary, in which he would normally have recorded the incident in meticulous detail, and within the hour he was considering how he should tell the story to Ruth, the aunts and his friends, embroidering it a little to make it more interesting. He certainly brought his swagger stick down on the desk with a crack and he shouted something, though it was probably incoherent, before rushing from the office and slamming the door behind him. The whole interview had taken hardly a couple of minutes, although it seemed much longer. Then he ran the half-mile from the lines (where the offices were) to his room in the barracks. It was a beautiful sunny day and he ran joyfully, breaking his run now and then for a skip and a jump so that passers by turned to watch him. He had done it! Sweating and out of breath he threw himself down on his bed. His roommate, who was just leaving, asked: 'Had a nice day?' 'Very nice, thank you.' A moment later he heard the telephone ringing in the Company office just below him. Within a couple of minutes the Major came clumping up the stairs, accompanied by an NCO bodyguard to whom he remarked: 'That chap will end up in the loony bin! Now,' he said to Gai. 'Most unfortunate, but I have spoken to the CO and he's prepared to be generous. If you will go to him and apologise he's prepared to overlook the incident'. This was completely unexpected, but Gai only answered: 'No. There'd be violence'.

He need not have worried. He need not have worried for a moment, although he only discovered this a month or so later. Shortly before he had arrived in Maidstone another subaltern had fallen foul of the CO and had been given a punishment not permitted for officers according to King's Regulations, the 'bible' of the Army. This young man had an uncle in the War Office, and the CO had received a reprimand for exceeding his powers. Now he had done something far worse. He had humiliated an officer in front of the men. This blurred the distinction upon which all discipline was assumed to depend. It would be difficult to imagine a more serious offence than this, and the CO was in trouble. He could only hope that Gai had no relatives in high places and dispose of him as quietly and unobtrusively as possible.

Later in the afternoon he was sent to the young Medical Officer who seemed rather amused by the whole situation and asked: 'How about a spot of sick leave? Would that be a good idea?' It would, so next morning he returned to Berkhamsted. A week later he was instructed to report to a Medical Board and three elderly army doctors talked to him, repeating, as a formality, what Major S. had said. All would be forgiven if he apologised to the CO. 'Impossible', he said. 'I'm afraid there will be violence if I ever see that man again.' The most senior of them, a full Colonel, asked him to wait in his car while they conferred, adding that he would find the *Faber Book of Modern Verse* in the glove compartment, 'though I expect you know it by heart'. When he returned they told him that they considered him too 'highly strung' for military service and he would be invalided out of the army. Soon afterwards, he received a letter from the War Office regretting that ill health had terminated his army career and thanking him for his services.

But he had not quite finished with the West Kents. A Regimental Ball was to be held a couple of weeks later, and Betty had spent half her year's allocation of clothing coupons on a gown for the occasion. He did not want to disappoint her. He was still technically a member of the Regiment while on sick leave and still entitled to wear his uniform, so why not go? He returned to Maidstone and took her first to a pub to get up some Dutch courage. In any case, she needed cheering up. She thought this might be the last time she would see him. 'I want to remember this always, unspoiled', she said as they hugged and kissed, adding later: 'You make me feel terribly maternal. I feel responsible for making you get all the things you want in life'. Then they went on to the ball. The CO and his 'lady wife' were dancing sedately in the centre of the floor. He guided Betty closer and closer to them, then pushed her gently to bump them. It amused him to reflect that this was his threatened act of violence. The CO's eyes were fixed on the ceiling as though he found something of great interest there, demonstrating a fine example of the British stiff upper lip.

Gai chatted with a fellow subaltern who had been a lion tamer in civilian life. 'What are you going to do now?' he was asked. 'Dunno exactly, but I think I might go into the theatre.' His colleague laughed so much that he nearly fell off his chair: 'Right job for you, old boy, definitely the right job. I bet you'll be good at it. Should I ask for your autograph here and now?'

Back in Berkhamsted Ruth was preparing her case against the Erringtons with Colclough's help. Was there some kind of parallel between his gesture of defiance and that of his mother, defiance of the old men? He still did not realise that the CO might have represented, not his father as such but one side of his father, the authoritarian, the 'little Colonel'. He would always find it easier to be angry with a 'type' rather than with an individual or with an opinion. An article in the press would infuriate him as no person ever could. Real people were too complex and too multifaceted to be objects of wrath, but opinions could be damnable.

K A Y

T ime stood still in the Red House, Janus-headed. The past
was set in stone. The future was indecipherable but frightening, overshadowed by the need to earn a living and by
the case against the Erringtons, soon to come to Court. Ordered
by Francis to destroy the correspondence which would have
proved Gai's parentage conclusively, Ruth had to find two or
three people who would swear they had always known the truth.
Among these was Laura Hillary, who had tutored Gai as a child
and become her good friend. Perhaps Laura really had guessed,
perhaps not, but she signed the necessary affidavit.

He had thought that he was unashamed of his illegitimacy,
telling the story to his friends with a kind of pride, but a small incident brought with it the shadow of shame which had probably
always been lurking in a corner. Mrs Hopkins, the owner of the
horses on the Common, telephoned one day asking if he would
do her a favour. A sixteen-year-old schoolgirl who had just returned from America, where she had been an evacuee for the past
three years, was staying in the area and wanted to ride. Would
he look after her? This was no ordinary schoolgirl. Lady Jane
Douglas was the daughter of the Marquis of Queensbury. She

was also far more mature than any schoolgirl he had ever met and far more intelligent. His fascination with the aristocracy — inherited from his father? — was aroused, but he was even more fascinated when she talked of her eccentric 'Uncle Alfred', Lord Alfred Douglas, better known as Oscar Wilde's 'Bosie' (the ruthless young man who had destroyed Wilde).

They went riding almost daily, comfortably at ease together. The diary: 'Another ride with the Queensbury girl this morning, a brilliant windy day. The horses fresh and frisky as we cantered towards the Beacon. She kept up a flow of interesting talk; America, modern painting (her mother is a well-known artist), gossip about Augustus John and other famous people. She sparkles and she's absurdly sure of herself for her age. Near the Beacon we came upon a young rabbit with a great wound in its belly. "We ought really to kill it," she said doubtfully. What followed seemed to me pure D. H. Lawrence. I dismounted, knelt and squeezed the little creature's neck. The warm body writhed briefly in my hands, one ear that had been rigid fell back, a little blood oozed and the back legs gave a last jerk. Jane had exclaimed: "Oh, it's horrible. I can't watch!" but I had been aware of her eyes on me. I thought I should have failed her if I had not done as I did and the incident had a kind of mythic quality; the young girl on her tall mount and the suitor kneeling at the horse's feet performing a blood sacrifice to the Virgin Goddess. We were silent for a while afterwards, galloping up to the Beacon against a tremendous gale, both her hair and mine wild in the wind'.

When Jane left the area she suggested they should meet again. Gai proposed lunch in Town, but soon afterwards Lady Queensbury telephoned Ruth to say that her daughter was too young to go out with a man but that Gai would be welcome to come to tea one day. He did not take up the offer, realising the absurdity of his little fantasy. Apart from the fact that he was too poor to mix with such people, he was a bastard and this would soon be public knowledge if the case attracted publicity. Believing as he did in the virtues of a stratified society in which everyone knew their place, he did not know his place. How could he entertain any idea of entering 'smart society', as he would have dearly liked to do, wearing this badge of shame? 'Go in peace, little Jane', he thought, 'and find love'.

He was writing. That was what mattered. Already at Maidstone he had started on a romantic novel which he called *Prelude to Tempest*. Now he was hammering out at least a thousand words a day and was caught up in the story. He was also reading voraciously: St Augustine's neoplatonic sermons, Meister Eckhart, the Hindu *Upanishads* and the Taoist sage, Chuang Tzu. He absorbed only what made an immediate appeal to a touchstone within himself and evoked a spontaneous, heartfelt response: 'Of course! That's it, that's true!' It was as though he had started out with a blank page, but a page with defined borders and representing what, in some strange way, he already knew but could not as yet articulate even in his own mind. What he sought in books of wisdom was the articulation of this innate knowledge. When he read, in the Maitri *Upanishad*: 'The Golden Person who is within the supernal sun and who, from his golden station looks down upon this earth, is even he who dwells consuming food in the Lotus of the Heart', he believed that he recognised this as a truth he had always known. To others this might appear as a fancy way of saying: 'God is present at the deepest level of the human heart', but if he was to absorb such insights he needed them to be expressed in a particular idiom which provoked what he called the 'click' of recognition.

He did not believe that life could be divided into separate compartments, hermetically sealed. The spiritual and the mundane, the search for truth and a kiss, even 'real life' and fantasy, overlapped. He did not yet know that this was the Islamic perspective, but in MEO, the friend he had made two years earlier in an Oxford teashop, the spiritual and the mundane came together. He could talk to her about mysticism and he could seek her help in finding a job. She had set herself to procure him an entry into the film industry through her contacts and she enlisted the help of a Polish woman friend, Jadwiga. Ironically, this women was assistant to Ian Dalrymple, the very man who had earlier destroyed Gai's confidence by his cruel comments on his novel *Curtain Raiser* and who was now a power in the film world. There followed a number of interviews, including a long one with Dalrymple who said he would 'adore to help if he could' but betrayed, by his subsequent comments on 'this precious young man' to Jadwiga, the fact that his declaration of support meant nothing. A meeting with the most powerful figure of all, Sir Michael Balcon, proved inconclusive. Other interviews were less negative, but Gai was always afraid of appearing 'pushy' and that was not the attitude he needed to adopt.

He made frequent visits to Oxford to talk with MEO, but there were several reasons for these visits, including the Keble girls to whose parties he was invited. Peter Heyworth was now stationed there, and Peter needed any support Gai could offer. A few weeks previously he had been arrested for soliciting. Two young off-duty policemen had been out for an evening's sport 'queer-hunting' and one of them had smiled at Peter in a public toilet. Peter had returned the smile. That was all, but when he emerged a heavy hand had been laid on his shoulder. Instead of protesting he had panicked and babbled something to the effect that he would 'never do it again'. He had been brought up before a magistrate notorious for jailing homosexuals and sentence was about to be pronounced when his CO had marched into the Court and announced in peremptory tones that this young officer was required for the defence of the country and must be released. The magistrate, looking—so Peter said—like a tiger robbed of its prey, had complied. Peter had been very lucky, but he was traumatised none the less and it took him some time to recover.

There was another Peter whose friendship would become equally important to Gai, Peter Gastrell. They had met first in the army when both were in the Intelligence Corps and he too had been invalided out. Like Peter Heyworth he had a Jewish mother and he compensated for a deep sense of insecurity by forming a close and very select circle of friends around him. As he now had a house in Chelsea and a live-in girlfriend (whom he later married) he provided a base for these friends to meet regularly. They were a varied group. Apart from Gai there was John Mortimer who eventually became a famous novelist and dramatist, at that time a svelte young man whom no girl could resist and an armchair socialist. Sebastian, on the other hand, was an armchair fascist, a passionate supporter of General Franco, the Spanish dictator. David was a morose artist of considerable talent, and then there was Freddie, who might have stepped straight out of 'Brideshead' and who dismissed most of the people he met as N.Q.O.C.D. (Not Quite Our Class, Dear). The two Peters never met and their destinies were very different. Heyworth went on to become an eminent music critic, settled down with a young German, whom he mothered with a mixture of severity and tenderness, and died of a stroke in his seventies. Gastrell was divorced by his wife, fell agonisingly in love with a young prostitute of mixed race, eventually married a simple Corsican girl and was killed in a motor accident in his forties.

Gai had another reason for returning to Oxford whenever he could. Quite by chance he had learned that Ann—'Paris Ann'— was now living there. In the four years since he had last seen her they had both matured and he felt at ease with her as he had never done in the past. She was a softer person now, less prickly, and he immediately christened her 'Teddy Bear', aware that he would like to cuddle her in a storm. After that he saw her frequently and he introduced her to Peter Heyworth who commented afterwards: 'She's delightful! She has a nice steadying effect on you. Of course, she's the girl you ought to marry'. This renewed friendship was important. What he wanted most from life was continuity, a pattern in which the threads diverged, then came together again, a life which could never be defined in terms of 'one damn thing after another' and in which the people he cared for might be lost in parting but would re-emerge from the stream of time renewed and yet still the same. Later there was another re-union, another healing of a past wound. He went regularly to stay with Eleanor and Goo in Bedford, his favourite aunt and her friend, to be spoiled and cosseted, always aware that Brenda was next door. Then, as was bound to happen sooner or later, he ran into her in the street. He invited her to dinner in the Bridge Hotel and she astonished him by saying: 'If I hadn't known you for so long and if I didn't remember telling you to keep your eyes closed when you were kissing me and all that, I believe I could fall in love with you!' Overwhelmed, Gai replied that, if he had to marry someone there and then, it would be her. 'I'd be a handful', she told him. Soon afterwards she disappeared into the 'FANYs', the elite women's army, but now she had made it possible to remember her over the long years with tenderness.

Such reunions were wonderful and fulfilling, but what mattered most was his writing. Was he a novelist? He was more than half-way through *Prelude to Tempest* and decided to send what he had done to Leo Myers in the hope of encouragement. Leo's verdict was devastating. 'The novel has bewildered me in relation to you. It's like a portrait that is very like the sitter, and yet very unpleasing. Your plan was good, but when it came to writing you took the primrose path of superficiality and Narcissism. In real life you have had deep experiences and must have suffered real despondencies. But your hero is a little worldling . . . One feels that the author is writing out of a necking party personality, as though the book were written by the wretched hero who is a gross libel on yourself, unaware of his own triviality'. The letter was signed, 'with irate love'. So Gai would never attempt to write another novel. It was clear that, when he wrote fiction, he exposed the contemptible side of his nature. No doubt he did the same in his diary and would again do the same if he ever wrote the story of his life. The trouble, he reflected, is that this is the real me coming out.

The term 'necking party' has fallen out of use and requires explanation. Current in the thirties and forties, it referred to parties at which young people, usually adolescents, got together in the absence of their parents and paired off to kiss, cuddle and whisper sweet nothings to each other. Many years later he would have known how to answer Leo, for whom the worst of sins was what he called 'trivial-mindedness'. Gai would have demanded a definition of 'triviality'. He would have claimed that it was in the eye of the beholder, an attitude of mind which attaches this label to certain events. No event, he would have said, is in itself trivial. In the Islamic perspective, at least as he would one day present it, not only is everything in nature a 'sign of God', a reminder of what lies behind surface reality, but every event which occurs in the course of a human life is similarly a sign, whether or not it is perceived as such. God alone can judge what is or is not significant. Every event is eternally present in the divine Record and there is no triviality there.

Gai's isolated childhood and lonely adolescence had one positive outcome. Every encounter with 'the other' seemed and, indeed, was important but, if an erotic element was added to the encounter, then it became almost miraculous. Even a kiss between a man and a woman—a boy and a girl—was among the great 'signs' since it prefigured the union of all opposites, all dualities, in the One. If a 'necking party personality' was required to see this, so be it. Reductionists might see the matter their way, but that was their misfortune. He was delighted to find in a book written in extreme old age by one of his most deeply loved authors, Gustave Thibon, the confession: 'Yet I still prefer the sweetness of a kiss to the radiance of a star'. Compared with a great spiritual writer such as Thibon, it was Myers who seemed trivial-minded.

If Gai was a worldling, he should at least have been better able to deal with the world. Leo had once blamed him for not taking a more active part in helping Ruth to prepare her case against the Erringtons, but he left everything to her as he had always done. At the end of 1943 the case finally came to Court. Ruth and Gai arrived early at the Law Courts, both of them fearful. Colclough had warned them against being too hopeful He fussed over them and introduced the Counsel he had engaged after long consideration and without regard for cost. 'Then Ralph, Barbara and Esmé filed in with their battery of Leader and two junior Counsel. Mr Justice Uthwatt entered on the dot of eleven and I almost had to lift *Maman* to her feet. Opposing Counsel asked that the case should be heard *in camera* to preserve my reputation and the Judge ruled that I should be referred to simply as 'A'. Opening, our man, Wynn Perry, concentrated on the sums of money involved. Not until the Judge began to read through Father's surviving letters to *Maman*—some fifty typed pages— couched in affectionate terms and with many references to 'A', did I begin to feel hopeful. The Judge seemed to be enjoying them, and his mood was benign when he joked with Wynn Parry about me being 'apprenticed to a fishmonger in Northumberland to learn fly-fishing'. Then the opposing Leading Counsel rose and insisted that the Act of Parliament merely referred to 'reasonable provision for maintenance' and this had been made in the Will. He wished, he said to cross-question *Maman*. I touched her icy hand and she jumped to her feet, a warrior going into battle, but the man promptly changed his mind. Had the look on her face alarmed him? She had never looked more formidable. His colleagues rose in turn and mumbled exactly what he had said.

'The Judge, glancing at the clock, gave his judgement. He awarded *Maman* an additional annuity of £350 a year with costs against the Estate, regretting that he could make no provision for me as I was over eighteen. The Court rose. It had taken just an hour-and-a-half. Colclough wanted to take us to lunch at the Savoy but it was full so we went to the Meurice for a splendid lunch with whiskey and lager. Then we went to the Brompton Oratory to light a candle as Ruth had done the previous day'.

A few days later Ruth had a letter from Colclough. 'A very great wrong was done to you and I am pleased beyond measure that I have been instrumental in getting that wrong to some extent minimised. I can honestly say that no case has given me greater anxiety or a greater desire for success. I think this is the first case I know of in which a Judge has seen fit to exercise the discretion entrusted to him by the Legislature. I am so very glad that you had the courage to let me fight it for you.' Then he added something that can only remain a mystery. 'The wheel has turned full circle since first we met and, by a strange turn of fate, it has fallen to me to come to your aid in time of need.' What could Ruth have done for him when he was in need, so many years before? Gai never asked her.

Early in the New Year, now twenty-three but still a mother's boy, Gai had a mild attack of flu and Ruth decided that he needed some sunshine—as much as might be available to England—to warm his bones. She sent him to stay in a hotel in Paignton, a relatively sunny town in Devonshire. In later life he asked himself again and again whether, if he had had a premonition that this holiday would change the course of his life for ever, he would still have gone. Would he have cowered at home, unwilling to face change or grasped the future in both hands? He hoped that he would still have had the courage to go.

The hotel was full of elderly people, but the bar was crowded with American airmen who were stationed near by. On his second day, however, he met two girls, Kay and Patricia, the one fair-haired, good-looking and, he judged, something of an intellectual, the other—much more his type—a dark-haired beauty. Within twenty-four hours Gai was their friend and constant companion. The two of them had driven an ambulance together right through the *Blitz* and afterwards, but Kay had gone down with pleurisy and her friend, Patricia, was keeping her company in her convalescence. It was one of the strange aspects of war that two young women with a privileged, sheltered upbringing should have found themselves, without preparation, dealing day after day—or night after night—with the dead and the dying while themselves risking a cruel death at every turn. There was a dance every evening in the hotel so he found himself dancing with each in turn and defending first one and then the other from the clumsy approaches of drunken Americans. To protect themselves Patricia, who was married to an officer fighting in Burma, claimed that Gai was her husband, Kay that he was her boyfriend. Not all the Americans were so crude. One evening a boy who could not have been more than eighteen, member of a bomber crew, asked if he might join them at their table. He confessed that he was frightened all the time. 'Before take off,' he said, 'they give us candy and an orange. I always eat my candy first. After all—you never know, do you?' When he wandered off to join his buddies both girls had tears in their eyes.

Gai was attracted to Patricia and liked Kay, but there was no doubt as to which was designed for him. Dancing with Patricia he made polite conversation, with Kay there was a meeting of minds and a compatibility of temperaments or so it seemed, and the discovery that she was interested in mysticism, loved the poems of St John of the Cross and had read Leo Myers seemed almost too good to be true, as indeed it was. He did not at once catch onto the explanation. Before the war she had been a debutante, presented to the King and Queen as was the custom in those days. She had hated the whole business and had little use for the young men she met, but the process of 'coming out' had left its mark. The first lesson a debutante learned was to find out within five minutes of being introduced exactly what a man's interests were, to encourage him to talk about them and to pretend a lively interest. If nothing else, this required a wide if superficial education. She must be equipped to discuss religion or golf, world affairs or which were the best night clubs. Kay had been to a leading girls' public school. She had hated that too, but her education could not be faulted.

Her childhood had been, in its way, as strange as his. Her father, Harold Clayton, had been Financial Secretary in the Burmese administration, in effect Number Two to the Governor, whom he was likely to succeed in due course. A colonial Governor must have a wife, so he had had married a woman entirely suitable for her future role. Unfortunately she had been unable to tolerate the Burmese climate and, having given birth to Kay, withdrew to England. It was clear that his daughter would have to be his hostess, the First Lady of Burma, and he had begun to train her. On trips up river the government launch would stop at each major village and the village headman would come aboard to do obeisance to the six-year-old child—enthroned in a chair too big for her—scattering flowers at her feet. Clayton however was a man of duty, a Bishop's son, and eventually his sense of duty to his wife had triumphed. What kind of marriage was this if he was only to see her during periods of home leave? He had retired in his early forties and his great talents had gone to waste. Apart from a period as Secretary to the Church of England Men's Society, he had done nothing with his life and had become an angry, embittered man. But how could Kay now fulfil her role? Sensibly, she had decided to become an actress. Perhaps she could at least be a princess on stage.

They returned to London where the two girls had rented a Mews cottage which soon became Gai's home-from-home while Ruth searched for a flat in Town. Preoccupied with his growing intimacy with Kay, he took little interest in flat-hunting, eventually paying the price for his irresponsibility. The 'doodlebugs' —pilotless flying bombs—had begun to fall on London and no one in their right senses was buying property, so this was the time to invest in property. A Mews cottage, offering peace and privacy, could probably have been had for £150. A small house in Chelsea, just across the King's Road from Drayton Gardens where Ruth finally settled, would not have cost more than £200. Before the end of the century these houses would be worth over a million pounds apiece. As it was, she rented a five-room apartment, quite unaware that, in due course, the rent would increase whereas her modest income was fixed. After being virtually bedridden for nearly twenty years, she was now in perfect health and had been ever since Francis's death. She joined the French Club and the exclusive Hurlingham Club, made new friends and enjoyed an active life. It seemed that the cause of her long illness had been, not 'bugs in her water works', but her husband.

Now that she had triumphed over him, exposing his hypocrisy to the world, she might perhaps have forgiven him, but forgiveness was not her way. Hatred fed on itself and every small act of meanness was recalled from the distant past in which it had festered unperceived. 'How I could have made that old man squirm', she said one day. 'He'd have doubled up—I can just see him—if I had once let loose at him. I wish I believed in an afterlife, I'd enter heaven like a whirlwind of rage.' The likelihood of a 'whirlwind of rage' entering heaven seemed to Gai improbable, and the 'old man' in question was his father whom he had forgiven— assuming that forgiveness was required—long ago, but he said nothing. He had to allow for a proud woman's belated reaction to the humiliations she had suffered.

While Kay searched for an entry into the theatre, Gai waited for MEO, Jadwiga or someone else to find him a job in films. He did not have to wait long. The diary entry for 9 February: 'It's fantastic! I've got a job. Feeling all "babes-in-the woodsy", scared, almost howling for Kay, but she's out of Town. I want her so! Just for her to hug me'. An interview had been arranged for him with Michael Powell, one of the most outstanding film-makers of the time and a cult figure among movie buffs fifty years later, a producer, director and scriptwriter all in one, a man of superabundant energy and inventiveness. The interview took place, not in an office but on the stage of the Piccadilly Theatre. Powell had decided to break into live theatre and had chosen, with his habitual daring, to produce the only play that Ernest Hemingway ever wrote, *The Fifth Column*, set in the Spanish Civil War.

The stage was crowded with people and Gai came face to face with a small balding man whose piercing blue eyes seemed to stare unblinkingly into his soul and who greeted him with little more than a grunt. He poured out his ambitions to be involved in film-making. There was no response except for that intimidating scrutiny, so he began to dry up and finally fell silent. For a few moments which seemed to last for ever Powell continued to stare at him, then he turned to the Stage Manager who was at his side and said brusquely: 'This is Gai. I like him. Assistant Stage Manager'. Always a man of few words, he turned back to Gai: 'Six pounds a week. Suit you?' 'Yes, yes OK. When do I start?' 'Now', said Powell. 'Could we make it Friday?' 'Yes.' And that was that. It was a start.

Rehearsals were in London and, having done nothing since leaving the Army, Gai found himself working up to ten hours a day, but he was a quick learner and, by the time the company set off on tour, opening in Glasgow, he was getting the hang of the job. By then he was already enthralled by the cast and loved them all. The star was Roger Livesey, possibly one of the most likeable men he had ever met, and included Frederick Valk, regarded by some as the most outstanding Shakespearean actor of his generation. There was Peter Cushing, the star of many horror movies in later years, and a sweet natured French actress, Yvonne André, and then there was the Leading Lady, a pretty Australian actress called Margaret Johnston with whom Gai was soon half in love. There was no hierarchy in the company and, since he was so young and so green, he was adopted as a kind of mascot and everyone was kind to him. The joke soon went round that 'our Gai is enamoured of the Leading Lady'. Always something of an exhibitionist, he played this role of humble worshipper to the full and was rewarded with many delicious smiles from the lady in question.

But it was Roger Livesey who soon became his hero. Roger was not a conventionally handsome man and, in general, he played character parts, but these he played superbly (as in Powell's film, *The Life and Death of Colonel Blimp*) and with an individual style that was inimitable. Equally inimitable was his voice. John Gielgud was considered to have a voice of uncommon beauty, but it was rarefied and a little unearthly. Roger's voice was no less beautiful, but it was powerful and earthy, with a tremendous range. Sometimes it was spine-tingling. In the course of one of his speeches in the play the words 'great flights of geese' occurred, and then his voice soared to the heights. Years later, when Gai was doing a good deal of public speaking, he would sometimes detect in his own voice, at moments of strong emotion, a dim echo of Roger's 'great flights'. As the company travelled from one town to another—Manchester after Glasgow, then Newcastle and other northern towns—he alternated between staying in theatre digs and spending a few days in the hotel in which the leading members of the cast were staying, and, on these occasions, Roger always invited him to join them at meals. He wrote a letter bubbling over with enthusiasm to Leo Myers and received a kind but slightly barbed reply. 'The Ancient Fathers of the Church held cheerfulness, the capacity to enjoy life and amiability to be of the first importance. You abound in these qualities . . . But to enjoy the company of play actors and —wonder of wonders!—to rejoice in a job connected with the stage, all this is to me a marvel.'

He missed Kay painfully. She had now got a job in the chorus of a touring production of an old but popular musical, *The Country Girl*. This was, to say the least, a humble beginning, but at least it, too, was a start and she had her Equity card. With her upper class accent and air of distinction, she made an odd chorus girl, but she was soon adored by the other girls. She was by nature immensely generous and she would go to any amount of trouble to help others. She became Mother Confessor to the Chorus and also their defender, able to speak to those in authority in tones that commanded their respect. If there was something of *noblesse oblige* in this, no one minded, and she had a deep conviction that her privileged background imposed on her a duty to fight for the less fortunate. She and Gai wrote to each other several times a week and love fed on absence.

He, meanwhile, was growing into his job which consisted mainly in checking the props before each performance and taking care of the sound system, a constant source of trouble. But the cast was becoming increasingly worried. In his search for a West End theatre Powell was constantly frustrated by the two London managements who had the field sewn up and did not welcome the attempt by an outsider to break into the magic circle, particularly such a formidable outsider. Judith Furse, who was in charge of the company in his absence, sent him a stream of telegrams demanding to know what was happening. The only reply she received was unhelpful: 'Yes, I know I'm the meanest man in trousers, but I love you all'. After eight weeks the show folded, no London theatre being available, and the members of the cast went their different ways. That was how it was in the profession.

Ruth was now settled in the Drayton Gardens flat. Early in April she showed Gai a letter she had just received from Leo Myers, who had been corresponding with her regularly, a correspondence usually concerned with the mystery and perversity of Gai's 'double nature'. This letter was different. 'I think he's going to commit suicide', she said. There was nothing in the letter to suggest anything of the sort, beyond his usual complaints about his health, the state of the world and the likelihood that Britain would become a fascist country. A few days later she came to him in tears with the news that Leo was dead. He had taken an overdose of Veronal after arranging his affairs in an orderly manner. Why had he done it? No one would ever know. Despair, certainly, but that explained nothing. As well as grief, Gai felt a touch of guilt. He had disappointed his friend at a time in his life when he was already beset with disappointments and when the horror of old age obsessed him.

But Leo's death taught him more than he could ever have learned from his books, though it required a long time for him to understand its significance. His wisdom had been only in his head and had never penetrated his human substance or been reflected in his conduct. A man might spend a lifetime reading spiritual books and studying the writings of the great mystics. He might begin to feel that he had penetrated the secrets of the heavens and the earth, but unless this knowledge was incorporated into his very nature and transformed him, it was sterile. When the real trials encompassed him it would desert him, leaving him naked to the cruel wind. Eventually Gai would see that a simple man of faith, praying to God with little understanding but with humility and with a full heart, might be worth more than the most learned student of the spiritual sciences. But it would be many years before he had this insight, and many more years before he would try to put it into practice.

For the present he had to live with his contradictions, more apparent to others than to himself. While on tour he had written exuberant letters to MEO, now he wrote in a more introspective mood and her response surprised him. 'How like the limbo that state of extraversion is,' she wrote. 'You were not even in the letters you wrote to me. A shade might have written them, the not-self. But where does the self go then and why does it suddenly live again?' Expressed more gently, this was similar to Leo's comments on the 'wretched hero' of the novel. The implication seemed to be that Gai was, on the one hand, a serious-minded young man with a wisdom surprising in someone of his age, on the other a worthless playboy, empty-headed and self-indulgent. The solution must be to kill off the playboy, and then he would be truly himself. He did not think it worked quite like that. He was one person, an introvert and an extravert, a man with spiritual aspirations and a playboy, a playboy with spiritual aspirations.

He could not divide the two, nor did he want to divide them, they were so closely interconnected. Kill one, he thought, and the other might die. Dismemberment was not the answer.

He thought Kay might have the answer, but all she could say was that she loved him just as he was. He was free now to travel to whatever town *The Country Girl* was playing and spend time with her. In Peterborough, after the show, they strolled hand-in-hand round the Cathedral. 'The reverse side of my dependency on people—nothing makes me feel stronger, closer to the heart of things than someone turning to me for comfort and reassurance, and my Kay did so this evening. She clung to me, her face ghostly in the darkness, her eyes pools of light.' Her grandfather had been Bishop of Peterborough and the present incumbent was a friend of the family. She told Gai that he had put the Cathedral at her disposal the day she got married. 'I thought to myself rather ironically that this was the only time the chance of being married in a cathedral would come my way. Such a noble setting would rather appeal to me!' He had finally overcome his terror of being responsible for a pregnancy and, on a visit to Manchester, their relationship was at last fully consummated. It made a difference, a greater difference than he had anticipated. Now she was a part of him, now they had bonded.

Even so, he had no thought of marriage. There was too much life to be lived before that; so many adventures, so many girls. They would part, but perhaps they might come together again one day. That would be the time to talk of marriage. 'I wrote her a very long letter concerning my 'destiny' and saying that happiness with her could only be a station on the way and so on'. In her reply she was too sensible to reproach him for this but wrote only of her love for him. He felt that everything was under control, always a dangerous supposition.

In May of 1944 an agent with whom Roger or some other member of the cast had put him in touch gave him an introduction to J. Baxter Somerville (always known as 'JB') who owned repertory theatres ('Stock' to Americans) in Brighton and in a Welsh town, Llandrindod Wells, as well as a London theatre. In contrast to Powell, JB was an avuncular character whom it would have been impossible to dislike and, after a friendly but perfunctory interview, he offered Gai a job with the Llandrindod 'Rep'. He also obtained an Equity card for him, making him a member of the actors' trade union. On 21 June he set off for Wales, having survived the previous night. 'I thought we were done for. In the early hours a doodlebug, throbbing closer and closer, cut out almost directly overhead. There was a swishing sound and I put my head under the bedclothes and wondered what it would be like to die. The explosion shook the building and my room was momentarily illuminated. Another soon afterwards. I'm told that poor old Miss Donovan, a neighbour, got dressed and sat, her bag over her arm, awaiting the call to Heaven.'

So now he was an actor. It was a very small company and he had a part in every play they put on, a different one each week, ranging from farces to serious drama. He had no fear of an anonymous audience, shadowy figures beyond the footlights—all the more shadowy because he was short-sighted—but, in the first play in which he had a part, he was briefly alone on the stage when the curtain went up. The small stage seemed to expand until he was reduced to a tiny figure in a vast expanse, a whole world isolated from the rest of the universe and self-sufficient. At Charterhouse he had learned reams of poetry by heart, so learning his lines was no problem.

JB had a farm with horses close to the town and invited Gai to ride whenever he wanted. Between learning his lines, rehearsing, playing whatever part he had been given, cycling over to the farm for a ride and getting to know the company, it was a pleasant life. But he was missing Kay dreadfully. They exchanged passionate love letters, and she often surprised him. 'If you want a nice singy-songy Welsh girl,' she told him, 'have her. It wouldn't worry me. I've never regarded physical fidelity in a man as of the slightest importance'. Later: 'Why have you taken away my peace of mind with you? I can't imagine a world without you to long for . . . I can do nothing for myself any more—so be very tender with me'. Later still: 'I love you, and you love me, but I don't see us married. I don't think it would work for long because you don't know yourself yet. I love you with my heart, my mind and my body, so I can be your mistress and love it, as I do'.

At the end of July she got a few days off from *The Country Girl* and came to Llandrindod for a joyful reunion. Gai did not remember ever before being so happy. They romped and played together like puppies, swam in the river and made love. He was aware of how impressed the rest of the company was with his beautiful girlfriend and he swelled with pride. He must, surely, be the luckiest man in the world. On their third night together, drowsy after lovemaking, they talked for a long while until she said something that must have been on her mind since her arrival. The 'secrecy and deceiving', she said, were becoming too painful for her. She loved him too much to go on in this way and had begun to think that it would be 'a very, very good thing' if they got married. Even if it lasted for only two or three years it would be worth it.

His body registered the shock even before his mind had fully grasped what she had said. 'I lay like a stone beside her, tears in my eyes. I couldn't speak or touch her, paralysed as every fear and every conflict I had ever known came to the surface at boiling point. She felt my misery and tried to comfort me while I felt self-contempt for needing this comfort. Still I lay, still unable to speak, while a battle royal in which I personally seemed to have no part raged independently in my mind. Gradually I relaxed, put the problem aside to be considered next day, and we made love again.'

After that he slept peacefully. Tomorrow would be another time, a new beginning or, perhaps, an end. He was too exhausted to know or even to care which it would be.

10

G U É N O N

Next morning they walked by the river in bright sunshine. At first he said nothing, waiting for his mind to make itself up. 'You looked so stern,' she told him later. 'I felt terribly frightened and about two years old.' After a while they began to talk. Having said, the previous night, that it would be worth getting married even if it lasted only two or three years, she now amended this to 'a year or two'. He had supposed that marriages were supposed in principle to last a lifetime so this put a completely different complexion on the matter. The war would soon be over, but travel might not be possible for a while afterwards. Taking what remained of the £1,000 Francis had left him, he would be able to set out on the Voyage and his life, the life he dreamed of, would really begin. As to sexual adventure, that would be no problem. She said again that she attached no importance to physical fidelity on the part of a man. She seemed to believe that husbands had mistresses much as dogs have fleas, although a mistress must know her place and never, even in thought, attempt to replace the wife. Meanwhile, he reckoned up the advantages. No more hiding in corners, no more clandestine meetings, no need to enter 'Mr and Mrs Smith' in hotel registers. They would be legitimate.

Gai was impressed by her knowledge of the world, her wisdom and foresight. She was eighteen months older than him, but in worldly experience she seemed old enough to be his mother. If she believed that a temporary marriage was possible without damaging anyone, she must be right. 'Only one thing matters', she said. 'Do you love me and want to be married to me?' Did he love her? He wanted and needed her, but he did not ask himself the key question: if she was suffering, would he care, would he share that suffering? He thought he knew the answer to her question. 'Like a sleepwalker,' he wrote in the diary, 'barely conscious of what I was doing, I said "Yes" with complete conviction. I didn't recognise myself, but I had a conviction of rightness. Some inner voice had made itself heard as a categorical imperative'. She set out certain conditions. There was to be no question of him keeping her financially. If either of them felt that the marriage had gone dead, they were free to end it there and then. She added that she had been engaged on two previous occasions because the men concerned could give her everything she thought she wanted. Now all she wanted was him. 'And that's all you'll get', he told her rather grimly.

Kay returned to *The Country Girl*, which was still on tour, and Gai sat down to write to Ruth, Peter, MEO and his aunts, Eleanor and Dolly. In the diary he wrote: 'What's happened to me? The snake has sloughed off its skin. Yesterday that old skin seemed as firm as ever. Today it lies twisted, yellow on the river bank. God save us all from imagining that we have any control over our own lives. I'm frightened and could easily cry again, but only a small part of me weeps for the cast-off skin. Let go!' Next day he chanced to run into JB and told him the news. JB had met Kay on one of her visits to Llandrindod and immediately offered her a job with the Company. So one problem was solved. They would have safe employment until something better offered and they would be together.

For a couple of days he was euphoric, quite unaware of the impending storm. When it broke he was crushed. Ruth's response to the news was savage. He had often admired the 'stinkers' that she wrote with such abusive eloquence to people who annoyed her. He had never expected to be the target of such a missile himself. Normally he copied excerpts from important letters into the diary, but in this case he could not bear to do so. He did, however, copy parts of a second letter received a few days later. This she said was the final tragedy of her life, after which there was nothing for her but to disappear from the scene. 'How can I make you understand the enormity of your behaviour? You hadn't even the decency to let me down gently. You've successfully administered the *coup de grace* to me. When you've made your plans you will let me know where to send your things. This spoiled, wilful, scheming girl has got you in her clutches.' He read the letter to Kay over the phone and she offered to release him from the engagement, adding that 'great love can renounce if it must'. It was too late for this, much too late. His mother, he firmly believed, had cast him adrift and would never forgive him. He knew how implacable she could be, and now she had associated him explicitly with the arch-enemy, his father. He was alone. To whom could he cling if not to Kay?

His aunt Eleanor wrote to him in similar terms, telling him that he was ruining his life. Some measure of relief came with a letter from Dolly, now living in the Sussex village of Etchingham on the small pension paid her by the publishers of *The Strand Magazine*. Consciously or not, she seized this opportunity to triumph over Ruth whom, as a small child, she had followed around bleating 'Dolly *aussi*'—'Me too'. Now she could effectively replace her elder sister in Gai's trust and affection, so she wrote with enthusiasm of how the love of a nice girl would stabilise him and give him a motive to succeed in life. Gai at once dismissed Eleanor, replacing her with Dolly as his favourite aunt (Violet and Rose did not come into the picture).

Kay's parents, the Claytons, were hardly less appalled than Ruth. With her background she should marry money or a title, not a penniless actor who happened also to be illegitimate. As she was playing Hereford at the time, a meeting was arranged there in August. Peter Heyworth, who had joined the chorus of disapproval, came too. They processed in pairs round the Cathedral. First Alice Clayton walked with Gai, warning him of the bitter suffering he was bound to cause her daughter, adding that Ruth's 'insults' (presumably those contained in the letter he had read to Kay) could never be forgiven, while Peter lectured Kay on the folly of this engagement in view of Gai's immaturity and irresponsibility. Then they changed partners and Peter took his turn to warn him that he was ruining his life and probably Kay's as well. Alice, meanwhile, begged her daughter to think again. So the whole world (except for dear Dolly) was against them and the unhappy couple clung to each other like orphans in a storm.

The storm cleared as suddenly as it had come, leaving behind it a menacing rumble of thunder. Early in September Gai had a telegram from Ruth saying simply: 'Withdraw all opposition. Love. Mother'. Soon afterwards she agreed to meet the Claytons, a chilly meeting. 'They make me think of two elderly tortoises,' she wrote, 'who cannot understand how they came to give birth to a butterfly'. When Gai went up to London, their first encounter since the storm broke, he hugged her and asked: 'Am I forgiven?' 'Of course you are, my love,' adding, 'We all rather lost our heads at the time'. He and Kay, she told him, could take over the Mall Chambers flat which she had rented since the beginning of the century, so at least they would have a home of their own. He wondered if he would ever be able to love Kay as he loved his mother. He doubted it. Soon afterwards she lunched with Kay who told Gai that she had been 'so easy to talk to, so sweet and kind'.

Plans for the wedding went ahead. Making the best of a bad job, the Claytons arranged a grand ceremony on 5 December 1944, in a fashionable London church, St Saviour's, with the Bishop of

Peterborough presiding. 'What a farce' was Ruth's only comment, and Gai felt rather the same since this would clearly not be a Christian marriage. There exists a photograph which would be comical if it was not so sad. Harold Clayton, who always looked grim, wears an expression that should have frozen the film in the camera. Alice looks as though she is suffering severe pain with a stiff upper lip. Ruth, tight-lipped, is the very image of anger only just under control, and Peter, the Best Man, may be trying to smile but cannot quite manage it. As for the photograph of the couple themselves, Kay has an air of triumphant happiness while Gai appears a little confused as to quite what is going on. There were no good fairies around on that day.

Ruth paid for their honeymoon in the grandest of grand hotels, the Imperial in Torquay. On their second evening, when the guests were assembled in the lobby for dinner, Kay made an entrance that turned every head. In a long black skirt topped with a hundred-year-old Burmese blouse, inset with iridescent beetle and butterfly wings, she came slowly down the main staircase. Gai swelled with pride, hardly able to believe that this beautiful woman was his wife. Not even the Imperial was allowed sufficient fuel to heat the hotel adequately and that night they made love on the carpet of their bedroom in front of a single-bar electric heater.

They returned to Llandrindod, now both of them members of the Regency Players. Kay charmed and delighted the members of the Company, and Gai basked in her reflected glory. Even his acting improved as he became increasingly confident, at ease with himself and with everyone. It was a bitterly cold winter but now he had Kay to keep him warm, both psychologically and physically. He was often intrigued by her opinions. In matters of social behaviour they were positively Victorian, but, when it came to sex, they were unpredictable; one evening she told him: 'Women like to be treated as animals, otherwise they feel something is wrong'. Would any Victorian maiden have said this? Life in

Llandrindod could not be better, although there were problems in the theatre. She was playing Principal Boy in the annual pantomime. On the day after Christmas he noted in his diary: 'Matinée a catastrophe. Icy theatre, no front tabs, Eric (director) having hysterics, revived with last of our whiskey, Kay going on twice to fill a gap when no one knew who was on next, Maureen with flu. A drink, dinner and then the evening show, all of us feeling mutinous; baton and tabs came down in one scene, just missing John. Kay's voice going to pieces, little dancer cut herself'.

The Company went on tour. In Weston-super-Mare, a small town distinguished by a vast expanse of mud where the sea should have been, Kay announced that, in spite of all their precautions, she thought she was pregnant. The next week, in Exeter—it was now mid-February of 1945—this was confirmed, and Gai saw all his hopes for the future crash down on his head. The 'perambulator in the hall' was now a reality, except that the Mall Chambers flat had no hall and, in any case, no pram could be carried up the four flights of uncarpeted steps leading up to the flat. They walked round and round the Cathedral talking. 'I wish you'd never met me', she said. 'Then you wouldn't be so unhappy'.

One mid-winter evening some fifty years later two old friends —a 'Bone' and a 'Boo'—who had once been married to each other would sit before a blazing log fire reminiscing, as they did from time to time. Kay ('Boo'), who paid him a visit whenever she was feeling depressed, had drunk a good deal of whiskey and was becoming sentimental. Suddenly she said: 'You know, don't you, that I got pregnant deliberately?' Gai did not believe her. She had always been something of a fantasist and he thought she might be unwilling to accept that the person she loved most in the world, now a successful documentary film producer in America, could have been the result of an accident. He made no comment. In any case, it no longer mattered.

Here and now they seated themselves on a bench by the Cathedral wall. She told him she would not have an abortion. A few minutes later she said that she would if that was what he wanted. The idea made him shudder. Abortions were what happened to servant girls at the hands of hideous old witches with knitting needles. But could this be the solution? If so, it must be her decision. He could never take the responsibility. Finally she decided to seek the advice of a third party, a friend in London. This was a curious choice. The friend in question, Denis, was an eminent psychiatrist with whom she had been in love for two years before she met Gai. In all that time he had never touched her and she had become increasingly frustrated. In the end she had summoned the courage to ask him what was wrong. Hugely amused, he had told her that he was homosexual. She had asked him why, in that case, he had led her on. Still amused he had told her that one of his greatest pleasures was to make a woman suffer. Nevertheless, it was to Denis that she went for advice the following day. He laughed at her and told her to make up her own silly mind.

That was what she did on the train back to Exeter and she came up with what seemed to Gai a brilliant solution. The baby would be handed over at birth to her parents who could well afford to employ a live-in Nanny. There was plenty of space in their house in the country and they might be happy to have a child around the place. Gai would be relieved of all responsibility and she could continue her career in the theatre as soon as she was on her feet again. He marvelled at her capacity to solve any problem that arose, reflecting that he need never worry about anything with such a wise woman at his side. The notion that she might be as foolish and impractical as he was never crossed his mind. It might have done so if he had consulted his memory. As a small child he had dreamed of having children and worried because he would have to share them with a woman rather than having them all to himself. When he was nineteen he had written in almost identical terms in his diary. It should now have been obvious to him that he would be intensely possessive over any child or children he might have. The thought of handing over his son or daughter to strangers—hostile strangers at that—should at once have struck him with horror, but he could not see beyond the panic of the moment.

In July they left Llandrindod for the last time and moved into Mall Chambers until, in advanced pregnancy, Kay went to stay with her parents. On the 26th there had been a General Election which, to Gai's horror and astonishment, brought the Labour Party to power with Attlee—a little man he detested—as Prime Minister. For six years of war the British had been schooled in obedience to authority, anything else being akin to treason, and now they were in no condition to resist an authoritarian government determined on a campaign of 'social engineering'. National Socialism had been defeated, but Soviet Socialism had triumphed and now British Socialism was in a position to be almost equally authoritarian. Even VE (Victory in Europe) Night on 8 May seemed to Gai less glorious than it might have been now that Churchill, the architect of victory, had been discarded although the spirit of the crowds around Buckingham Palace that night, with complete strangers kissing each other passionately, was probably unprecedented in British history. Crushed in the vast mass of people at the gates of Buckingham Palace he felt himself one with them.

Money was now once again the obsessive problem. He got some work as an extra in various films, on one occasion dancing for ten hours in a ballroom scene with a partner who stole fruit from the tables, thrusting a plum and an orange into the pockets of his dinner jacket. Jadwiga got him another interview with Michael Powell who promised him 'something' in his new film, *A Matter of Life and Death*. Powell kept his promise. Raymond Massey, who played the American inquisitor, had to rush back to Hollywood before all his scenes with David Niven had been shot. Gai was given the job of standing in for Massey in the back shots focused on Niven and given six weeks to study Massey's mannerisms before the scenes were actually shot. He was thrilled to stand face-to-face with a famous Hollywood film star and even more thrilled by the presence of Roger Livesey, friendly as ever, who played the doctor in the film. He earned enough to last him some three months.

On 12 October 1945, Kay gave birth to a healthy boy after a difficult labour. She had no views on naming him, so Gai chose 'Leo Francis', not without a sense of irony. Leo Myers, had he still been alive, would have joined the chorus of disapproval over the marriage and denounced Gai's irresponsibility. Now Myers was saddled with a posthumous godson, and 'Francis' was an acknowledgement of the father who had never acknowledged him.

He was now writing again, this time in a serious vein. He thought best on paper rather than in his head and he needed to sort out what he had learned over the past four years of reading on Hindu Vedanta, Chinese Taoism and Zen Buddhism. He began a series of essays, to be called *Affirmations*. The floodgates were opened and he found that he understood much that had previously been obscure. It was as though this raw material had been through a selective process of digestion and what emerged was his personal interpretation. He surprised himself. 'Divine possession', he wrote one evening in the diary. 'Joy and assurance!' On a visit to the Claytons in Grafham to see the 'Boolet', as he and Kay called their offspring (she was 'Boo' and the baby had a bullet head), he gave one of the essays to Harold to read, feeling sure of his approval. The following evening the proud author was summoned to his father-in-law's study. 'I was out of touch with reality and real people,' he told me. 'I seemed to have no interest in real people, and my lack of rough, lived-through experience vitiated my writing. It was all very well to sit on a river bank having beautiful thoughts, but I must row on the river. The tone of my essay was both patronising towards ordinary people and didactic.' Gai took all this like a lamb brought to the slaughter and said nothing. What could he say?

As soon as she was well enough Kay began a round of auditions and, in December, got a small part in a touring pantomime. In mid-January she wrote to say that she was pregnant again. Gai began to wonder if there was some truth in Ruth's conviction that 'Nature' had designed him to compensate for a barren family The precautions available at the time could not, it seemed, frustrate this destiny. There would always be one little sperm—one out of millions—clever enough to circumvent the defences. In the event, an older woman in the company plied Kay with drugs which, after two weeks, induced a painful miscarriage, but Kay had told her parents of this. Gai could no longer go to see his son unless she was with him. The only time he tried to do so, he was told that it would be inconvenient. His dreams, however, were troubled. 'Dreamt last night of the Boolet, a dream which released a flood of feeling for him and a confused sense of guilt and rage that we can't have him with us and bring him up ourselves. Then, longing for Kay, I felt the most damnable desire to hurt her.'

The next time they went down to Grafham to see their son he was seized with an intense fit of jealousy, knowing only too well how ungrateful this was. Alice Clayton and the Nanny seemed to take it in turn to pet 'the dear little thing' and fuss over him, and one or other always appeared just when he wanted to be alone with the infant and try to establish some kind of unspoken communication with him. They both seemed to resent his presence. In the afternoon there was a tea party with a neighbour who lived at the top of a small hill. When they returned Gai remarked on how pleasant it must be to live in a house with such a wonderful view. This, Harold told him, was clear evidence that he wanted to be in a position to look down on ordinary people from a position of superiority. After that he should have learned to keep his mouth shut but, on another occasion when some friends were visiting and the conversation turned to the wonderful new world of peace and friendship which lay ahead for humanity, he felt the need to say something and suggested that there might yet be problems with the Soviet Union. This, Harold, pointed out, demonstrated his malevolence. It was clear that he hoped, not for an age of peace, but for conflict and misery. From now on, if he wanted to see his son, as he did with desperate longing, he must take his courage in both hands and plunge into poisoned waters. Harold, as a committed Christian, could not permit himself to feel hatred for anyone, but there are times when human nature overcomes good intentions.

On yet another occasion, when he had still not found work, he was again summoned to the study to be told: 'I would like to be proud of my son-in-law, but you make it extremely difficult for me'. Nowadays the young are seldom in awe of their elders, but in the 1940s the authority of the old men was still unchallenged. Perhaps, if Gai had shown the arrogance of which he was accused and proclaimed himself a genius, or if he had said to Kay, 'To hell with your father, tell him to shut up', he might at least have retained some shreds of dignity, whatever the cost. As it was, the self-confidence he had acquired before his marriage had seeped away and this affected his search for work. He had interviews with the BBC, the British Council and, finally, with UNESCO (the United Nations Educational, Scientific and Cultural Organisation), a job which would have taken them out of England with the Boolet, but he went into each interview expecting rejection and he was, of course, rejected.

Meanwhile the marriage was fast deteriorating and there was no peace or reassurance in Mall Chambers, nor was there any consistency on Kay's part. One day she would be full of reproaches, declaring that she hated him and threatening to leave him. She had no feelings left for him, she said, except physical passion, and that was not enough. Within 48 hours she would be contrite and apologetic, affectionate and comforting. He never knew where he was with her from one day to the next. They had no rows. It takes two to have a row and, at the slightest sign of hostility, he retired into his shell, but this shell was a miserable place in which to live. Kay went to one audition after another, always returning in floods of tears, reducing Gai to bleak despair, but she usually recovered within an hour or two leaving him still sunk in the depths. One day she had a talk with Ruth who appeared sympathetic to her complaints and agreed that Gai was a hopeless case, only to tell him soon afterwards of his wife's 'treason' and to remark bitterly on 'what a cuckoo he had brought into the nest'.

Then, late in May, there was another pregnancy, and this time there was no simple solution. They were given an introduction to a certain Dr M. who had been struck off but still insisted on keeping the title of 'Doctor', a man in his fifties, partially paralysed by polio. His passion was for oriental philosophy, and on the two or three occasions that they met to discuss the abortion he was happy to talk with Gai about Hindu Vedanta. This, however, did not stop him from charging a huge fee. In due course he injected some substance into Kay and sent her home to await the outcome. It was bloody and painful, but by then she was with her parents in Grafham. Their family doctor took charge of her. He tried to get Dr M.'s name out of her so that he could be prosecuted and, when the miscarriage was over, brought the foetus to show her, saying to her: 'He might have saved the world'. 'I felt quite sorry for the poor little thing!' she said afterwards.

Now he could only make love to Kay when desire overcame the fear of another pregnancy. That happened fairly often, but afterwards he was invariably riddled with anxiety until she had her next period. This was probably the lowest point, after which things could get no worse, but evenings in Mall Chambers were mostly passed in silence since they had nothing to say to each other. Gai wished he could interest her in the ideas which he poured into his essays, but her only comment when he showed her one of them was that it seemed like a 'rehash' of all he had read. Once—and only once—she made a suggestion which might have saved the marriage. As a young girl she had been left a sum of £6,000 by an uncle. This capital was not to be touched under any circumstances, but on this occasion she debated whether to take something from it so that they could go abroad, taking the Boolet with them. He had hardly assimilated the idea before she shook her head, asking what she could possibly do with herself in such a place. The theatre was her life and there could be no other life for her. Like thousands of actors and actresses who are not quite good enough, she was now addicted as surely as if some drug had taken her over.

In July, while she was on tour, he went to a small party given by a friend. He noticed a young woman standing on her own and went over to talk to her. She asked him what he did and, unwilling to confess that he was an unemployed actor, he replied: 'Well, I sort of write'. She asked what he was writing and what he intended to do with it, then told him that she worked in the poet T. S. Eliot's office, adding that, if he sent her his essays and if she liked them, she would show them to Eliot who was, at that time, head of the publishing firm Faber & Faber. A month later he was summoned to meet the man who was one of his heroes. Eliot told him that there was material here, well written and interesting, which would make a publishable book if he could tie the essays together and he suggested ways in which this might be done. He also gave him an introduction to a well-known literary agent, A. D. Peters.

The sun was not out yet, but it was beginning to emerge from behind the clouds. Soon afterwards MEO introduced him to a woman who headed the J. Arthur Rank Story Department and he was taken on as a 'reader'. Every Thursday he went to the offices to collect, from the piles of novels—some published, some in manuscript—which had been submitted for filming, as many as he thought he could read in a week. He was paid £1 for each brief report and £2 for a *précis* of any novel he thought might be of interest. This provided a weekly income of seven or eight pounds, ample for his needs.

Surprisingly, visits to Grafham were becoming a little less painful. Perhaps Harold had simply given up on him. They avoided each other as much as possible. In September he noted in his diary: 'I spent most of the morning sitting with the Boolet (now with seven teeth), who crowed and coo'd and smiled at me, held out his arms for a cuddle and rubbed his face against mine. I sat and adored him, determined that, at all costs, he must not be sent to a school where he would lose the capacity to show affection'. A friend of Kay's had firm ideas on the boy's education. Anthony, an old Etonian Guards Officer who had been hopelessly in love with her for years—a gentle, uncommonly dull army officer—explained that 'one goes to Eton' and that the boy must be put down for the College at once. They went ahead with this farcical procedure to which Gai could have no objection since there was not the remotest possibility that they would ever be able to afford the fees, even assuming that this was what they wanted for their son.

Soon after this, wandering round the flat when Kay was out, he noticed a letter on the mantelpiece and, although he knew this was absolutely against the rules, he picked it up. She had written to her friend Patricia to say that, out of compassion and in return for his dog-like devotion, she had spent a night with Anthony. She had not enjoyed it, but she felt that she had paid a long-standing debt. Confused and upset, Gai dared not admit to her that he had read the letter since only the lower classes—so she believed—read each other's private correspondence. The thought that she could have left the letter there (not even in an envelope) for him to read did not cross his mind. At least he was saved from being obliged to react when he did not really know what his reaction was.

The essays were now in the hands of the agent, A. D. Peters, whose enthusiasm was a balm to an old wound. Gai left it to Kay to inform her father that two such eminent literary figures had praised the work which he had treated with contempt. The time had come to make a book of them, and he chose a quotation from Thoreau's *Walden*: 'My instinct tells me that my head is an organ for burrowing, as some creatures use their snouts and forepaws and with it I would mine and burrow my way through these hills. I think that the richest vein is somewhere hereabout . . . and here I will begin to mine'. So the title would be *The Richest Vein*. It fitted his intention so well. He was not a 'seeker'—a term he disliked—but a 'burrower', doing what came naturally to him.

By now, however, a new influence had come to mould all his thoughts. If the course of his life had been changed by the encounter with Kay on a dance floor, a second and more decisive change took place in a London bookshop. Waiting for the assistant at Watkins to find a volume of Meister Eckhart's sermons for him, he browsed through the shelves and picked up a book with an uninteresting title, *Figures of Thought and Figures of Speech*, by Ananda Coomaraswamy. He read it in two days, re-read it sidelining almost every paragraph, then rushed back to the bookshop to find anything else they had by the same author.

Coomaraswamy, at that time Curator of the Fine Arts Museum in Boston, was the son of a distinguished Ceylonese lawyer and an Englishwoman hardly less distinguished as a scholar and intellectual. He was not only a man of two worlds, he was a man of many worlds, at home in all of them and equipped with a knowledge of Sanskrit, Pali, Greek and Latin as well as a number of contemporary European languages. Long afterwards his son told Gai that he had come upon him one day reading a Chinese book and expressed his surprise. 'I never claim to know Chinese,' said his father, 'because I sometimes need to use a dictionary'. As an interpreter—one might say a 'penetrater'—of the symbolism of many different cultures he had no equal. It would be fair to say that, in his own field, he was the greatest scholar of the twentieth century and his field was as wide as the earth itself. He could link Greek and Hindu myths, Buddhist iconography and the symbols amidst which so-called 'primitive' tribes lived their lives, link them so that their transparency to a universal truth was apparent. Reading him was like watching one veil after another fall away, revealing an underlying unity.

From all this a convincing doctrine of traditional art and its significance emerged. 'Aesthetic experience', he wrote, 'is of the skin you love to touch or the fruit you love to taste, but art is an intellectual, not a physical virtue; beauty has to do with knowledge and goodness, of which it is, precisely, the attractive aspect'. An art which did not spring from profound spiritual knowledge and did not express this knowledge both effectively and beautifully was mere frivolity. The crafts, however humble, belonged to this category of art, which was why he condemned modern industry in scathing terms as a symptom of degeneracy. In place of a life of which unity was the guiding principle, modern man led a disintegrated existence in which many things that could only function properly in unison had fallen apart into sterile separation. Everything made by man in the past, from the Stone Age until quite recently, had been made by art to serve a double purpose, at once utilitarian and spiritual. Until modern times it would have been unthinkable that anything, whether natural or man-made, should have a use but not, also, a meaning.

Coomaraswamy led Gai inevitably to discover the co-founder of what would become known as the Traditionalist School of thought, René Guénon, who had converted to Islam as a young man and lived the rest of his life in Cairo as the widely respected Sheikh Abdul Wahed. There were three possible reactions to the many books he wrote. Some people found him unreadable, others incomprehensible, while a few found their lives changed irrevocably. Over the next fifty years there would emerge a dozen or more writers whose lives had been changed in this way. Among them were the Franco-German 'sage' (in this rare case, the term is apt), Frithjof Schuon, the Swiss Sufi and expert on Islamic art, Titus Burkhardt, the English writer on Sufism, Martin Lings, the agriculturist, Lord Northbourne, and the leading exponent of Islam in the West, Seyyed Hossein Nasr.

Guénon, although a Muslim of strict conformity, wrote for the most part in terms of Hindu Vedanta and his radical condemnation of the modern world, from the Renaissance onwards, was based on the Hindu doctrine of the four cycles into which each 'Great Age' is divided, and he identified the present age as the *Kali Yuga*, the dark age which precedes the end of the cycle. As he saw it, all the principles which had guided humanity in earlier times had now been turned upside down. Quantity had replaced quality, and time had speeded up as it does in the old age of an individual, racing towards the end. The gulf which separates his work from that of any of his contemporaries is too wide to be bridged by any compromise, so contrary to the whole trend of European thought since the Middle Ages are the doctrines which he expounded—and so strange to the contemporary mindset—that, had he been anything less than a consummate master of lucid argument and forceful exposition, his books might have sunk without trace. As it is, they are still widely read.

His critique of the modern world is summed up in a passage from *The Crisis of the Modern World*, published some eighty years ago. After deploring the loss of any sense of hierarchy, particularly in the spiritual realm, he continues: 'Nothing and nobody is any longer in the right place; men no longer recognise any effective authority in the spiritual order or any legitimate power in the temporal; the 'profane' presume to discuss what is sacred and to contest its character and even its existence; the inferior judges the superior, ignorance sets bounds to wisdom, error prevails over truth, the human supersedes the divine, earth overtops heaven, the individual sets the measure of all things and claims to dictate to the universe laws drawn entirely from it own relative and fallible reason'.

The principle of 'orthodoxy' was at the centre of his work. First there was a transcendent orthodoxy expressed in many different forms through the traditional religions, secondly there was the specific orthodoxy which was the necessary framework of each religious form. He had no use for contemporary liberal ecumenicalism. The adherent of a particular Faith must practise it without any flirtation with other Faiths which, on their own level (the formal level), could not be reconciled. He abhorred what he called the 'mixing of forms'. An intellectual recognition of the universal and transcendent truth did not water down the truth of each religious form, its essential dogmas, rituals and moral principles which were to be followed rigorously by its adherents. 'It is very difficult,' he wrote, 'to make our contemporaries see that there are things which, by their very nature, cannot be debated. Modern man, instead of raising himself to the truth, tries to drag it down to his own level.' But it would be useless to attempt to summarise such a vast and coherent structure of spiritual insights, interpretation of traditional symbols and demolition of modern thought.

Gai tried to explain to Kay something of the perspective argued so persuasively by Guénon and Coomaraswamy. Her reaction was one of fear and rejection. This, she thought, would isolate him more than ever from ordinary people and from the world in which he lived. She was not entirely wrong, but, unlike his mentors, he was a creature of compromise, never inviting dispute. He would speak of these matters only when he met someone already sympathetic to the traditionalist perspective and he seldom challenged opinions which conflicted with it. Some might say that this was another of his deceptions. But he included a chapter on these two authors, together with chapters on Leo Myers, Aldous Huxley and Max Plowman in *The Richest Vein*.

1947 came, and it was an improvement on the previous year. Kay was almost constantly on tour, and Gai worked slowly on recasting the book in the way Eliot had suggested, confident now it had been accepted for publication that he had found his true voice. In bitterly cold weather, when the single gas fire was quite inadequate to heat the flat, he took refuge in Harrods store which had a bank on the ground floor surrounded by comfortable arm-chairs and no one disturbed him. He would lunch off a sardine sandwich in the snack bar, but in general he was fed by Ruth who prepared delicious meals for him. Otherwise there was always unrationed whale steak, though it tasted like an old boot impregnated with rancid fish oil. Rationing was now even more strict than it had been during the war. British socialism was rooted in the puritan tradition with all its meanness, intolerance and self-righteousness, and the Labour Government seemed to rejoice in a regime of austerity. Sixty years later a journalist would write of that period: 'The British were hungrier, colder, dirtier, sadder and more hopeless than anything we can imagine from our pampered vantage-point in time'.

Early in the year Chris, his Sandhurst friend, returned from Egypt where he had been a senior official in the administration of the Canal area. After he had lost an eye at the Battle of al-Alamein his mother, whom some people thought the most beautiful, certainly the most attractive woman in England, had taken advantage of the fact that she was on familiar—sometimes over-familiar—terms with most of the generals in the British army to ensure that her son was given a good job. Although completely inexperienced, he had been put in sole charge of an area of recently conquered Libya. While Gai was at Maidstone Chris had written to say that he was living in a hilltop villa with a tame gazelle and an Italian mistress, arousing painful feelings of envy. He had made such a success of the job that he had ended the war as a Lieutenant-Colonel in the administration of the country. Now he was preparing to take his examinations for entry into the Foreign Office.

Chris had a problem in which Gai became deeply involved and which provided him with light relief from his work on the book. The problem had a name, Maureen, a 'blonde bombshell' who was passionately in love with him. Unfortunately she was married and a divorce would have ruined his career prospects. He tried to end the relationship but she was both determined and irresistible. One night around 3 a.m. he telephoned Gai in a panic to say that Maureen, who lived with her husband in the same apartment block, had got into his flat through the rubbish hatch and refused to leave. Gai took a taxi there and found her sitting stark naked on the bed in floods of tears while Chris sat in the living room with his head in his hands. No one who has not had the experience—and it cannot be common—could guess how difficult it is forcibly to dress a young woman against her will, but finally he got some clothes onto her after which, each taking an arm, the two of them dragged her to the door of her husband's flat, rang the bell and fled.

As Kay was again on tour, Chris came to live with Gai in Mall Chambers, thinking he would be safe there, but a few days later Maureen moved in with them. She brought an element of passion, gaiety and outrage into a flat redolent of misery and provided a merry background to his metaphysical speculations. She had a dislike for clothing, perhaps because she rejoiced in showing off her superb body, and she had a habit of wandering around in the nude whether or not Chris was there. She liked to chant a little ditty, two lines of which were far from politically correct: 'If I'm asleep, take me/If I'm awake and don't want to, make me!' The couple left when Kay returned and the girl's husband forgave her, not once but a hundred times, so there was no divorce.

Someone else out of the past had now come back into Gai's life, 'Paris Ann', Ann the lovable 'Teddy Bear' whom Peter thought he should have married. She was now sharing a London flat with her friend, Cecilie, and soon Gai and Chris were going out with the two girls as a foursome. Returning to their flat or to Mall Chambers afterwards, they would settle down to some gentle kissing and cuddling, and by then it could be said that Gai had been teetering on the edge of 'something' with Ann—whatever that 'something' might be—for six years, and Chris was not alone in urging him to take the plunge. Kay, about to set out on another tour, more or less ordered him to sleep with Ann. It might, she said, cheer him up. Once again she had demonstrated a singular blindness to the realities of human nature and of his nature in particular.

One evening they shared a bottle of wine in her flat, Cecilie being away, and she told him: 'It's no good trying to seduce me tonight'. She was starting an important new job the following morning and had to get up at the crack of dawn. Gai took the point or thought he did, but asked if he might at least share her bed for a few hours if he promised 'not to do anything' (the conversation was meticulously recorded in the diary). She undressed and stood before him with a curious mixture of pride and innate modesty, astonishingly beautiful at that moment. So they lay together like brother and sister, agreeing to meet the following week when, by unspoken agreement, they would consummate the relationship. The next week Kay returned unexpectedly from her tour, and that was the end of the matter. In any case he was a little scared, sensing vaguely that this could have been a momentous event.

For ever after he referred to her as 'the nearly girl'. Eventually he named his youngest daughter after her as an ironic tribute to what never happened, aware that things which do not happen in life can be just as important as those which come to a conclusion. In retrospect he would understand that, had they taken the final step, he would almost certainly have fallen seriously in love with her. Given the state of his marriage, he was ripe for this and the marriage would probably have foundered. The warm embrace of his 'Teddy Bear' would have triumphed over the chill that had come into his relationship with Kay. But it was not to be, and soon afterwards, events took over.

Thoughts of the Voyage had always been at the back of his mind. Late in 1947 they came to the fore when several different factors merged, all pointing in the same direction. The Arthur

Rank Story Department was about to close down, depriving him of his livelihood, such as it was. The Government was proposing to introduce Direction of Labour, which could mean that he would be conscripted into industry. Three different friends just happened to mention Jamaica in one context or another, and, finally, a new airline called British South American Airways had just been established, offering direct flights to Jamaica stopping only in the Azores to refuel. What had, until then, been little more than a daydream was now a real possibility. Very soon it consumed him and then he remembered Bruce Barker, the Jamaican boy who had been his friend at Charterhouse.

When he discussed the idea with Kay, saying that he had it in mind to go for two years provided he could find work there, she agreed that this might be the best solution to their problems. 'When you come back, either our marriage will be over or else we'll start off again on a new footing', she said. His only real worry was over abandoning his son but, in effect, he had already done so and saw him only on the rare occasions that Kay brought him up to London. His book was now with Faber & Faber and they agreed to send the proofs to him in Jamaica for correction.

He was about to escape from his 'cold, hungry, dirty, sad, hopeless country' and it was as though the blank wall blocking the end of the alleyway in which he lived had suddenly vanished to reveal an open landscape, a landscape of blue skies and palm trees, a barely imaginable new world, freedom at last. In November 1947 he wrote to Bruce Barker.

11

F L O

Ocho Rios, Oracabessa, Tegucigalpa, Chichen Itza, Shu-nan-tunich ('The Maiden's Rock'), Yucatan, Port-au-Prince and, of course, 'The Land of Look Behind' . . . The place-names were mouth-watering. Bruce Barker replied promptly to Gai's letter, welcoming him to Jamaica, assuring him that he would be able to find a job and enclosing a book called *Black Caribbean* by a British officer who had served on the Island during the war and fallen in love with it. The place-names which the author so clearly relished were chosen, not only from Jamaica but from its environs, all within easy reach: Honduras, Belize, Mexico and Haiti. But it was the wonder and mystery of the Blessed Isle that the writer expressed with such naive enthusiasm, confessing that everywhere else he had felt himself to be a misfit, but not here. He marvelled when girls came up to him in the velvet darkness to whisper: 'Please Sir, give me a white baby'. He marvelled at everything and, reading the book, Gai could hardly believe that such a place existed on earth. He had been imprisoned in England for six years, long enough for the outside world to seem unreal or, at least, for ever out of reach. Approaching his twenty-seventh birthday he became a child again,

198

bursting with excitement at the prospect of the most wonderful adventure he could ever have imagined, hugging himself as the days dragged by.

He had hoped to join the inaugural flight of the new airline but it was reserved for very important people so he booked on the next one. Somewhere over what is now called the 'Bermuda Triangle', the inaugural flight disappeared. No wreckage was ever found nor any bodies, and, years later, there were those who believed that it had been taken by an alien space craft. That would have been an adventure too far even for him. If the airline was to survive, they could take no risks with the next trip so, in place of the state-of-the-art Tudor aircraft, they rented a converted York bomber left over from the war. It could not cross the North Atlantic, so they planned a crossing at the narrowest point where the bulge of West Africa faces the bulge of South America, and then they either said a prayer or crossed their fingers.

Gai set out on 3 February 1948, turning his back on an England in the grip of an uncommonly bitter winter and of an austerity regime without precedent. They flew to Lisbon and were put up for a night in a five-star hotel in the suburb of Estoril while the pilots got up their courage to make the next hop. To pass the time he went to the Casino, prepared to throw away £5 on the roulette wheel. He could not lose on *rouge et noire* — a good augury? — and ended up with £40 in his pocket, half what the entire trip cost. Next day they flew to Dakar in Senegal (a French colony in those days) where the contrast between the squat, sweating French officials and the tall Africans in their white robes gave him a new understanding of what human dignity means. They crossed the Atlantic to Natal in Brazil and there they stayed two nights while the engineers checked every nut and bolt on the aircraft. Swimming in the tropical sea for the first time in his life he felt his leg lashed by a whip. Quite prepared to die on this great adventure, he went over to the young woman who represented the airline in Brazil and told her casually: 'A funny thing just happened to me'. He had been stung by a Portuguese Man o'War jellyfish, which simply added to the fun. Back to the airport, squirted with ether on their way by a Carnival crowd, and the good old York lumbered off the runway for the most dangerous stage of the journey, over-flying Amazonia to land next morning at Port of Spain, Trinidad.

The final hop to Kingston, Jamaica, provided its own wonder. The aircraft seemed to be stationary, enclosed in a vast blue envelope, the sea indistinguishable from the sky. The whole world was blue, the colour of Paradise. He was met by Bruce Barker, little changed in the ten years since they had last met, and driven to the Manor House Hotel in Constant Spring where Bruce left him to rest. He sat in the scented tropical garden as dusk fell and his attention was caught by a penetrating voice coming from one of the rooms, a voice which could only be that of a Dowager Duchess or someone of that sort. To judge from the meek, barely audible replies she must have been addressing her paid companion or lady's maid. She had a serious complaint against her creator. Her husband had recently died and it had been her intention to die with him. Now here she was, still lingering on against her wishes. She spoke of God as she would have spoken of an upper servant who had gravely disappointed her. So this was a life ending just as what Gai thought of as his real life was beginning.

The following evening he went round to the Barkers'. Bruce's mother, Lady Nina, surprised to hear that he wanted a job, picked up the telephone: 'Henry, I have a young man here who would like to teach at your school. Please take him on'. 'That's fixed', she told Gai, and then they went to dinner at the Liguanea Club where life again became a dream. The war had never happened. This was pre-war Britain at its most extravagant. The food on a single plate would have fed a British family for a week, and the women's gowns, even if they had been available, would have exhausted any number of clothing coupons. This was not just another world, it was another planet. Next morning he met Henry Fowler, the owner and Headmaster of an exclusive private school attended by the Governor's two daughters, *The Priory*. They got on together at once (and later became close friends). Henry was in his late thirties, an outstanding educationalist, involved in the arts, the Little Theatre and St Andrew society as such, St Andrew being the elite area of Kingston. Gai began work the following week, teaching History and English Literature. He also bought himself a car for £60. The man from whom he bought it died of a heart attack shortly afterwards, possibly from the shock of selling a piece of junk fit only for the scrapyard.

Now came the anticlimax. The Barkers fixed him up as a paying guest with a Mrs Dignum, a widow with a grown-up daughter, almost next door to the St Andrew tennis club. He had travelled all this way only to find himself in what might have been a middle-class suburb anywhere in England. What he thought of as 'real Jamaica' lay somewhere behind an invisible barrier. He did however receive an education in local sensibilities at the Club. One evening a white-skinned man sat down for a chat. 'You see my friend Joe over there,' he said, 'you'd take him for a pukka white man wouldn't you? But if you saw his aunt in Mandeville—black as my hat, old boy!' Later on Joe joined him. 'I see you were talking to my friend Mike. He could pass for a white man anywhere, couldn't he? Don't you believe it. His Dad raised his colour by marrying white.' Someone else explained: 'If you're black and rich here, you're brown. If you're brown and poor, then you're black'. A rich black man would always take care to marry a girl fairer than himself, thus raising his children's colour, as would a brown man in a position to do so. Shade prejudice replaced racial prejudice in Jamaica.

His new friends at the St Andrew Club were full of useful advice for the newcomer, recommending the best brothels out of the 370 such institutions said to exist in the town. Bruce Barker, when he drove him round the Island, had a particular warning.

The most beautiful girls, he explained, were the 'Chinee-Royals' (half Chinese and half Jamaican), but they were also the most dangerous and to be avoided if one wanted to keep out of trouble. 'Coolie-Royals' (half-Indian) were safer. The fact that Bruce kept a revolver in the glove compartment of his car demonstrated the fact the Jamaican ruling elite were becoming a little fearful and not without reason. His uncle, so he said, had been in the habit of relaxing on his veranda with a shotgun beside him in the mango season, taking pot shots at the little black boys climbing the mango trees to steal the fruit. The police had never disturbed his sport.

Soon afterwards a heavy parcel arrived and six copies of *The Richest Vein* spilled out of it. Ruth had already received a copy and wrote to say that she had jumped up and down with joy till she was exhausted. This should have been one of the great moments but somehow, here in Jamaica, the book seemed remote from him, written in another place and another life. In due course he received several enthusiastic letters from readers and he found them a little alarming. Had he, scribbling away in the freezing flat and in Harrods, taken on a new kind of responsibility? One man wrote to say that he had been trying to picture the author and had an image of a wise old man with a long beard meditating on a mountain top. Some time later a Catholic priest came to the Island to stay with relatives and told them he had just been reading 'a fascinating book' written by someone called Gai Eaton. His hosts told him they had met the author and could probably track him down. They did so and took him to a party given by friends of theirs. The priest was led up to a slightly tipsy young man sitting with a girl on his knee who rose unsteadily to his feet to be met with a look of baffled astonishment. 'You couldn't have written that book', the priest said. As the years passed Gai would become increasingly puzzled by the contrast between certain spiritual writers and their human characters, their human failings. It was as though earthiness took its revenge on those who concerned themselves with the heights, or was it simply a matter of compensation, one extreme balanced by another? But how to be whole, let alone holy? Wisdom in the head did not necessarily imply wisdom in the belly, let alone wisdom in the heart.

When the book was reviewed in the local newspaper, *The Daily Gleaner*, the Editor invited him to a downtown bar to see if he would accept thirty shillings (£1.50) each for contributions to the paper. Theo Sealy was the first black editor of the paper, an outstanding journalist respected far beyond the coral reefs. Gai was also invited to tea by the First Lady of Jamaica, not the Governor's wife but Edna Manley whose husband, Norman, was the Island's leading politician and who was a distinguished artist in her own right. Her favourite pupil was a young artist called Corah Hamilton whose self-portrait appeared soon afterwards on the cover of *Spotlight* magazine. The text described her as 'the most beautiful black girl in Jamaica' and her self-portrait fascinated Gai, although he could not guess why. If some agent from beyond time, an angel perhaps, seeing both what has been and what is to be in a single vision, had whispered in his ear: 'That is your future wife who will bear you three children', he would certainly have been astonished.

He had not, in those days, heard the saying: 'If you have lost days in your past, you will spend the rest of your life making up'. He had too many lost days, weeks, months in his past, lonely idleness in the Red House (watching life go by in the street), timid isolation in Paris, opportunities ignored and adventures missed. He was hungry to make up for them. One evening, walking along North Street in Kingston and wondering how he would ever make contact with real Jamaica he almost bumped into a young black girl with an enchanting smile who barred his way, her arms outstretched. She took him to a shack with a corrugated iron roof and they made love. He still believed that the way he saw an event was the way it was. If he chose to transform this girl into a princess, then she was indeed a princess. Afterwards, still smiling, she teased him about his absurdly white skin which she thought almost unnatural. Brown was the normal colouring for the human creature. Then a tropical downpour drumming on the iron roof prevented further talk and she fell asleep curled up in his arms. He lay awake reflecting that he had now travelled as far as it was possible to travel from the Red House, the Erringtons and the Claytons, and here was someone who would not judge him or criticise him. They arranged to meet again, but, a few days later, he had a letter from Kay saying that she was coming to Jamaica.

Two disastrous affairs had left her feeling that her life was a mess. 'To whom should I turn,' she asked, 'if not to my husband?' This seemed logical. She arrived a couple of weeks later, and Gai was soon aware of a subtle change in the way he was regarded by St Andrew society. They had not known what to make of him in relation to their idea of the conventional Englishman but his wife was easy to place and met with instant approval, moreover she was a glamorous actress. She was particularly welcome to the Little Theatre Movement which depended on talented amateurs, and that meant she was welcome to Greta Bourke, the social lioness who presided over it. Greta, although married to a gentle and complacent husband, had been the lover of Henry Fowler (Gai's Headmaster) for a number of years and the relationship had by now been so completely accepted that they were frequently invited as a couple to King's House, the Governor's residence. One could be sure that Henry and Greta—their names indissolubly linked—would be at every fashionable party.

Doors were opening, doors at which Gai had never attempted to knock. Kay, in a few weeks, had taken him into the centre of local society. They were always welcome at the Theatre Arts Club, and she made friends with the British Council representative, Martin Blake and his wife, whose parties were attended by some of the most interesting people in the Island. She was asked to play Principal Boy in the Little Theatre pantomime and invited to sing at King's House, popular wherever she went, and she persuaded a group of singers, musicians and comedians to form a concert party which she took to the Leper colony, setting an example to the others by shaking hands with the inmates. She caught the attention of the editor of *Spotlight*, Evon Blake, famous for having broken one of the major taboos as the first black man to swim in the pool at the principal hotel in Kingston, the Myrtle Bank. He took them to the Press Club, opening a door into a different world. Gai hardly noticed the tall half-Chinese girl serving behind the bar, having, as usual, no premonition that he had glimpsed the person who would re-direct the course of his life.

They went to an exhibition of painting at the Institute of Jamaica and, while Kay was talking to some people, Gai was introduced to Corah Hamilton and, a little later, he pointed Corah out to her as 'the most beautiful black girl in Jamaica'. 'I can't tell the difference between them', she said. The Island and its people were fascinating but alien to her. This was not her place, whereas to him it was beginning to feel like home. He had a recurrent dream—or nightmare—which would return often enough without variation over the next year. It started with a Jamaica that was all fruit and flowers, dazzling light, enveloping warmth and smiling faces. He dreamed that he went aboard a ship in the harbour to see a friend off to England, only to discover with horror that the ship had sailed. Watching the ship's wake he wondered if he could jump overboard and swim to the shore, but soon the sea turned from aquamarine to grey and he found himself in the grim half-light of England climbing the steps to Mall Chambers, steps covered in garbage. On each occasion he woke in despair, only to be flooded with joy as he realised that this had only been a dream. In this case he really had been given a glimpse into the future.

Away from their parents, he and Kay now seemed to be in love again, all the more as the time for her departure drew closer. The

Theatre called and there was no question of her staying on. She told him that she would, of course, have affairs until he returned home, and she selected a suitable mistress to keep him happy, a young girl called Cynthia who performed exotic dances at the Theatre Arts Club. Early in February 1949 Kay sailed away on a banana boat. Gai was devastated. That same evening he was due to take part in a radio discussion on Jamaican artists with the British Council representative and Corah Hamilton. He wiped away his tears and performed as best he could, after which Bruce Barker collected him and took him round the clubs, deliberately getting him drunk. Kay was not simply crossing the Atlantic; she was disappearing into the Dark Continent, the sad continent of Europe. The *Gleaner* seldom carried any overseas news since the outside world was of little interest to islanders content with their narrow horizons. The discovery of the horrors beyond the ocean came, therefore, as a shock.

Martin Blake invited Gai to accompany him to Montego Bay for a meeting with Marcia Davenport, a well-known American novelist. Traumatised, she had come to Jamaica to recover from the loss of her fiancé, the Czech statesman Jan Masaryk. The Communists were in the course of taking over Czechoslovakia and he stood in their way. He had decided to escape while he could and sent Marcia to Vienna where he would meet her in a couple of days time. She never saw him again. He was alleged to have committed suicide by jumping out of a window in Prague, but to Marcia it was obvious that he had been pushed. Was it likely that a man about to be reunited with his beloved and in a position to make his voice heard throughout Europe would take his own life? Now, on this peaceful veranda overlooking the tropical sea, she talked of a continent devastated by the war and its aftermath; the ruined cities, the bleak roads crowded with 'displaced persons', the shortages of food and of the most basic amenities, a civilisation destroyed and chaos come again. Martin felt guilty over being where he was, out of it all. Gai did not. He was where he wanted to be, the only place he wanted to be. He returned to Kingston in search of an anchor.

Cynthia was a delight and they flirted evening after evening, but she was an intense, passionate virgin and Gai's innate caution warned him against becoming more involved. There were other flirtatious girls whose company he enjoyed, and whenever Martin and his wife were giving a party they asked him to pick up Corah Hamilton who had no car. He did not know at the time that she was partially deaf, probably due to her mother's habit of boxing her ears whenever she noticed her and was diverted from performing good works among her neighbours. But he found her rather reserved, uninterested in flirtation and awkward in conversation. He spent much of his time in congenial company at the Press Club and began to notice the half-Chinese girl, Flo Tai Chung, since she was difficult to ignore; a big girl (she told him that her father came from Hangchow, 'the city of tall men'), exuberant and full of life. One evening she mentioned that she was organising a party for a couple called Milner, whom Gai had met briefly, and suggested that he should come along. Once the party had got going he danced with her. They danced together almost without a break until dawn and, as he remembered that night, the other guests gradually faded away until it was as though they were alone in each other's arms.

At this point memory and the diary conflict. Memory suggests that it was then that he fell irrevocably in love with her and she with him. The diary does not support this. 'I wouldn't describe her as pretty in the conventional sense. She's full-bodied and warm-hearted with Chinese features framed by glossy black hair cascading over her shoulders. Attractive? Oh dear me, Yes. I've noticed her before, mothering the Press Club, and she was making herself miserable at the party trying to solve people's problems. "Someone must have made you very unhappy once", I said. Between dances we cuddled up on a sofa. Something I had said about Kay, whom I'm still missing, induced her to say: "You love her very much, don't you!" I said I did and she hugged me, exclaiming: "I love you for that!" It was as though I had shown her a firm foothold in a landscape of quicksands. We danced on and dawn came up, fresh and clear. I drove her home, hoping that the demonstrative affection she had shown me would not evaporate with the onset of sobriety.' The next few entries are taken up with Cynthia and meetings with friends. There is no mention of a *coup de foudre* or of undying love.

Within a few days, however, he wrote: 'I don't know what this is that I'm plunging into with Flo Tai. It may be trouble or it may be what I have been looking for in Jamaica. This evening at the Press Club she protested herself so unworthy that she could not understand why I should be interested in her. When we parted she even said: "Thank you for wanting me", and I certainly want her'. But where and when? It could not, she insisted, be a brief scuffle in the back of a car. Their first time must be perfect, the right time and the right place. He discovered that she was as much of a romantic as he was. In Paris Ann had sworn she would cure him of his romanticism, an impossible task. The true romantic's will to romanticise is stronger than the force of circumstance and, as she began to unfold her life story—the most fascinating he had ever heard—he realised that he was falling in love with her, wishing he could, so to speak, assimilate her past into his own, thereby participating in an alien world of experience.

Her story began with the arrival in Jamaica of an impoverished family from Haiti, 'Golden Haitians' as they were sometimes called, the result of exactly the right mixture of races. The family was soon deeply in debt to the local Chinese shopkeeper who had his eye on their fifteen-year-old daughter, Avis, a child of quite exceptional beauty. They gave her to him, and the debt was cancelled. She was soon pregnant and, in due course, gave birth to a daughter who looked pure Chinese, a monster from the mother's point of view. She could see nothing of herself in this strange creature, nothing but the image of the man she hated.

Avis fled and became the most sought after courtesan in Jamaica, adored and well paid by some of the most important men in the Island. She died of TB in her early thirties, devotedly nursed by Flo, the daughter she had rejected who, none the less, refused to grant her the forgiveness for which she asked and who would suffer for the rest of her life from an almost obsessive sense of shame because her mother had been a prostitute.

She claimed that her father had not been unkind to her, but on at least one occasion he locked her in a cellar for 48 hours, leaving her with a permanent fear of being alone in the dark. On her sixteenth birthday he pointed out that she could not expect him to provide for her any longer. It was now time for some other man to take over her maintenance and he had the right man in mind. This was a fellow shopkeeper in another village, rather a weird little Chinese man who was content to forgo normal sex so long as she encouraged him to dress up in her clothes, parading happily before the mirror in drag. Less than a year later, her Knight in Shining Armour appeared out of nowhere and swept her up. Ramos de Moya, a South American journalist who had lived most of his life in Jamaica, took possession of this treasure for the next eleven years and set about transforming her. Her ignorance was unacceptable and would have shamed him in front of his friends, so he set about educating her. She was a good learner, eager for education, and he prescribed a number of books on history, literature and the arts, examining her regularly on what she had read. She was also ordered to take an interest in world affairs, and he taught her the rudiments of journalism. After some years of this, she was probably better educated than the vast majority of Jamaican girls and could hold her own among his friends at the Press Club.

Ramos also imbued her with his faith. A lapsed Catholic, he had adopted a religion of erotic mysticism, preaching that the true and complete union of a man and a woman was the apex of human life beside which everything else was secondary. He was

209

a handsome man and had a host of young girls on the side but they did not matter. Flo was his woman, and he swore that he would kill her if she ever looked at another man. She believed him, but he was becoming more and more possessive as time passed, while she was developing a sense of independence. He demanded constant proofs of her love and, on one occasion, insisted that she must be prepared to die at his hands. He told her that he was going to strangle her until she lost consciousness without knowing whether or not he would desist before she died. She submitted to this, but she had had enough and left him soon afterwards. She tried to hide, but he tracked her down and, by the sheer force of his personality and the power of his love, drew her back to him She had to admit that she would never meet another passion like this, and erotic love was her deity.

At the time Gai met her she had just left Ramos for the second time and was determined never to return, but she was in need of a comparable passion and of someone who shared her faith. Now she seems to have sensed that she had met the right person, if only she could release Gai from his English restraint as she believed she could by giving herself totally to him. Ramos had not neglected her education in opera so, with *Madame Butterfly* in mind, she took to describing herself as Gai's Chocho San, which he found flattering as well as romantic. In mid-June her friend Hyacinth, a black girl notorious for defying every taboo, suggested that they should go to stay with her uncle who was overseer of a coconut plantation near Morant Bay. It seemed a long journey since the car had a maximum speed of 20 mph and, when they arrived, Uncle Percy insisted on taking Gai to a local bar where he plied him with one rum after another, most of them emptied into the nearest flower-pot. Protests were of no avail. *'Yuh mus' always keep 'ooman waitin','* his host told him. *'That way she respec' yuh.'* Finally he was released and hurried to join Flo in a bare room; bed, chair and small table, with a single scarlet hibiscus in a jam jar. The time had come at last.

He would never quite understand what happened to him that afternoon, that night and in the days that followed. Looking back, he thought he had changed in some profound way, emerged from his chrysalis. It was as though he had been obliged to travel to the ends of the earth—China in the Caribbean—to find his true home and as though he had cast off a great weight from his shoulders and from his loins, a burden of fear, anxiety and uneasiness in every human relationship. He had dreamed of a perfect union with a fellow creature, as most people do in secret, and he thought he might have found it. 'I want to become a part of you', she had said, and now he told himself—I am Flo and she is me. At the same time she had struck a humorous note, having shared the common Jamaican idea of the English gentleman, shy and inhibited. 'I thought,' she told Gai, 'that you might say: "May I— er, um—with your permission of course—if you don't mind—er —well, if it's alright, may I perhaps insert my . . . ", and she shook with happy laughter. He was glad not to be that sort of Englishman. They drove into the coconut groves with a large bag of mangoes, a species so juicy that it is best eaten in the bath, stripping off and letting the rich juice spill over their bodies as they sucked the fruit.

They returned to Kingston, effectively homeless since there was nowhere they could be together. At the Press Club, where there were no secrets, his friends asked if he needed a bodyguard in case Ramos tried to knife him. He could imagine no more romantic death than to be killed by a passionate Latin American on account of a woman, and he repeated to himself those lines from *Othello* which he had recited many years before after a night with Louise: *If it were now to die, 'twere now to be most happy* . . . Soon afterwards they were in a downtown bar when a stockily built man with a neat moustache wandered up to Flo and began talking to her in an undertone. Gai moved away so as not to eavesdrop on a private conversation. The man raised his hand apparently to caress her cheek and then left the bar. 'That was Ramos', she said, rubbing her cheek where he had stubbed his lighted cigarette.

Her friends the Milners encouraged her to live with them and made Gai welcome whenever he wanted to stay overnight, and it was as though his bond with her carried with it a bond with Jamaica. Even before she confessed to him, with bitter shame, that she was infertile (what Jamaicans called a 'mule') he did not worry about the possibility of pregnancy. Perhaps he had already adopted the Jamaican belief that *'Ebery pickney born wid him own pudding bowl'* (Every child is born with his own sustenance). Life seemed to be getting better and better. One day he was asked to do a broadcast on the local radio. 'Flo and the others listened to it in Miss Joe's Bar, and I was told she was jumping up and down with excitement, telling everyone: 'That's my man!' When I joined them she smothered me with kisses, confirmed in her opinion that there was nothing from making love and using chopsticks to broadcasting and writing (an article of mine had appeared in the *Gleaner* that morning) that I couldn't do well. This is making me conceited and I don't like that. It always means something will happen to drag me down to my accustomed place, the outsider, the focus of blame.'

It was Henry Fowler who solved the problem of where they could be together on their own. He was going to England for six weeks in the summer holiday and asked Gai if he would like to live in The Priory School for that time and 'keep an eye on things'. Now they had a perfect setting, an idyllic setting, for their perfect love. The wooden veranda to their bedroom looked directly onto the Blue Mountains without any obstruction and, when the moon was full, silvering the palm fronds in the garden, the shadowy outline of the mountains took on a magical quality. Here they could sit happily for hours, closely entwined, and only their voices disturbed the silence together with the rustling of dry palm fronds in what was called 'the Undertaker's Wind', the light breeze which carried all the ills of the day out to sea leaving the Island cleansed.

But the idyll could never be perfect since Gai had made it clear from the start that he would be returning to his wife, his son and his mother in the New Year. Flo seemed to understand that, once his mind was made up, he was incapable of unmaking it, and she never tried to do so directly, hoping that the force of her love would ultimately hold him in chains as strong as his own fixed resolve But she could never say this since he had told her that he would hate anyone who threatened his independence. Perhaps she also sensed that his mother was more important to him than his wife and, in the early hours of one morning, after a night drinking with the Milners, she burst in to curse the God who would inevitably part them and she transformed the Litany of the Virgin into 'Holy Ruth, Mother of Gai'. She also confessed that Harry Milner had offered to buy him for her by setting him up in business. After that she became sad and sober, shedding a few tears, and he wept with her. As always, love-making was the only refuge from life's complications. Only then did the present moment suffice.

She was frightened as Kay had been by his spells of remoteness and puzzled by his inability to lose his temper under any circum-stances. An angry quarrel is at least an intimate encounter, and she wanted there to be no bounds to their intimacy. One evening, when she was looking particularly splendid, her magnificent breasts pointed at him like cannons, she began to mock him. At first he remained distant, as though superior to such nonsense, but then something snapped in him and he slapped her as hard as he could, amazed at himself. She threw her arms round him crying: 'Now I know you love me—you hit me, now I know you love me!' After that it seemed as though every barrier that could ever have existed had dissolved. Perhaps they had, for soon she began to exhibit an intuitive understanding of his nature and an insight even into his thoughts that astonished him. He knew that people were usually puzzled by him, as Kay had been, and he had a longing to be understood as he was, the good and the bad of him.

The first occasion, trivial and yet memorable, was at the Glass Bucket club. She had an unlighted cigarette in her hand and Gai drew a box of matches from his pocket, then noticed that the barman had done the same. He put the box back, reflecting that even a match costs money. Flo reproached him gently, aware of every brief thought that had passed through his mind, aware of his meanness. He remembered Ruth telling him how, soon after she moved to the Red House, Francis had said that he would give her a piece of his former wife's jewellery. As he rifled through the jewel box he had given her a quick, sidelong glance, and she had known that he was calculating how cheaply he could get away with his promise. 'I'm my father's son', Gai thought, and he was glad to have been found out. There had been too many deceptions in his life, and he could never deceive Flo.

Lack of money was an obsessive concern and one day, when he had fallen into despair over the prospect of a penniless future, she took his hand and said: 'I wish I could cut my belly open and put you in where you'd be safe!' This pierced him to the core, as it would any mother's boy. Another time, when they were standing at the window after making love, watching the lights come on in neighbouring houses, she said: 'Don't you think—I mean, do you think that, when two people have been together like that, it's so powerful—it must make everyone around better people?' Among an earlier generation, the generation to which Gai might have belonged had his father and grandfather been quicker in begetting, a mystical approach to the sex act was not uncommon. They had sensed that it was something not quite of this world, a break in the carapace which covers us, and Sufi poetry frequently relates it to the intercourse of man with God, but this is probably incomprehensible to the present generation in the West for whom the act is either recreational or else related to principles of commitment and domesticity, mundane in essence and in practice. None of this had to be explained to Flo, and Gai always had the memory of Wagner's *Tristan and Isolde* at the back of his mind.

Flo frequently referred to love as 'sweet pain'. They began to torment each other, although this was always followed by a passionate reconciliation, never acknowledging that behind these torments lay the fact that their love would be terminated on a given date in the coming year. She could do nothing about this, and he would do nothing about it. One evening, when they were with the Milners at Miss Joe's bar and Flo had already drunk too much, Gai tried to drag her away and she fought him off. He left and went back to The Priory, leaving the door open, but he was soon overcome with fear. Where was she and with whom? Hours later he heard her wandering round the house, calling his name. She wept and then broke into an impassioned paean glorifying sexual love as the one thing that mattered in life and alone gave it meaning. 'She tried to persuade me that she loved me as no one else ever had or ever would. Then we came together and, after that, talked till dawn. I read her something that seemed relevant from my book and she listened wide-eyed before saying: "All I can do is love and wag my tail. Can that ever be enough for you?" It is, Oh I think it is.' Another evening she prayed: 'Oh God —if You exist—strike us both dead here and now' and was immediately overcome with terror that He might take her at her word. Pressed between the pages of the diary is an undated scrap of paper: 'I love you. Come to me! Flo. P.S. I hate you'.

Henry Fowler was due back soon and the question of where they would live was pressing. The Milners insisted that they must come and live with them. On Harry's side this was simple friendship and generosity, but Rona had more practical motives, though these were never spelt out. Flo would be their unpaid housekeeper and Gai, when he was not teaching, their unpaid chauffeur. This was a most unhappy household. Harry was commonly referred to as a 'remittance man', that is to say a man whose family, to avoid scandal, had shipped him off to some distant colony with an adequate income to keep him from bothering them. He was also seen as an effete aristocrat whose class was his only asset, and this was unfair. He had many talents but no capacity for coping with life, which is where Rona came in. A tough black girl—now a woman in her thirties—she had started out at fifteen as a nightclub dancer. She and Harry had got together early in the war and had stayed together, but his family would never have tolerated their marrying. A black woman could not be the wife of General Milner's son. In Jamaica they presented themselves as a married couple and everyone addressed Rona as 'Mrs Milner', but even so far from England and South Africa, where his mother lived, there could be no question of marriage. His funds would have been cut off, and he was quite incapable of earning his own living. Rona's resentment had now boiled over. She battered Harry with verbal abuse, day and night, while he either remained silent or murmured, with quiet dignity: 'Please don't be so unkind to me'.

Gai and Flo walked open-eyed into this situation without a sensible thought between them to act as a buffer between the warring parties. Had Gai possessed a spark of initiative he might have found an alternative to living with the Milners. He was paid little enough by the school, but even so he should have been able to find cheap accommodation where he and his beloved could be together. Since Ruth was not there to tell him what to do, he never even thought of this. Perhaps he was rather like Harry, another mother's boy (though ten years older than him), who, if for some reason he was required to wear a tie, dithered for half-an-hour over the choice until Rona made it for him. Within three weeks, however, a real crisis arose. A neighbour had threatened to go to the police over the noisy late-night parties held in the house, a universal phenomenon throughout most of Kingston but not in this smart suburb. Rona confronted him with a stream of abuse. His reaction was to go to Henry Fowler and tell him that one of his teachers was living in a brothel. Deeply upset, Henry Fowler told Gai that he would have to insist he did not go near the house in the future.

This spelt disaster, but for once Gai was spurred into action instead of falling into despair. He went round to the neighbour's house, knocked on the door, introduced himself and began to talk. Afterwards he could not remember what he had said, but he discovered for the first time that he had inherited his father's ability to charm when required to do so. He had scarcely left the house before the man telephoned Henry to congratulate him on having such a fine man on his staff and withdrew his complaint unconditionally. He had, he said, seldom met with such transparent sincerity and honesty. The curious thing was that Gai had seldom felt less sincere, and he was a little scared to find that he could put on such an effective act. Yet, can an actor be described as insincere when he throws himself into his role? Henry Fowler was both relieved and amused. 'For God's sake, how did you do it?' It was Greta, Henry's mistress, who came up with a discreet solution, although whether such a formidable, not to say regal lady could be described as a 'mistress' is another matter. Until the end of the year (he was supposed to be leaving Jamaica in late January), Gai would live in her home only a stone's throw from the Milners. What he did in the nights was his business, but it would be a good idea if he breakfasted there. There was a touch of irony in this, since Greta herself lived with her husband only for the sake of appearances.

Gai was now considering the possibility of postponing his departure until April in the coming year. Since he would no longer have his school salary, Flo decided to revive the magazine *Cathay* which she and Ramos had produced some years earlier. She was sure that, with Gai's help, she could sell enough advertising space to bring in the money to keep him for the three months. So New Year's Eve, the dawning of 1950, was not as sad as it would otherwise have been. They escaped from the Milners, usually so inescapable, and went to Cable Hut beach where they lay on the sand beneath an incomparable display of stars, their brightness unchallenged except by a few wood fires on which people were cooking sucking pigs. Gai took the opportunity to talk to her about his metaphysical beliefs, about time and eternity, the impermanence of all things under the sun, the Absolute and the relative. She found all this cold and rather frightening, so distant did it seem from flesh and blood. What did it have to do with her life or his? 'Everything', he murmured with conviction. Shivering a little and holding onto him, she said: 'It's not your coldness I want, it's your warmth'. She turned to lie over him so that a curtain of sweet-scented black hair blotted out the stars.

Y O U N G   G A I

Once upon a time Jamaica, like the Gold Coast, had been 'The White Man's Grave'. Rows of crosses in forgotten graveyards bore witness to the swathe that Yellow Fever —the same 'Yellow Jack' Gai had feared as a child—had cut through young soldiers and sailors, some no more than sixteen years old. By the twentieth century the Island was as healthy as anywhere in Europe, but it still held a sting for Englishmen (the Scots seemed to be less susceptible). There were those who had come originally as teachers, businessmen or government officials, cocooned in their British values, and had succumbed to the girls and the rum, lost their jobs but still been unable to tear themselves away and return home. They were often to be found in downtown bars—gentle, broken men—waiting patiently for someone to buy them a drink. Gai was reminded of one of the best of Simenon's many novels, *Touriste de Bananes*, the story of a young Frenchman who goes to pieces in Tahiti.

He met the headmaster of a local school, a Methodist lay preacher from the North of England, when he had only recently arrived and who found the Jamaican way of life 'completely disgusting'. He had never suspected that such dreadful immorality existed in the world. Gai chanced to meet him a couple of years later, by which time he had divorced his wife, converted to

Catholicism, acquired a Jamaican girlfriend and developed a taste for the best rums. Up in the foothills lived a wealthy English homosexual (what in Jamaica was called a 'botty man'), a former senior official, who was attended by a staff of three or four handsome black youths. Friends who visited him reported that the house was dirty and uncared for, but a time came when they were turned away at the door by one or other of the servants. Some said that they had heard feeble cries for help, but did not want to interfere. Eventually the police broke in and found the owner's decomposing body naked on the floor. The youths had disappeared, taking with them everything of value that they could carry. Gai thought there was material for a novel here, but he was overwhelmed with material and yet lacked the confidence or the talent to use it.

Whenever, in the final months, he was tempted to cut loose and stay on, he thought of the broken men he had known and the abyss into which they had fallen. That was not for him, although he could not think of England without fear and a bitter taste on his tongue. Meanwhile, he was receiving mixed signals. Back in October letters from Kay and Ruth had arrived by the same post. Kay had written of the 'awful fleetingness of time'. 'Come home soon, my darling. All my memories of our marriage seem, in this dying season of the year, to overflow the flat. More and more do I realise that, for good or ill, my life is bound up with yours. Somewhere and somehow our stars were bound together. I love you very much.' His mother had struck rather a different note. 'Although I long to see you back, there is nothing very cheerful to come back to. I can't see you living in that little flat again, doing the shopping and cooking and washing up which is what Kay intends that you should do. She says so openly.'

Later, as the time for his return approached, Kay wrote in terms that could have made him change his plans. He would have to face the real world, she said, and the fact that 'life is grim and life is earnest'. Flo, she acknowledged, had been an important and delightful episode in his life, but it was an episode which had nothing to do with reality. 'You are going to have to face facts', she repeated. There seemed to be a difference of opinion as to what the facts were. She wrote in the New Year to say that her parents had found a wonderful boarding school for Leo Francis, now five, and she was sure he would be very happy there. Ruth wrote on the same subject. 'I'm horrified and so are all the aunts to hear that Leo Francis is to be pushed into some dreadful home for small children. We all think it's cruel and disgraceful. Well, the less I see of that **** Kay the better!' Gai wondered if there was some way he could rescue the boy when he got back. Could he steal him away? It all came back to money, and he had none.

Life with Flo was now a torment of extremes. At one point she begged him to free her so that she could get on with her life and possibly find a husband who would give her some security. In response he turned his back and began to walk out to the car, but she ran after him reproaching him bitterly for doubting her love. He tried to define what it was that seemed to bind them together almost against their will. The cynic would have said it was sex and nothing else, but he knew that it was something more than that. Long afterwards Corah Hamilton—by then Corah Eaton— told him of an evening she had spent at the Glass Bucket club with some other girls, watching the dancers. Her attention had focused on one couple, Gai in a black dinner jacket and Flo in a long black dress, and she had experienced an overwhelming impression that they were one person. It was not just the merging of black with black, she said, but something inexplicable. They seemed to her to exist in a different world to that which the other dancers inhabited.

Flo had been slow to recognise his ruthless selfishness—he always said that 'it takes one to know one'—but now she could not ignore it. 'You're a very peculiar person', she said. 'One can see right through you and still love you very, very much'. He remembered Kathy in Cambridge saying to him: 'One always has

221

to excuse you. That's the trouble'. And he remembered Peter grumbling that he always 'got away with murder'. He wondered how he did it and was frightened. Surely he would have to pay for this one day when his sins caught up with him? But soon he had reason to think that they had already done so.

He had supposed that the matter of the neighbour who told Henry Fowler that he was living in a brothel had been settled, but he had not reckoned with Rona. She decided to sue the man for defamation since it was to her house that he had referred, and, dipping into Harry's funds, she was prepared to hire Norman Manley as her Counsel. This was soon common knowledge in St Andrew society. Even before the end of his final term at The Priory, Gai had overheard one of his pupils talking of 'the Winston Avenue brothel', and Lady Barker let it be known that she was distressed to hear that he had fallen into bad company. Evon Blake, himself the centre of constant scandals, told him that he was 'losing his moral reputation in Jamaica', and others chattered behind his back. Years later when he, Flo and Harry were, each in their different ways, respected figures in the Island, he could laugh about this, but here and now it was no laughing matter. He cared for his reputation. Eventually the case petered out with apologies all round.

On 5 January 1950, he wrote in the diary: 'Every day seems to draw us closer together and makes the thought of parting more bitter. We find it increasingly painful to be apart for more than a few hours (I long ago gave up even the pretence of sleeping at Greta's). This parting is the prototype of all partings. Doesn't the fact that I shall forget and that I shall re-attach myself to Kay make it possible to face the prospect of April with equanimity? It does not!' One evening soon afterwards, when Flo had been imagining to herself his first night at home with Kay, she became abusive and they ended up fighting on the living room carpet, Gai pummelling her, though half-heartedly, while she bit and scratched him, after which they fell to lovemaking in which there was more despair than joy. Soon afterwards he wrote: 'I must remember her as she was before the stresses of the Milner household and the prospect of our parting scraped her nerves raw. It was foolish to think we could pack a lifetime of sweetness into these final months. We have both been miserably unhappy, more so with every day that passes. Looking back at this diary, I hope I haven't given the impression that Flo is some kind of primitive, moody jungle cat. By nature she is sensible, even-tempered and very balanced, but unnatural circumstances produce uncharacteristic reactions'.

Rona claimed that Flo was her best friend and confided in her, but she treated her as a servant. As for Gai, he was expected to earn his keep. Rona and Harry, with Flo in tow, spent the greater part of most nights in one bar or another, quarrelling. When this became intolerable to Gai he would drive back to the house and doze on a couch until they phoned to be collected. If, for Flo's sake, he managed to tolerate it, he would fall to sighing and gazing at the ceiling as the hours passed, making his displeasure only too obvious, after which Rona would embarrass Flo by grumbling to her about his ingratitude. He would also complain of exhaustion or did so until Flo pointed out, with mild sarcasm, how odd it was that she had never known him too exhausted to make love. Harry was also a trial. He was a compulsive talker, but he talked at people rather than with them and required no response. His topics covered art, literature, the theatre, politics and, sometimes, philosophy. He was knowledgeable, but this monotonous and unbroken monologue eventually became almost unbearable. It was probably years since Rona had heard a word Harry said but he did not seem to care. He would have talked at a block of stone if there had been no other audience available.

Flo and Gai had a refuge of sorts, somewhere that they could get away from all this. Frenzie Fook, who was vaguely related to her, owned a bar called Shanghai Lil's at the wrong end of Harbour Street, and they were always welcome in the back room, away from the clientele but often joined by Flo's friend, Hyacinth and by the London *Observer's* Latin American correspondent, Jock, who was based in Jamaica. But even here there were tensions. Frenzie was in love with Hyacinth, and Hyacinth with Jock who, Gai suspected, was at least a little in love with Flo. The bare room with its whitewashed walls and naked bulb made him think of the setting of Sartre's play *Huit Clos* and the line: 'Hell is other people'. None the less, Frenzie, with his brown belly overhanging his trouser top, was so sweet-natured and so placid that his simple presence was calming and, whenever Gai returned to the house to find Flo missing, he thought he knew where to find her and drove down to Shanghai Lil's, terrified that she might not be there this time, his hands trembling on the steering wheel. Harry and Rona kept away from the place, perhaps because they sensed that Frenzie Fook, who liked almost everyone, did not like them.

The time had come to make practical arrangements. Gai was afraid to book passage on a banana boat, which would have given him twelve days in which to brood and grieve. It would be better to have an eventful journey, so he arranged to fly on 18 April to Miami and travel up to New York by train, continuing after a break to Quebec where he would board a trans-Atlantic liner. A man called Robert Allerton Parker whose praise of Coomaraswamy he had quoted in *The Richest Vein* had written to him inviting him to stay if he was passing through New York, so he wrote taking up the offer.

Flo saw that they must have a little time alone together if they were not to part in the midst of quarrels and under the shadow of the Milners, so she rented a little wooden cottage at Guava Ridge, three thousand feet above Kingston, for five days. Rona at once objected. This would inconvenience her, she needed Flo for this or that, it was Gai's job to chauffeur them in the evenings, they were ungrateful even to think of leaving her on her own with Harry at such a time. They ignored her and got a friend to drive them up into the hills on 7 April.

'This seems like Paradise to me,' he wrote next day. 'The cottage is primitive but comfortably furnished. Oil lamps, an earth closet, water brought to the kitchen through a bamboo conduit from a little spring, the bath a natural pool under a waterfall, orange trees and bananas. It's on a hillside completely covered in wild nasturtiums—their scent is everywhere—and Blue Mountain Peak is in sight. Flo transformed almost instantaneously into her old self, gentle and loving. Not only our bodies but our hearts too are linked. Kingston seems far, far away.' And so it was, the City of the Plane with all its fevers and its ugliness. At night, hugging each other for warmth in the unaccustomed chill, they could watch the twinkling lights far below, beautiful now that they themselves had risen to the heights. The first thing they saw when they woke next morning was an emerald green humming-bird darting among the nasturtiums. A flash of beauty, perhaps an omen. The air was pure and fresh after the smog of bars and night clubs, and there was never a cross word between them. It almost seemed that the bad times had brought them even closer together. But never for a moment did it occur to Gai even to hint that he might return to her or, assuming he found a job in England, send for her should things not work out with Kay. His conditioning excluded her as a possible wife.

They returned to Kingston and, on the morning of the 18th, accompanied by the Milners, were driven to the airport (or, so they felt, to execution). There was no lingering farewell. The flight was called sooner than expected and there was time only for a desperate, hasty embrace before Gai made his way to the aircraft. As it left the ground something happened which he could only describe afterwards as the lifting of a veil. It seemed to him that, up to this moment, he had been living in a fantasy, the real-isation of his adolescent dreams with a beautiful dusky maiden centre stage. Quite suddenly, all that had evaporated. Flo was a real woman, his woman, the only woman he wanted and—as in that recurrent nightmare—he had made a dreadful mistake. If he had been equipped with a parachute he might have been tempted to jump while the plane was still over the Palisadoes and, as it headed out to sea, he was so empty that it was as though he had left himself behind in Jamaica. Now he was nobody, nothing, no more than a shell.

He tried to look forward to Miami. He had always wanted to visit Florida and now he was on his way there. Miami was horrible, not a town but an urban mess made up of used car lots, building lots and huge advertising billboards. Under the exchange regulations, having paid his fare, he was allowed $25 spending money for the whole trip. He was hungry but could only afford a miserable sandwich, and he filled in the six-hour wait for his train walking the desolate streets. Here he was in the America of his dreams, except that America had now turned into a nightmare. At least on the thirty-six-hour train journey to New York, people would talk to him—Americans were always friendly to strangers, weren't they?—and he might even be able to tell them about Flo. No one spoke to him, except for an official who shouted at him when he went to the 'Coloureds only' coach to take a photograph of a wayside station. For the first and probably the last time in his life he let loose a stream of savage abuse, including some obscene references to 'your filthy country', before returning to his 'Whites only' place feeling a little better.

He arrived at Penn Station unkempt, unshaven, wearing an old army duffel coat with wooden pegs instead of buttons. He was met by the immaculate figure of Robert Allerton Parker, an American gentleman of the old style, a true patrician with impeccable manners, and taken to a grand apartment overlooking the East River to meet Mrs Parker who turned out to be one of the Editors of *Vogue* magazine. Neither she nor her husband so much as batted an eyelid when faced with this scarecrow, their disreputable guest, but, on his second evening, when they took him to a show on Broadway, Robert suggested with exemplary tact that Gai might care to borrow an overcoat. He suspected it came from Savile Row. After four days of sight-seeing under Robert's guidance and a trip on his own to Harlem, just for the comfort of being surrounded by black faces, he set off by train for Quebec. At least he had something to which to look forward, a voyage on a trans-Atlantic liner. He knew from films he had seen what a wonderful experience this would be.

The *Samaria* was no ocean liner. It was a small troop ship which the Cunard Company had not yet got around to converting for passenger use. Fifteen hundred passengers were packed into it, sleeping on two-tier metal bunks without even enough chairs to go round. Every possible discomfort was provided, and everyone looked as miserable as he felt. The ship sailed down the St Lawrence river, pushing aside grey ice-floes under a grey sky, no colour anywhere and no warmth. Remember this? he asked himself. This is called 'cold'. It's what happens when the atmosphere —the surrounding air itself—becomes an enemy, obliging the frail human creature to cringe under a pile of clothing just to survive.

Chairless (as well as cheerless) he spent most of his time in his bunk trying, by an act of will, to transfer all that he felt for Flo to his wife. The trouble was that Flo refused to withdraw. She kept coming to him when he did not want to remember her. The bleak Atlantic—not a sliver of blue in it—rolled by and, if there were storms, he did not notice them. On his last night at sea he wrote in the diary: 'This has brought to the surface all the confusion and contradictions in myself. I don't know who I am or what I want, and my philosophy is useless to me, meaningless. If this comes from my selfishness, thinking only of myself, what use is that knowledge since I don't know the language of unselfishness?' The ship was six hours late docking at Tilbury and, during the short journey into London, he was at last able to think positively of Kay, remembering the good times and looking forward to a warm, welcoming embrace which would make everything alright. When he reached the door of the Mall Chambers flat he found a note pinned to it. She had waited as long as she could, but she had been obliged to go to an audition. 'Welcome home. Key under mat'.

When he let himself in he faced the mantelpiece on which three bulky envelopes with Jamaican stamps were displayed. He tore them open immediately and began to read, and at once it was Flo, not his wife, who was present in the little flat. She had found a hundred ways to express her desolation, her loss and her loneliness. A couple of hours later a complete stranger entered the flat, an interloper intruding upon his sad communion with his woman. He went through the motions of greeting Kay with affection and, after she had poured drinks for both of them, they sat in front of the gas fire talking. After a while she suggested shyly that, perhaps, they should put off sleeping together for a few days till they had really got to know each other again and he experienced a huge wave of relief. Eventually she put him to bed on the converted couch in the living room and fussed over him. Finally she asked: 'Is there anything more I can do for you, anything at all?' He knew exactly what she meant but pretended not to understand, adopting a tone he might have used in thanking Mrs Allerton Parker in New York for her hospitality: 'So kind . . . Most grateful . . .'

That was how it started and that was how it continued. Over the weeks that followed she tried every way that a woman could find to arouse him, from provocation to tears to mockery, and he reacted with an excruciating politeness, so remote that she could not touch him. It was his politeness and gentleness that were almost unbearable. Any show of emotion, even angry rejection, would have been preferable and less humiliating, but he seemed to be enclosed in a wall of ice which she could not penetrate. At one point she even offered to raise the money to pay his fare back to Jamaica. 'Flo obviously represents life and freedom from inhibitions to you,' she said, adding: 'I feel that everything to do with England and with me fills you with distaste'. He felt more ashamed than he had ever felt before, more guilty and more help-less. He could not understand what had happened to him. Here was an attractive woman—his wife, moreover—offering her nakedness freely, generously, and, although his body was quite ready to respond, he froze. He was making two loving women un-utterably miserable. What sort of man was he? A monster?

Later he wrote in the diary: 'I feel smothered. She asks me con-stantly, do I like this, do I like that, am I happier? She takes my hand and resents my not taking hers first. She complains of my coldness. And I can do nothing about these things, but wish—outrageously—that she would leave me alone. I feel also (a small voice, but persistent): If only she hadn't been so constantly 'un-faithful', if there hadn't been a 'blond beast' in Germany so soon after she left Jamaica. If only my woman, which was what she was supposed to be, had not been handled quite so freely. She might have been wiser not to tell me all this, but when was Kay ever wise? Unfair of me, I know, but there it is'. The situation reached a climax when they went to Bedford to spend a weekend with his aunt Eleanor and her friend Goo. Brenda had married a Frenchman and gone to live in France, but another neighbour of theirs happened to meet Gai and Kay in the street, a friendly character who had worked for many years in what was then Malaya.

He remarked jokingly to Kay that he hoped she had put black sheets on the marital bed. This was a colonialist joke which would not be understood today. The implication was that a husband who had worked in the tropics would have become accustomed to the pleasing contrast of black or brown bodies on white sheets (even Harold Clayton had owned a Burmese mistress in the old days). His wife, when he returned to her bosom, might be well advised to offer him the comparable contrast of a white body on black sheets. Kay was not amused, but that night she made her last attempt to provoke him into taking her. He did not know what it was that held him back, but he sat on the bed grim, silent and unresponsive. After that they settled down to a miserable existence as a divided couple imprisoned in a block of ice.

Meanwhile, of course, life outside their prison had been going on. The day after his return he went round to Ruth's flat. Leo Francis, now five years old, was staying with her for a few days. 'An enchanting small boy, obviously intelligent with perfect manners. In fact everything one could wish in a son. A nice little person—a stranger.' He wished there was someone who could tell him what to do, how to recover his son, but there was no one. Ruth had resigned herself to loving him without attempting to intervene in a tangled life with which he himself could not cope.

A couple of weeks later Kay brought the boy to Mall Chambers for the night and Gai shared a small camp bed with his son who slept in his arms while he lay awake, his mind full of crazy ideas. He would kidnap Leo Francis and take him to some far-off country or, perhaps, he would take him to Jamaica and they would live with Flo there. Since she was childless she would make a wonderful step-mother, he was sure of that. But—this was the brick wall against which all his hopes died—he still had no money, thanks to his father. He could only wonder what his life would have been had he inherited the third share of the Estate which had once been intended for him.

He had written to the Cunard Company complaining of conditions on the *Samaria*, threatening to go to his MP (this was 'a disgrace to Britain') and take the matter up in the press. He was reimbursed his total fare, £58, and that would keep him for a few weeks. Some time later he got a part-time job as a salesman for a magazine publishing company, tramping the streets with his wares for a small commission. Soon afterwards he saw an advertisement for an assistant lecturer in English Literature in the English Department of Fuad I University (later Cairo University). Since he had taken his degree in History this was a very long shot, but he was prepared to try anything. To his surprise he got an interview with the Egyptian Education Bureau in London, staffed, of course, not by Egyptians but by Englishmen. Although Egypt was nominally independent it was treated, in effect, as a protectorate and, when King Farouk had tried just once to act independently, his Palace had been surrounded by British tanks.

He had no friends to whom he could turn as Chris was learning Arabic at the Foreign Office language school in the Lebanon and Peter was in Germany. He had lost touch with others, but in mid-June, Jock, his former companion at Shanghai Lil's, turned up in London and they dined together. Gai had just received a letter from Flo: 'My sweet, I miss you more each day. Funny — I should miss you less, shouldn't I? No other man measures up to your standard. I shall love you always'. Now he could talk to a friend who knew and admired her, someone who spanned the two worlds. 'A joy to be with someone who knows and admires my Floflo. He said he thought we would make an ideal couple.'

Had he known it, two other meetings were of far greater significance. One of the people who had written to him after the publication of *The Richest Vein* was Marco Pallis, a Buddhist of the Tibetan school (and a traditionalist) whose book, *Peaks and Lamas*, had been — for a book of that type — a bestseller. Marco had been astonished by the fact that Gai had discovered the traditionalist perspective on his own and written of it so eloquently.

He himself had learned from Tibetan monks in Ladakh that there was a real alternative to the beliefs which dominated the western mind, an alternative that was timeless and liberating. He had embraced it with conviction and intellectual rigour, strongly reinforced by a reading of René Guénon's books. This was a man whose powerful personality influenced everyone he met and whose gentle severity cut through self-deception and all the illusions of the time. Some years earlier a woman doctor had come to him with a simple question. 'How,' she had asked, 'can anyone really believe in God in this modern age?' He had told her to read Meister Eckhart, the fourteenth-century German mystic 'from whom God nothing hid', and to come back to him in a year's time. When Gai met her long afterwards she at once asked him: 'Did Marco change your life?' She was by then a Benedictine tertiary and, as soon as she entered the Catholic Church, she had mounted an onslaught on the Vatican to persuade it to acknowledge Eckhart as a true teacher of the true Faith rather than a purveyor of heretical opinions. She was so formidable a woman that she had at least partially succeeded.

Gai spent an awkward evening with Marco. It was one thing to write about the traditionalist perspective, quite another to meet one of its principal exponents. He had never before met anyone like this, so uncompromising in his convictions, so rigorous in his arguments and so dismissive of everything that other people took for granted. Later, when they knew each other better, Marco told him that he had been baffled by the fact that Gai had only wanted to talk of Jamaica rather than of spiritual matters. Was this really the author of the book he admired? However, he introduced him to a certain Peter Townsend who had been instrumental in getting some of Guénon's books published in England. Townsend, a senior civil servant of rather intimidating gravity, invited Gai to lunch and put to shame his frivolity. It was all very well, he told him, to write such a book as *The Richest Vein*, but surely it was now time for him to put into practice what he clearly knew and understood, in other words to embark upon a spiritual path. Of course he was right. But the idea was terrifying, shattering. It would require the rejection of everything that, here and now, he wanted. I'm too young, he thought. There is so much life still to be lived. Above all, there was Flo who could not conceivably be fitted into a life of prayer and austerity, but neither Marco nor Townsend were trying to impose this on him. It was he who should be imposing it on himself if he was logical, consistent. He was not.

There was, however, one positive result of these meetings. Townsend had pointed him in the direction of Sufism, the inner dimension of Islam. The argument was compelling. Assuming that one was unable, for personal or temperamental reasons, to follow a Christian monastic path, then what was the alternative? Marco himself had never recommended his own way, Buddhism, recognising that it was too alien for most westerners. Hindu Vedanta offered many keys to spiritual understanding, but one had to be born a Hindu—born into a particular caste—to belong. Sufism, on the other hand, offered all that could be found in the other traditions (including Christian mysticism) and, at the same time, belonged to the Semitic monotheistic stream of revelation. A westerner could feel at home in it. But Guénon and the others always emphasised that one could not follow a Sufi path without being a Muslim in the full sense. The inner dimension could be approached only through the outer one. Kay was on tour, so Gai had an opportunity to read intensively about the Islamic tradition.

She returned from her tour refreshed and prepared to try again to re-establish the relationship. She admitted that at one point she had thought of taking one of Gai's revolvers—he had brought two back from his army service, moreover he still had the little handgun with which Francis had threatened to kill himself—and shooting him, then herself. Perhaps she had forgotten that there was no ammunition for these guns. But now, coming home drunk one evening, she told him that she felt the failure of the marriage was all her fault; she had 'picked up his love and then thrown it away'. A few days later a registered letter arrived offering him the job in Egypt. 'I feel so grateful,' he wrote, 'for the generous attitude Kay has taken to this, although it is a bitter blow to her. She asked me: "Do you think, when you're in Cairo, a visit from a Boo would be welcome? You wouldn't send me packing?" That depends, doesn't it? Depends on Flo.' But Flo's letters had ceased a month earlier and he was in an agony of uncertainty.

Jock had told him that Rona Milner was in London. This meant that Flo and Harry were alone together in the house. She was,

he realised, destitute although he had succeeded until then in putting the fact out of his mind. It was not difficult to guess what had
happened, but he refused to guess and, having written to her,
wrote again and then again demanding to know. Just before leaving for Egypt he received a reply. 'Believe me, I have been trying
for weeks to write to you. I still don't know what to say or how to
say it as the whole thing is so damned complicated. Now that I've
mustered the courage and hinted that everything is not what it
should be, I hope you will write to me and give me enough pluck
to explain just what has happened.' He sent her a cable at once,
writing it with a shaking hand. He knew but did not want to know
the truth. A few days later another letter came, written before
she had received the cable. 'By now you may have seen Jock, who
can tell you more than I dare. How can I explain what bitchery
and want have done to me? In time, dearest, I promise I will, but
give me time. My mind is in such a dreadful state that I don't
know if I'm coming or going. I want you to let me know how one
gets to Egypt. Does one have to show any money on entry? Let me
know the details. It's very important. If I get fed up enough I'm
leaving . . .. I can hardly get to write to you, Harry is so insanely
jealous.' So it was Harry, but there was still hope.

He went down to stay with his aunt Dolly, whose quiet, undemanding affection was a balm to his wounds. He told her nothing
of his troubles since she was in no position to offer advice. In any
case, he had no need of advice since there was nothing he could do
about anything. He had written to Flo asking her to come to Cairo
and now it was up to her. Kay was sad by this time rather than
emotional, and his mother, who insisted on doing all his packing,
was sad over his departure. Everyone was sad. The world was a
sad place. On 29 September 1950, under grey skies just like those
which had greeted him when he had arrived on the *Samaria*
nearly five months before, he boarded a plane for Cairo.

Kay had remarked that he seemed to find everything to do with England distasteful. Of course he did, since it was not Jamaica. Egypt filled him with the same distaste, and for the same reason. Perhaps he was by nature a territorial creature. He had never been given the chance to sink roots in the country of his birth, although he would always love Switzerland and defend it as the only true democracy in Europe, but the fertile soil of Jamaica had invited rooting and there he had rooted himself. Now, with what he saw as characteristic incompetence, he had doubled the distance from his adopted home and from his delinquent beloved.

He was here under false pretences to lecture on eighteenth-century and early nineteenth-century novelists although he had read none of them except Jane Austen. He went to the Assistant Professor and confessed. 'Don't worry, old boy', he was told. 'It does them good to talk to an Englishman.' On the plane he had sat beside a young academic, Dennis Hurrel, who had a First Class Honours degree in English Literature and who, like him, had been appointed an assistant lecturer in the English Department of the University. Dennis immediately lent him a book which told him all he needed to know and included summaries of the novels in question together with useful comments on them. Overnight he was equipped for his task.

A couple of days later he sat in his office interviewing potential students. A tramping of boots signalled the arrival of two soldiers, armed to the teeth, dragging between them a boy of seventeen or eighteen. Gai ordered the soldiers out—in those days Englishmen with a Public School background expected to be obeyed—before talking to the youth who explained in halting English that he was imprisoned as a member of the 'fundamentalist' Muslim Brotherhood but had been told that he might soon be amnestied. This was definitely not Jamaica.

Gai was suffering culture shock, but there was a compensation of incalculable value. Among the letters he had received when his book was published was one from Egypt. The writer was a certain Martin Lings, a lecturer in the English Department at the University, a member of the traditionalist group which included Townsend and Marco Pallis. Twelve years older than Gai, he was an adherent of a Sufi Tariqah, so here was a man who was wholeheartedly on a spiritual path, the Path. He had arranged Gai's accommodation in a small hotel and, on arrival at the University, Gai asked a student about him. 'Oh Sir,' he was told, 'that is the gentleman who talks to the flowers and is loved'. Later, as he got to know him better, he recognised in this man a quality he could only identify as holiness and a faith that was neither intellectual theory nor passionate emotion, but simply a state of being. There was nothing strange or dramatic about this. Gai was struck by the ordinariness—the normality—of this excellence, and he remembered reading in a book by a Catholic priest that the only failure in human life was the failure to be a saint. Without attributing sanctity to Lings—how would he recognise sanctity if he met it?—he had to acknowledge that this was how one was supposed to be as the fulfilment of human identity and human potentiality.

Over the coming months he would have two supports, as different from each other as any two men could be. On the one hand there was Lings, a man of the Spirit, single-mindedly dedicated to the Islamic faith and to the traditionalist perspective, on the other was Dennis, clever, tough, warm-hearted and cynical, coming from a working-class background (his mother had been a domestic servant) which was marvellously strange to Gai and, for that reason, like a breath of fresh air. Between quiet evenings with Lings and his wife in their home in a sandy little village at the foot of the Pyramids and touring the Cairo bars with Dennis, getting drunk together, the two poles of his nature were satisfied or would have been had he not been obsessed with Flo.

The beginning of an obsession, like the beginning of a grave illness which starts with almost imperceptible symptoms, cannot be dated. It creeps up on the patient until the condition is irrevocably established. The early entries in the diary are unusually brief. 'Busy learning Chinese (200 characters so far), hating Cairo, wanting Flo, sexual fever, reading Mircea Eliade, the Rumanian anthropologist who shares our point of view.' Soon, however, the entries expand to monstrous length although what he did with his days, whom he met and where he went are hardly mentioned. Page after page circles—a vicious circle—around the simple questions: 'Will she, won't she? Shall I, shan't I? How can I best break her will?' Revisited after fifty years, these pages have the smell of sickness about them. The best that can be said is that they served as a safety valve, though emitting a noxious vapour.

The first letter he had from Flo begged him, quite gently, to accept the situation. She was not coming to Cairo but hoped they could remain friends. She now owed Harry both gratitude and loyalty, so Gai must put aside his disappointment and think of her rather than himself. He at once sent her a cable: 'Good luck my love'. But in the diary he wrote: 'The void of "nothing to live for" is filled with the fantasy of getting back to Jamaica as soon as I have some money and taking her from Harry'. He had too much pride to plead, so he took the line of what can only be called emotional blackmail or what he described at the time as 'pounding', but first he sent her another cable asking her, at last, to marry him. In his first three months in Cairo he wrote her fifty-four letters. He kept no copies, but a five-page undated draft is stuck between the pages of the diary.

It opens with a blatant lie: 'I came to Cairo so that we could be together, I never thought of this place except in relation to your being with me'. He no longer knew that this was a lie. It continues: 'Don't you understand, my Flo, that I have been nearly going out of my head with jealousy? How could you expect me to feel well-disposed towards Harry when I think of you in his arms? You said you would "teach me to live" and I broke off the lesson. Now I don't know how to live in my own way and cannot, without you, live your way'. After that the anger breaks through. She had, he reminded her, given herself totally to him and she did not have the right to withdraw this gift to suit her convenience, the implication being that she should have been prepared to starve rather than abandon him. He was now so bereft of reason that the fact that it was he who had abandoned her counted for nothing. How, he demanded, could she have betrayed not only him but also herself by forgetting so soon her promise to love him for ever? She would destroy herself in this foolish relationship with Harry, a useless man incapable of love. And so it went on. In December there was what he described as a 'wise' letter from her, stressing her obligation to Harry and Gai's to his wife and son, but wisdom was not for him and he continued to pound her.

He had time on his hands. The University required of him a seven or eight-hour week, spread between Mondays and Thursdays, and standards even at third-year level were at best those of The Priory school in Jamaica. All he could do with first and second-year students was to teach them enough English for them to read the course books, but it was a small group of third-year boys and girls who gave him real joy. When he read them English love poetry tears came into his eyes and his voice was often choked. This had a sensational effect and, after a while, one of the students took him aside and said: 'We did not know there were Englishmen like you, Sir. We thought all Englishmen were cold-hearted with no feelings. We love you, Sir'. This was a comfort beyond anything he deserved. At the end of the university year they did well in their exams and the Head of the Department told him: 'You must have taught them very well'. This was astonishing, considering how little he knew about the subject he was supposed to be teaching. All he had done was give them his love in return for theirs, and this raised some interesting questions about the very nature of teaching young people. Was it possible that giving affection was more important than bestowing knowledge which, with encouragement, they could pick up for themselves?

Pounding Flo took up only a small proportion of the oceans of time at his disposal. He borrowed from Lings, who had himself recently published a book called *The Book of Certainty* as well as some poems, a pile of back numbers of the *Etudes traditionelles*, a journal for which Guénon and others of like mind wrote regularly, and he spent hours translating and typing out these building blocks of the traditionalist perspective. He needed to be well equipped to hold onto beliefs which denied and rejected everything that westerners had believed since the Renaissance and the so-called Enlightenment, in other words since the incursion of Roman paganism and the triumph of 'Reason' over Faith. In a sense it was his scepticism that made this possible. The schoolmaster at Charterhouse had been right in describing him as 'a universal sceptic'. He doubted the competence of the human mind to access truth unaided by a light from elsewhere and this opened him to the possibility of faith.

What he believed and would always believe was that a single truth, in itself inexpressible, had found expression under a vast diversity of forms and images. Only in the modern age had one sector of humanity gone astray, losing both the sense of the sacred and the intelligence to see through forms, myths and symbols to what lay behind them. A similar loss of spiritual intelligence was responsible for idolatry, whether in ancient Rome, in popular Hinduism (among those who failed to see the deities as Names of the One God) or in tribal Africa. The divine powers or attributes had been separated from their source through a process of decadence until they came to be worshipped as 'gods'. There had, then, been what amounted to a human consensus until quite recently. This fitted comfortably into the faith of Islam which teaches that no people on earth has been denied a message of truth from heaven suited to their needs but that these messages had been changed and distorted in the course of time. As for the scientific perspective—the claims of modern secular science—he had no problem with this. If, as the scientists believed, man was a part of nature, a clever animal and nothing more, then it was inconceivable that the part could ever comprehend the whole or observe that whole objectively, so the scientific presumption contained within itself an insoluble contradiction.

So Gai, who always found conviction difficult, was reading to convince himself or to fortify a nascent conviction while, at the back of his mind, the obsession with Flo was always present. Years later, when he wrote about the 'perpetual remembrance of God' which is the cornerstone of Islamic spirituality, he used this experience to counter the argument that no one could achieve this uninterrupted remembrance or 'God-consciousness' and still live a normal life. If a man in love could have his beloved constantly in mind while working, playing and socialising, then he could certainly maintain a constant awareness of the divine presence. But nothing he had read so far compared with the works of an author to whose early books Martin Lings introduced him, Frithjof Schuon, one of the most extraordinary and the most challenging spiritual writers of the twentieth century. A sage in the line of Coomaraswamy and Guénon, he towered over his predecessors as a visionary. In the course of his long life he would publish more than twenty books and he transformed the lives of thousands of men and women. The mystery is why he did not make the same impact on millions, but the fact is that such men are unfashionable in the present age, as are all those who write out of certainty rather than speculation, those who know through direct intuition the answers to the perennial questions which human beings ask. His particular achievement was to solve again and again the contradictions both within the religions and between them. There were many—not only Muslims but also Christians—who attributed this to a visitation of the Holy Spirit. How else could they explain a vision which pierced through these contradictions, a gift from heaven in compensation for the spiritual darkness of the times?

Gai's problem was simple. He was a child of the twentieth century, not a throwback to an earlier and better time as were some of the people he met later in life. He had to struggle and would always struggle against the modern man within himself and he was able to do so because he knew, at heart, that Schuon was right. He had to accept this duality and live with it, but that too had a positive side. When he came to write about these matters he understood only too well the doubts which he was likely to provoke in the minds of his readers and appreciated the need to answer them. Walking the streets of Cairo night after night he sought to resolve the problem, if necessary by compromises which some might have called 'fudges'. He walked the streets because he thought this was all he could afford to do. He seemed to have inherited from his mother's family, the Muddocks, an incapacity to deal sensibly with such money as he had. His annual salary from the University was £600, which should have been ample. He could have rented a small flat for £8 a month and probably employed a servant for the same amount, but this would involve making arrangements which he could not bother to make. He ended up as a paying guest with a French-Jewish-Lebanese family in a smart apartment in the centre of Town. This ate into his income while he had to save what he could for a return to Jamaica.

In the early months he dreamed of returning there after two years, by which time he might have saved a reasonable sum and his contract would have expired, although in fact he never received a written contract so this was irrelevant. Flo's letters were few and far between and, on one occasion, he went to the Central Post Office and insisted on seeing the head man to complain that important letters from Jamaica had gone astray. In December 1950 she had written: 'I don't know if you understand what you have, and always will, mean to me, believe me dear' (she had written 'darling' and crossed it out). Next month she slipped up badly. Before finishing a painfully sensible letter assuring him that they could never be together again—'If I let Harry down, do you think we could ever trust each other?'—she must have got very drunk and she finished it off with an almost illegible scrawl: 'Darling, darling, I'm stupid, I'm a bitch, I'm no good. Curse me, damn me, but forgive me. I love you and always will'. That was enough for Gai. It is by such small things—even the slip of a pen—that destinies are determined. He began to consider the possibility of breaking his non-existent contract and heading for Jamaica in the summer. Provided he could save £100 by then, what was stopping him?

Ruth, he felt sure, would not send him another 'stinker'. He had received a relatively mild one after writing her a crazy letter about his miseries, but she had followed this up by writing: 'Surely you realise by now that my bark is worse than my bite'. Later, she told him: 'Do as you want. That's alright, I did the same at your age. I don't blame you for that, but if I criticise or disapprove, you're down on me like a ton of bricks.' It was true that he demanded unqualified approval from her, whatever he did. He demanded it of others too, but he was surprised by Dennis's reaction when he finally told him the story of Flo and spoke of his bitter suffering. Instead of sympathy from his good friend, what he got was a peal of laughter. 'You're the most cheerful person I've ever known. You're really enjoying this drama, aren't you!' This was confusing and might even be true, but it was also true that his state of mind when he was alone was very different to his state when he was with Dennis and his wife. With them he could be happy. They both hated Cairo and talked sometimes of going back to England in the summer. From time to time Dennis accompanied him on his night walks and, one evening, he was made aware of the difference in their backgrounds. They were passing Shepheard's hotel—the grand old Shepheard's that was later burned down—and Gai suggested they drop in for a drink. When they had sat down and ordered, Dennis said quietly: 'That's the difference between us. I would never have dared come in here on my own. You walked in as though you owned the place'. It was the first time Gai had ever given a thought to the privileges he had enjoyed.

With Martin Lings he visited the great mosques of the City and soon began to feel at home in them as he had never felt at home in a church. He knew that, sooner or later, he would have to enter the community of Islam and mould himself to its requirements. 'Not yet', he assured himself. There was a vast gulf to be crossed before he could submit to imposed rules and a strict discipline, and he doubted whether he was capable of crossing it. Yet he suspected that, under the fripperies and behind the play-acting, there was something genuine in his nature, a core of faith, still inarticulate and lacking form. Lings had promised to introduce him to Guénon who lived with his family in a district of Cairo called Dokki and with whom Lings and his wife had been close friends for a number of years. Gai was puzzled by the delay, unaware of the fact that there had been a serious disagreement between the two men. Then, on 8 January 1951, Guénon died quite unexpectedly. When this happened, his cat howled for an hour, then lay down beside its master and joined him in death. 'Martin talked to me about this extraordinary man, so different to what one might have expected of such a rigorous metaphysician; a simple man, passionately interested in the little individual details of people's lives and even in household matters (looking after his children's toys and so on). When Mrs Lings had considered keeping chickens he had been full of wise advice on how to rear them.'

Meanwhile, light and air were beginning to penetrate the dark cell he had made for himself. Just the thought of going to Jamaica in a few months' time cheered him up and would have done so even more if he had found a flat for himself. He sensed that his hostess disliked him, which was not surprising since she lived for her food, supervised her cook in the preparation of huge, over-rich meals, and she was obviously distressed to see Gai leave half of every meal on his plate. Moreover, his room was circular and he read somewhere that living in such a room could cause madness. Nothing fitted, since furniture is not designed to fit against a curved wall, and this might even have been a reminder that the furniture of his mind did not fit. For a while he had a fellow paying guest, Monsieur S., a Lebanese who, so he was told, had once been the strongest man in the Lebanon. One evening, soon after his arrival, this strongman had a little accident. A taxi driver, mistaking him for a fat middle-aged tourist and unaware that the flab was really muscle, drove him to a deserted area and threatened him with a tyre wrench. Monsieur S. hit him only once, but the single blow killed the man, and he complained for weeks afterwards that this had cost him £100 in bribes to the police to overlook the incident. But he had a soft centre. Gai told him the story of Flo and of how he pined for her. 'The same thing happened to me,' said Monsieur S., 'and I was most ill for six weeks with much suffering. I thought I would die. A doctor cured me of my love with a course of *picures* (injections)'.

Gai doubted whether *picures* would solve his own problem. The solution could only be action, so he wrote to the Jamaica Banana Producers Company telling them that it was 'a matter of life and death' for him to get to Jamaica in July but he could only afford a maximum of £45. He was prepared, he said, to hang a hammock in the engine room if necessary. After an agonising wait of a month, he received a reply. They were delighted to be able to tell him that the smoking room on their ship the *Jamaica Producer* had recently been turned into a eight-berth cabin. He could have a bunk for £45. So how was he to get to England? He discovered that he could get from Alexandria to Venice for £10 if he travelled on the deck of a steamer, and another £10 would cover the train journey from Venice to Calais and the cross-Channel ferry. He was on his way and able to announce his intention to Ruth and others. She appeared to take it in her stride, but his aunt Eleanor told him he was mad, as did his old friend Peter Heyworth.

The unexpected reaction came from MEO, the friend he had met in a teashop in Oxford nearly ten years before. She wrote that he was obviously 'possessed by a devil' and was ruining his life as well as destroying his mother. He would never get another job because this breaking of his contract would always remain on his file. She had become a close friend of Ruth, and he suspected that this echoed his mother's real reaction to the news. It seemed absurd that anyone should imagine he might change his mind. He never changed it once it was made up. He found it too much bother to do so.

There was another decision to be made, and this too would be irrevocable. Whether or not Flo returned to him—and he doubted that she would—he knew the kind of life he was going to in Jamaica and he was aware of the abyss into which he might fall. He must anchor himself to avoid this shipwreck. He did not think he was ready yet to embrace Islam, but the opportunity to do so might never come again. He faced an open door which would close the day he left Cairo. Could he at least sow a seed which, God willing, would eventually germinate? Could he make the *Shahada* (the declaration of faith) in full awareness of the fact that he was not going to become a real Muslim, a practising Muslim, for some time to come? No one needed to tell him that this was an outrageous proposal. To put the Faith on hold amounted to an impudent toying with God, yet he sensed that, once this step was taken, he would be on his way although he might have felt less confident had he known how long it would be before the seed, sown on such stony ground, germinated and grew into a healthy plant. One of the Names by which God has named himself in the Quran is *as-Sabúr*, the ever-Patient, 'He whose Patience is never exhausted'. Gai would put his trust in the divine Patience and hope for the best.

The saying that 'the fear of God is the beginning of wisdom' is common to both Islam and Christianity which suggests that it is worth considering. In his generation and in the preceding one there were a number of men and women, usually of high intelligence, who, while rejecting organised religion, adhered to what they saw as the spiritual dimensions of Hinduism, Islam, Buddhism or, occasionally, Christianity (Eckhart and the Rhineland mystics had a particular appeal for them). Whether aware of this or not, their attitude probably derived from an ingrained belief in progress. The nitty-gritty of religion—the rituals, laws and morality associated with a particular Faith—were seen as primitive and, of course, inconvenient, so they could be ignored. It was the heart that mattered, as though the heart did not depend upon the body as a whole. What these people lacked was any fear of God. Leo Myers had been one of them. Gai was, or had been until recently, another. Now, immersed in the world of Islam, he felt the first faint whisper of fear. He reminded himself of the saying of Saint Thérèse of Lisieux: '*Je suis trop petite pour me damner*', 'I am too little to damn myself'. Surely, he was too insignificant to merit the divine Wrath? In any case, he would chance it.

The legalistic aspect of Islam had no appeal for him, but the spirit of Islam had such an intense appeal that he thought had always shared in it. The idea of God as a caring father-figure was incomprehensible to him. God as the Real, God as Splendour, God as Light, God as Beauty and the source of all beauty; in this he could believe. It made sense, as did the awareness that Reality sweeps away all illusions. Splendour reduces triviality to dust, Light drives away darkness and Beauty consigns all ugliness to the category of the *bátil*, 'emptiness'. He had found his homeland.

But it was in the writings of the Sufi Masters that he found answers to the questions that had troubled him from his school days and which had been answered only partially by the complex doctrines of *Vedanta*. His reading of Ibn Arabi had been fragmentary and superficial but it already seemed obvious to him that the writings of the *Shaykh al-Akbar* contained a key which might eventually unlock the ultimate mysteries. He realised, albeit dimly and with limited understanding, that a mere taste of that wisdom—that illumination—was worth more than a thousand books of philosophy. It was as though this extraordinary visionary of the thirteenth century had been writing for the modern age which is tormented by questions which the Master's contemporaries were unlikely to have asked.

Some time later he would try to define what was, for him, the essence of the Islam:

Religion stripped to the bone. Religion as such.

Other religions soften or mitigate the encounter with the One, for who dares look directly at the sun? The terrible encounter is softened for Christians by the God-man, for others by 'idolatry' (the refraction of the One in the manifold) and, in the Far East, by a discrete unwillingness to look.

A religion for the end of time. Only when the play is almost over and the theatre about to close can such an encounter take place.

A single statement: God is. Substitute for 'God': ultimate Reality is, ultimate Truth is (eg: Bible — 'I AM THAT I AM'). Apart from Him there are only shadows, mirages, dreams. Only with Him, in Him and through Him do they take on a measure of reality.

To glorify That which is and bow down before the splendour of the Real in which we participate by our very existence.

Islam adds that there is communication (the ultimate miracle) between His Being and our existence. There is Revelation. Since communication implies reciprocity, there is, on our side, Prayer. He speaks. We speak.

The Muslim, having cleansed himself from the worldly stain by ablution steps out into empty space to stand, beyond time, before his Creator. He speaks words revealed for his use. He dares to look ('A cat may look at a King!').

Quran: HE IS THE FIRST AND THE LAST, THE OUTWARD AND THE INWARD. Before time He <u>is</u>. After time He <u>is</u>. In the midst of things seen, felt and heard, He <u>is</u>. In the depths, within and again more deeply within, He <u>is</u>. Quran: WHERESOEVER YOU TURN, <u>THERE</u> IS THE FACE OF GOD.

He went to Martin Lings to ask to be received into Islam, but first he would have to recount the whole story of Flo and tell him of his intention to return to Jamaica. Lings was riding in the desert, so he spilled out the story to Mrs Lings. She listened in silence, then said simply: 'You will have to tell Martin all that'. He did so, painfully and awkwardly, adding that he could not promise to give up rum for some while to come. Finding him immovable on this point and after much hesitation Lings, who had now grasped the urgency of the matter and who had been taken completely by surprise, told him to come to the house the following morning after taking a bath. He added that, if Gai was able to recapture Flo, he should perform a simple marriage ceremony, giving her a coin in lieu of a dowry and saying to her three times before witnesses: 'I marry you'.

On 29 May 1951, he made his *Shahada*, witnessing to the divine Unity and to the fact that Muhammad is the Messenger of God. This, at least, he could accept with complete sincerity. In the diary he wrote: 'Martin—I should now call him Sidi Abu Bakr—taught me the bodily movements and a few Arabic verses from the Quran. Then I followed him in the midday prayer (my mind seized up with panic). Never having prayed until now, never in any way, I feel as though I am using a limb that has never been used before. I'm aware of the murmurs of revolt in my own nature. What have I done—this terrifying leap into commitment? Oh dear! Life was complicated enough without adding this dimension to the complications'.

Next day he wrote: 'I feel like a new boy at school, very aware of my own smallness compared with my inflated importance as an exponent of theory. As Hasan abdul-Hakim (servant of the Wise), my Muslim name, the great metaphysician prays less well than the simplest peasant. Poor, clumsy Hasan'. It was Ramadan, the month of fasting, and this presented him with a weird experience. Till now he had never known what hunger or thirst were, and he had seldom awaited anything as eagerly as he waited for the boom of the sunset gun which announced the end of the daily Fast. The exercise of a self-imposed discipline was so contrary to his nature that he could hardly recognise himself. He felt marvellously at peace and acknowledged in the diary that 'it may be the attraction of Jamaica is a satanic one as MEO suggested, but it seems to be *maktúb*, written on the tablet of my destiny'. In a recent letter Marco Pallis had told him: 'You are not just a leaf in the wind!' but that was precisely what he thought he was and he would go wherever the prevailing wind took him.

It would be many years before he again encountered Martin Lings, discovering that this good man had never given up praying for him while he himself wandered far astray, neglecting 'the one thing necessary', and this encounter would finally set him on the Path which he had always known it was his destiny to follow as best he could.

At their invitation he went to stay with Dennis and Rosamund for his final three weeks, warmed by their friendship and untroubled by Dennis's incomprehension of the reasons for his conversion and unembarrassed to pray in front of them. They and the Lings were the only people who knew he was leaving. He told no one else, not even the Head of Department, out of a vague fear that the authorities might try to stop him from going. His absence would not be noticed for another three months as the university year had now ended, and his final function was as one of the invigilators of the annual examinations which were held in a vast tent beside the Nile.

He packed up all his worldly possessions, including nearly a hundred books, and took the train to Alexandria where he boarded a ship appropriately named *Esperia*, 'Hope'. Afraid to spend even a small sum on a porter, he had to make four journeys lugging his things up to the top deck, then down a number of staircases almost to the ship's keel, and finally up again to the aft deck where he slept for three nights under the stars, joining the sailors at meal times. 'This journey', he wrote, 'will take ten years off my life, but I'll remember it till my (probably premature) death. I have a wonderful sense of fulfilment. When I had a swim in Alexandria and the waves knocked me over I laughed from sheer joy. When did I last laugh so freely?' The ship docked in Venice on 7 July and he spent two nights in a cheap hotel. He knew he was in the most beautiful city in the world but he was too preoccupied with his ultimate destination to appreciate it. On the long train journey he could only afford a single sandwich, so he arrived at Ruth's flat famished. She fed him and cosseted him, making no reference to Flo.

He talked to Kay who told him that she and Ruth had thought he might be going to Jamaica to kill Flo and had discussed which of them should go out there to stand by him. He had involved a lot of people in his private drama but, after all, what was a drama without an audience? He went to stay with his aunt Dolly for few days, 'peace at last', then with Eleanor and Goo in Bedford, and he met MEO who had been astonished and, perhaps, discomforted when Ruth told her on the phone that 'it was years since she had seen Gai looking so well and cheerful'. So what about his 'satanic possession'? In all this there was one victim, one innocent, and that was his son. Kay, still half persuaded that he might soon lose the father he had never really had, brought the boy to Ruth's flat. 'He was looking fine, but a bit lost and nervy, poor kid. He may have been aware of his mother's screaming nerves and, for that matter, of mine. He is staying the night, and I helped Ruth bath him and get him settled, then read to him till he dozed off. Why can't I be with him? Why can't I have my cake and eat it?' He felt obliged to ask forgiveness of God for such foolishness, but it was a folly deeply ingrained.

The strange interlude—neither here nor there—was soon over and, on 3 August 1951 he boarded the steamship *Jamaica Producer* in the West India Docks on the River Thames. Immediately surrounded by Jamaican voices and by the dear, familiar accent, Cairo was truly behind him, as was England. As soon as they sailed he and his cabin mates observed that one of their number appeared to be less than sane if not raving mad. They complained to the Purser who assured them that the man had probably drunk too much at a farewell party. During the night Gai, who was in one of the upper bunks, was woken by a weight on his chest. The madman had climbed on top of him, but at the moment of waking he sensed that this was for refuge rather than for attack and the gruff words, 'Someone gwine kill me! Help me! All men brothers, and God too', told him that he was right. After much gentle persuasion he eased the man off him and got him into his own berth. Next morning he and his companions went again to the Purser, who told them they were making a fuss about nothing but went straight to the cabin looking smug. A moment later he popped out like a cork from a bottle, pursued by the man who now had in his hand one of the heavy iron instruments used for raising and lowering the cabin windows. The Purser was chased twice round the deck, while the passengers cheered and clapped their hands, until some sailors came to his rescue.

After that it was an uneventful twelve-day voyage as the sea changed gradually from grey to blue. Gai found a space behind one of the lifeboats where he could put down his mat and pray undisturbed, but there were other places too. 'This evening, right up at the prow of the ship, the scene was superb with a quarter-moon just rising over the darkening sea. I rushed back to the cabin to do the ablution, then returned to pray the Sunset Prayer there.' He spent most of his time with three young women from Port Antonio who had been to London on a shopping spree. 'Spent the day with the girls. In the evening we got up an impromptu sing-song on the boat deck, the English passengers (except for me) sitting on one side, the Jamaicans (and me) on the other'. He knew where he belonged.

He was up before dawn on 15 August to see the lights twinkling on the south coast of the Island. 'We passed Port Royal at six and docked an hour or so later. I couldn't help searching for Flo's face on the quay, saw her half-sister and little Norma, her adopted daughter, waving an envelope, and there was my former headmaster, Henry Fowler. As soon as I landed Norma handed me Flo's note, apologising for not meeting me herself, but saying she had sent Alva (her half-Chinese chauffeur and friend) with the car to take me to the lodgings she had found me at £3 a week. I asked Alva how she was: 'Much better, in fact she getting too big'. Henry Fowler offered to help in any way he could and suggested a loan of £50 so that Gai could buy some kind of transport at once. The offer was gratefully accepted, and then Alva drove him up to the guesthouse where he was to stay.

Flo phoned, sounding awkward, and arranged to meet him that evening at a club by the sea. Having settled in, he sat down to write up his diary. 'The fantasies end. The reality begins.'

14

T H E   I S L A N D

Greta and Henry Fowler took him out to dinner, perhaps to assess whether he was as mad as he was said to be. Apparently they found him quite sane, but they were uneasy when they drove him to the Springfield Club and left him there to face Flo. He did not have long to wait. As Alva had said, she had put on weight but it suited her; she looked magnificent and yet in some way changed. This was no longer the girl sleeping under the counter in a little shop in one of the lanes who had said to him: 'Thank you for wanting me'. This was a formidable woman, sure of herself and of her sexual magnetism.

Next morning he wrote in the diary: 'Difficult to know how to describe that extraordinary evening. If it had ended at 2 a.m. this would be simple; a theme of joy and adoration but, as it is, I'm left with a confused impression. For the first quarter-of-an-hour we argued. Then, sitting on the veranda overlooking the moonlit sea we forgot our prepared speeches and talked as easily as though we had parted only yesterday. We held hands, she slipped her arms round my neck, I kissed her smooth alabaster shoulders and inhaled the familiar scent of her body. I was sublimely happy. It was for this that I had travelled 8,000 miles over land

253

and sea. Even if nothing comes of it, the decision to return has been vindicated. She said that she loved Harry and me equally, but she had to say that. She could never hurt him, she said. He was less able to take it than I was. But more than once she remarked quite casually: 'If you and I come together again . . .' Then she ordered champagne and soon became fairly drunk'.

She phoned for Alva to pick Gai up and the car arrived with Harry, ashen-faced and trembling. 'You don't really mean to kill me, do you?' he asked Gai. Flo turned on him savagely, accusing him of spying on her, her face contorted with anger. This was a Flo Gai had never met before, and it was not surprising that Harry quailed under the onslaught and was reduced to dithering excuses. Then the Polish barman, a vicious character at the best of times, made insulting references to her past and her rage overflowed in a torrent of abuse. The gentle night had turned ugly.

Next morning Gai awoke to find himself famous. He never discovered where the rumour had started. Perhaps at the Press Club, where Flo had read out passages from his Cairo letters, perhaps through Greta who loved drama as much as he did, but everyone seemed to believe that he intended to murder Harry. A couple of days later, when he was having a coffee at a pavement café, he became aware of a tall young man looming over him. 'You Mr Eaton?' he asked, then sat down beside him and explained that he was an oil worker from Venezuela on his way home to the States. He was spending a few days in Jamaica and finding it expensive. Up to this point Gai was completely baffled. Surely this young tough was not begging and, anyway, how had he known his name and identified him? 'I'm told there's a guy you'd like never to see again,' said the man, adding after a pause: 'Give me £100 and you won't see him again'. This seemed a modest fee, but then the killer would be taking no risk. He would be back in the States within a few hours of doing the job. Gai thanked him nicely and declined the offer. In the days that followed people he hardly knew crossed the road to welcome him back. He suspected that they hoped to be able to tell their grandchildren that they had met the celebrated murderer before he went to the gallows. An American singer who had been staying with Flo and Harry had moved out when she realised that her bedroom window faced an ideal sniper post in the house opposite.

On 18 August the worst hurricane of the century struck Jamaica. The roar of the wind was beyond anything Gai could have imagined, overwhelming every other sound so that sections of the roof above him flew silently away, and the deluge — reminiscent of Noah's flood — had nothing in common with rain; it was as though a bucket of water as big as the globe itself was being emptied onto the Island. In the next room to him a woman who had recently acquired a record player in a fine wooden cabinet passed most of the night lying on top of it, preferring to be soaked rather than see her treasure ruined. A Chinese man with a room on the comparatively dry ground floor who could not sleep offered Gai his bed in the early hours. He slept through the rest of the storm, waking to a world cleansed and refreshed amidst the wreckage.

All communication with the North Coast was down so stories of utter devastation spread quickly; all the bananas were destroyed, the coconut palms had snapped when the wind changed direction after the eye of the hurricane had passed, several people had been beheaded by flying tin roofs. Gai had never actually wept for Flo, but now he wept for his Island, feeling exactly as though a beloved woman had been torn limb from limb. 'If only I could encircle Jamaica in my arms and comfort her', he wrote. The first letter that came through when the postal services were re-established was from his friend Peter Heyworth in England: 'I know you have to fill your life with drama, but weren't you overdoing things this time by conjuring up a hurricane?'

It was in this emotionally charged state that he went out with Flo on the evening after the storm. There were no street lights and he cut his leg on some unseen metal object. She took him into the nearest bar and poured over-proof white rum on the leg, cauterising the wound but leaving a permanent scar as a reminder. 'Four hours with her,' he wrote on getting back to the guesthouse. 'Four hours that were a lifetime. Nothing else matters but the fact that I love her. And now she says she'll sleep with me when the time is right! Nothing is as I foresaw it. This is thunder and lightning, out of any world. She is beyond everything wonderful and I would die for her. My God, she's Flo, Flo, Flo. Nothing like this ever was or will be again.' This and similar passages in the diary were obviously fuelled by rum but that does not completely account for what looks, in retrospect, like a reversion to adolescence at the age of thirty. Perhaps he had to be an adolescent to avoid responsibility. He had never really believed that she would come back to him, but now this began to look like a possibility and that possibility was rather frightening. What would he do with her if he had her? In fact they would never again recapture the magic of that evening in the aftermath of the Big Wind's terror.

For some days however magic ruled his heart. The woman in the next room to his in the guesthouse appeared to have only one disc to play on her precious gramophone and she played it over and over again. This was music from the show *The King and I*. Sitting on his balcony he drank it in and could never have enough of it. The song 'Getting to Know You' moved him to tears. Obsessed with a selfish love when they were together, he had never really known Flo. Now perhaps he would truly get to know her so that their roots were intertwined inseparably.

One summer's evening half-a-century later he would hear, as he passed a London house with its windows wide open, the strains of 'Getting to Know You' and he would be transported back to that balcony, seized by the memory of love. But this would be a love transformed by time, untroubled and cleansed of dross, although Flo and all the rest had by now gone ahead of him into the strangeness of death. It would seem to him possible that, when all was over, *Rahmah*, the divine Mercy, might transform turbulence into peace and pain into joy.

The best way to counter a rumour about oneself is to spread a counter-rumour so that people can say they have had the facts 'straight from the horse's mouth'. One's own version of the story —whether true or not—then takes precedence over all others. He found a ready audience. 'What is it that makes people who should disapprove—might be expected to see this as common-place—listen to me and take me seriously? Perhaps they perceive a little of the glow of this fire and respect it.' As time passed and it was realised that there would be no murder, the opinion of the community took shape. Bob Verity, an influential figure whom Gai called 'the Sage of St Andrew's', pronounced on the situation: 'Gai is the lover and Harry is the Father figure and also the child'. This did not contradict something that Flo said to him: 'I want you both rolled into one. I want love so much, I want you to go on loving me always'. There were some who obviously thought that this was the beginning of a stable three-part rela-tionship comparable to that of Henry Fowler, Greta and Greta's complacent husband.

Flo, like Gai, was now thirty. She was drinking very heavily and must have had a powerful constitution for she would, in the event, live on into her mid-seventies, but drink made her increas-ingly unpredictable. One night she got Alva to drive her up to the guesthouse and called Gai's name under his window. He came down in his pyjamas and they sat on the wooden steps talk-ing while Alva stood at a discrete distance. He kissed her breasts while she stroked his hair, murmuring: 'My Gai! My Gai!' A few nights later she was back, but this time shouting abuse. She had seen him dancing with a girl at the Glass Bucket. 'If you really loved me you wouldn't want to dance with anyone else.' Next day she told him: 'I don't love you, I don't love Harry. I hate you both'. To Gai's old friend, the *Spotlight* Editor, Evon Blake, she said: 'If I were to say to Gai "I love you" I'd have to leave Harry at once and sleep on the racecourse if necessary'. Evon told Gai: 'She obviously wants to come back to you. Help her to make up her mind.' As it was, they were both living in torment and confusion, and she said one evening that she envied Gai his sweet pain, adding: 'It must be better than the dreadful boredom of having all I could want'. Alva, chauffeur and confidante, told her it was time she made up her mind what she wanted, love or money. It seemed that everyone had got into the act.

Within a couple of weeks, however, sweet pain was giving way to anger. 'I think I must call her Your Majesty', he wrote. 'She gives orders and I obey, obliged to fit in with her changing moods, to accept cruelty and abuse or be humbly grateful for her kindness. It won't do.' There were moments when he came close to hating her. One day she would tear him to shreds with her bitter tongue, the next she was loving and apologetic. He met and talked with the American singer who had been staying with Flo and Harry at the time of his return, a big, kindly black woman. Her account of conditions in the Milner household appalled him. If he had been living a dog's life, so had Harry. It seemed that Flo was completely out of control, venting her bitterness on Harry as she did on Gai. He began to understand that he was the one who would have to end it before he was destroyed. There was one comfort: 'The prayers this evening were wonderfully refreshing, a great mercy, unfit as I am at present to pray. My miseries will soon be seen for what they are — small things of no consequence unless they instruct me and rectify me'.

The end came suddenly. She had told him to find himself an apartment or small unfurnished cottage for which she would provide furniture. Perhaps she had decided to 'share' herself, in which case he would find himself sitting at home evening after evening in the hope that she might deign to visit him, just like the old-style mistress of a powerful man. He needed no one to tell him that this would not work, but one morning he was joined for coffee by Tommy, a down-and-out Englishmen who was in Flo's entourage and who mocked him for imaging that she cared for him. This implied that he was a pathetic supplicant and his pride made that intolerable, so Gai told him briefly of her proposal regarding the cottage.

Tommy did not believe him and lost no time in going to her, telling her that Gai had boasted she was renting a cottage where she could sleep with him. She telephoned, incoherent with rage, and told Gai to meet her at a bar on Harbour Street. She accused him of being a psychopath. 'You don't love me. It's just some sort of complex you have!' Then she mocked him cruelly as, no doubt, she was accustomed to mocking Harry. When he tried to explain what had happened with Tommy, she told him not to whine. This was the last straw. It was time to take Evon's advice and help her to make up her mind. He told her to go to hell, tossed his drink in her face—enjoying her look of shocked incredulity—and walked out of the bar a free man. It was just eight weeks since he had returned to Jamaica.

Still wounded, but recovering at remarkable speed, Gai now had time to ask himself what had gone wrong or, more specifically, what had happened to Flo since she went to Harry. Greta, though she had hardly known her, said she had never before seen a girl go to pieces in the course of a year and congratulated him on his escape. Frenzie at Shanghai Lil's spoke with more authority, having known Flo since childhood. 'I t'ink she sick in her mind', he said. 'She was so nice, you know, so kind and jolly. Now she worser than Rona, she turn into nasty bitch.' No one guessed at the probable answer, which hinged on her deep shame over her mother's prostitution and the feeling that she too had now sold herself to a man. There was also the enigma of Harry himself. Could he be to blame for having turned Rona into a harridan and for having done the same to Flo? Had he, quite simply, been the wrong man for both women, too weak, too negative, altogether too much an English gentleman in decay, without passion and without warmth?

In any case, no one had a good word to say of fat Flo, but no one should judge a person until the end of their story. Many years later, when Harry's funds had run out and he was a sick old man, she started up a little video business. Still in correspondence with Gai, she took immense pride in the fact that she was able to keep Harry in the manner to which he had been accustomed and to pay his medical costs when he needed a major operation. By the end of his life she loved him. Time always holds surprises for those who wait patiently.

Gai was shaking himself like a dog that has emerged from a cage and is beginning to wag its tail. The University in Cairo had got his address, presumably from Lings, and, to his astonishment, paid him his September salary. There was also a letter from the Head of Department almost begging him to return, and this was flattering. He had enough money now to see him through until he got another teaching job and he bought himself a second-hand motorcycle which gave him the joy of freedom. He was glad to be where he was and even more thankful when he had a letter from Ruth abusing Kay more bitterly than ever before and cursing Alice Clayton. 'It seems,' he noted in the diary, 'that my mother-in-law (if I must call her that) sent Ruth an angry letter objecting to Leo Francis staying with her and with the aunts; 'a foul old woman', according to Ruth. I'm well out of it, but why do people have to hate and hurt each other? Don't they know how short life is? And don't they understand that they will be judged in terms of the mercy they have shown or withheld when it is over?' A letter from Kay congratulated him on escaping Flo's spell and advised him to 'pick a better one next time'. Meanwhile he was surrounded by friends, most of them women, who welcomed him back into the world of the sane and set themselves to rebuild his confidence.

Felicity Palliser, a white Jamaican married to a very sweet-natured Englishman, was sure she could find him a job, much as MEO had done in the past. One evening she invited him to a dinner party to meet Dr Simpson, Headmaster of Wolmers, the leading boy's school in Kingston. He had no vacancy until the second term in the following year, 1952, but was prepared to take Gai on then. Nothing daunted, Felicity contacted a friend who was Chairman of the Tichfield School Board in Port Antonio, a small town on the North Coast. She got him a job there for the January term. Late in November he had a letter from Dennis in Cairo. The entire English staff of the University had been dismissed, their October salaries unpaid. Some of them, he said, believed that Gai must have had inside information as to what was going to happen and had got out in good time, which would explain his mysterious disappearance. This was ironic. His 'mad decision' was now more than justified. 'Thank you, Flo', he thought to himself.

Some two months later he had another letter from Dennis, now in England. Expulsion from the University had been followed by the anti-British riots which preceded Abdul Nasser's Revolution and, out of the ten English colleagues Gai had left behind, four were killed while the remainder cowered in their apartments, afraid even to go out to buy food and without the funds to pay their fares home. He felt sure that he would have been among the dead since he would not have been able to resist the temptation to go into the city and observe the drama, just as he had gone out into the *Blitz* in London. As for MEO's prediction that his job prospects would be ruined, this too would turn out well in the end. Some twenty years later, when he faced a Commonwealth Office board, the Chairman remarked: 'I see you didn't stay very long in Cairo, Mr Eaton'. He was prepared for this and looked down modestly before saying: 'You may recall, Sir, it was a difficult time politically'. The reaction was immediate. 'You poor fellow, you must have had a dreadful time'. A good mark, he felt sure, went down on his file. This chap had been through fire and coped. After that, whenever he met some young man agonising over a decision which might determine his future, Gai would tell him the story to illustrate the impossibility of foreseeing the outcome of any decision.

The year 1952 came in quietly, and on New Year's Day he was full of optimism and prayed that his mother might find peace of mind, that Kay might at last find happiness, that Flo might turn back from the precipice of self-destruction, and that his son might grow straight and true after his wretched beginning. 'May God in His mercy grant me the right to intercede for them', he wrote. 'I have done them no good in my living. But I do believe that to pray for them is, in a certain sense, to bring them to the attention of the All-Merciful and, since His mercy is limitless and all-encompassing—Well, who knows?' With his future more assured and with the prospect of Alice Clayton dying soon, he began to fantasise about Kay allowing him to have Leo Francis and to bring him up in Jamaica. Short of carting him from one theatre dressing-room to another, she could not look after him herself. On 17 January he left Kingston to take up his appointment at the Tichfield School.

Port Antonio was the only town in Jamaica that had real charm. It belonged to the age of 'green gold'—the banana boom in the early years of the twentieth century—and had slumbered peacefully ever since. Mass tourism had not yet got off the ground in Jamaica but, already, in Ocho Rios, three big hotels were either completed or under construction where, two years earlier, there had only been a guesthouse called Dunlookin. Port Antonio was unaffected, partly because it had the reputation for being the rainiest place in the Island and partly because the beaches could not compare with those further along the North Coast. There was one hotel, the Tichfield, which had been bought by the film star Errol Flynn whose parents lived nearby and who was often to be seen dining with his wife in the hotel, both of them looking bored out of their skulls.

Gai was not the only new arrival at the school. The former headmaster, an Englishman, had retired at the end of the year and it had been taken for granted that he would be succeeded by his deputy, a Jamaican well qualified for the post. This man was passed over in favour of another imported Brit, in this case a Welshman who had never before left the UK and for whom the culture shock of Jamaica was overwhelming. He was bitterly resented by the staff as an interloper but must have hoped for Gai's support, while referring to him privately as 'that heathen', but he did not get it. The 'heathen'—the Muslim—sided with his Jamaican colleagues on every issue and quickly earned their friendship. He also earned the affection of his pupils through a small incident. He had in his class a fifteen-year-old Chinese girl of whom it could only be said that she was not very bright. One day, passing by, the Head noticed her staring out of the window instead of attending to the lesson. He scolded her severely, and she at once burst into tears. Gai jumped up from his desk and hugged her, stroking her hair. Today, in a dehumanised Britain, this would presumably have resulted in his immediate dismissal, but it was the natural thing to do and the Head pretended not to notice.

A pretty twelve-year-old black girl, Yvonne, sat directly in front of his desk and, whenever he extended his long legs, she bent down and used a piece of chalk to inscribe crosses for kisses on his shoes. He treated this as a joke, but six or seven years later he met Yvonne in Kingston. She glimpsed him passing her office and rushed out to greet him with a kiss. She told him: 'You were terribly shy, weren't you! We were all in love with you and you never did anything about it'. Considering her age at the time this was rather startling, but he was told later by someone that Jamaican villagers often considered 'Teacher' the best person to initiate their pubescent daughters as an authority figure, more responsible than the local boys and wiser in the ways of the world. In retrospect he realised that at least one of his male colleagues had taken full advantage of this custom.

It was a good life in the sleepy little town with the lush countryside, friendly colleagues, pupils who only wanted to please him and an undemanding five-hour-day teaching. He shared accommodation in a pleasant guesthouse owned by two sisters, retired teachers, with Mike, a clever young Guianese who soon became a good friend. Mike was a Communist and, although this was just as bad as being a Nazi, it could be forgiven on grounds of youth and immaturity. The two elderly sisters mothered both of them indulgently and waved to them every morning when they set out for school on Gai's motorbike. There was a Maroon settlement a few miles from Port Antonio. The Maroons were the descendants of escaped slaves who, by a treaty made long ago with the British authorities, enjoyed a measure of independence from central government. The diary records 'a glorious morning'. 'I rode the ten miles over dirt tracks through superb scenery to the Maroon village of Moore Town where I was joined at the local bar by the D.C., a grand character who keeps four women by whom he has eighteen *picney*. Good talk, mainly political. Speeded home bumping and skidding over the rough surface, wildly happy. Prayer this evening was full of sunshine, greenery and rolling hills.'

At weekends he rode over to Kingston to stay with James Michie, a young English intellectual (in the best sense of the term) with whom he had made friends in the previous November and who was to join Peter and Chris as one of his only lifelong friends. He had a charm and personal warmth which were a joy to his companions and irresistible to women. In London James had started an affair with a Jamaican girl, Daphne, and had followed her out to Jamaica. Daphne was the rarest of beings, the living embodiment of Gai's ideal woman — his *anima* in Jungian terms — and he adored her, but he could not let himself think of her in erotic terms as she was his friend's girl. The couple visited him in Port Antonio, accompanied by Daphne's younger sister, Lola, and he was free to fancy the sister. He thought she might be the person he was seeking, the person he needed if he was to feel complete as a human being.

The ride over to Kingston on the Junction Road was itself a joy. It was often raining on the north side of the mountains and dry on the south so he always left a change of clothes with a bar-maid at Castleton, the high point of the ride. Having changed, he would set off on the descent to the plane, swinging rhythmically round the successive hairpin bends, excited by the danger as the motorbike gathered speed. One day, as he drew up at the house, having broken his own record time crossing the mountains, the front wheel of the motorbike fell off just as James came out to greet him. He hardly gave a thought to what might have hap-pened if the wheel had come off on the Junction Road. He felt protected. It was not time for him to die and it seemed to him that he would need a long life to come to any good as a Muslim. In this he was right.

The end of term was approaching and, with it, his return to Kingston to teach at Wolmers. One of the girls asked him: 'Will you remember us at all? Please remember us'. He was sure that he would. There was something magical about these young girls and he realised how happy he was and how unhappy he might soon be. He feared Kingston and what it might do to him, quot-ing from St Augustine's *Confessions*: 'To Carthage then I came where a cauldron of unholy loves buzzed all about my ears'. He knew how slender was his hold on Islam. Most converts to a par-ticular faith start with an intense emotional commitment which carries them through the inevitable period of reaction when the disorderly elements in the soul are in revolt and urge the new believer to free himself from constraint. His conversion had been through intellectual conviction and there is neither power nor depth in such a conviction. He was sure he would never turn his back on Islam, but he lacked the strength of faith.

In mid-April he left Port Antonio, this *Darusalam*, this 'House of Peace'. James had suggested that they share the apartment on Hope Road and Gai agreed to this gladly. He and James had be-come so close that they could often read each other's thoughts and there was never the smallest disagreement between them. He started work at Wolmers, but within a week or so he received an offer he could not refuse. He was invited to become head-master of the Chinese Public School in Kingston the following term, and, under the circumstances, Dr Simpson was prepared to release him. The school had been going for some years but had never prospered. Those in the Chinese community who could afford to pay reasonable fees were not prepared to subject their children to a second-rate education. Now the leader of the community, an elderly millionaire named Tai Ten Quee, had come up with a practical proposal. They would employ an English head-master, preferably with a degree from Oxford or Cambridge, and hire the best Jamaican teachers, paying them a little above the going rate. The school would then be able to offer the wealthy members of the community standards equivalent to those at the best Jamaican schools with the added attraction of lessons in Chinese culture. Gai was interviewed by Mr Tai and they got on well together. He was appointed to the post.

He was entering a strange and secretive world. Outwardly the Chinese community was peaceful and harmonious, free from the disputes which troubled more 'barbaric' communities, law-abiding and hard working. In fact there were bitter rivalries, fed by jealousy and resentment of slights, whether real or imaginary, but all this was kept well concealed. They were proud to manage their own affairs without interference. When, as happened quite often, a man gambled away his shop or his business, he was soundly beaten and then given the funds to start up again. If outsiders were allowed to see him destitute this would shame the whole community. 'We look after our own', Gai was told and, as he soon realised, his presence as a licensed insider was sometimes resented. He might discover secrets which should never be revealed to the general public, so every effort was made to keep him in ignorance of what was going on. Mr Tai died just before he took up his appointment and matters were now in the hands of a Mr Yap as Chairman of the School Board. As a young boy, a new immigrant, Yap was said to have traded in Kingston with a tray of cheap goods hung round his neck. Working an eighteen-hour-day, seven days a week, he had risen to become a factory owner and he had a simple view of life. It was work, work and more work, leading to the accumulation of money and the respect of the community.

In their first serious talk, Yap explained to Gai that fear was the spur. No one worked as they should unless they were perpetually frightened. 'You mus' make staff fear you and children too, Misser Eaton. If you not make them afraid they not work, school not succeed', he said. 'You be strong Misser Eaton, so they trembling when they see you.' In this and subsequent interviews Gai adopted the tactics he had used as a child when dealing with his aunts: never argue, never defy, always ignore. In any case, it would be a waste of time to try to argue with this man. As usual, he would go his own way behind the shield of vagueness and amiability, impossible to pin down and a bit of a mystery.

The term he spent teaching at Wolmers is scarcely mentioned in the diary, probably because it held no interest for him. The boys had nothing in common with the Tichfield children and did not inspire him with any affection. Many were the sons of wealthy middle-class families and expected to have knowledge forced down their throats rather than opening their beaks like small birds waiting to be fed. He did what he could, but his heart was not in it. In any case, his prediction that he would encounter 'a cauldron of unholy loves' came true. His evenings were spent downtown searching among the bar girls for jewels among the pebbles. He found or thought he had found several, and he learned a great deal from them, not only about women but also about his own sex, their secret lives, their urgent needs and their search for love. He could not see these relationships as in any way sordid. He had been brought up without any sexual morals, and the fact that Islam had strict rules on the subject could, for the moment, be forgotten. These girls were basically no different to their respectable sisters, just as ready to give affection

generously when they met with it. The fact that they were despised by polite society gave Gai—still only too aware of his illegitimacy—a certain fellow feeling. He could be totally at ease
with them as they were with him, neither judging nor judged,
and the stories they told were endlessly fascinating.

He could empathise with the elderly man who wanted only to
lay his head on a young girl's breasts, lamenting the wasted
years and empty future, as he could with the American sailor
dying of lung cancer whose desperate death-defying lovemaking
was so vigorous that the girl he frequented could hardly stand
after a night with him. Gai remembered that, when he was a
child, Ruth had shown him how a dying plant might use what little energy it had left to produce a single superb bloom, driven to
reproduce on the edge of death. Above all there was the sixty-
two-year-old Dutch captain of a freighter who had fallen in love
with a marvellously pretty young girl of mixed race (a 'Coolie-
Royal') and taken her home with him to Holland. After a few
months she fled back to Jamaica but, some three years later
when Gai knew her, the captain wrote her a letter in stilted English describing the loneliness of his life since his mother and
brother had died and offering her the alternative of marriage or
adoption as his daughter if only she would come to him. Gai was
so moved by the letter when she showed it to him that he drafted
a kind reply which she copied out by hand with appropriate
spelling mistakes. But, with so many human stories to stimulate
his imagination, why could he not write a novel (or many novels)? What was wrong with him?

James and Daphne had got married and gone back to England,
and Gai began gradually to move towards a serious relationship
with Daphne's virginal sister, ten years younger than himself.
Lola had a confused identity. Her mother, living in a small town
on the other side of the mountains and isolated from contemporary Jamaica, regarded herself as a brown-skinned Englishwoman and brought up her daughters as such. They must, of

course, marry English gentlemen, not uncouth Jamaicans, and Lola—darker-skinned than her sister—referred to black men as 'frogs'. She had been taught from infancy not to show her feelings and always to act as the English girl that she was under the skin. Her mother was unaware that English girls had changed in the past fifty years and that English gentlemen were no longer so respectful of a young woman's virtue. Warning signs were posted all over the landscape, but Gai was so desperate to fill the vacuum left by Flo and to enter into a lasting, intimate relationship that he ignored them with dire consequences both for Lola and himself.

In the course of time he would find himself working for or with Indians, Pakistanis, West Africans and Arabs, as well as Jamaicans and Chinese. This satisfied his passionate desire to embrace all humanity in his experience, but there was no doubt as to which were the most problematic and the most alien to him although the Arabs would confuse him by the lack of connection between their minds, their hearts and their tongues. Flo had imbued him with a romantic love of China at a time when everything associated with her was dear to him but these were the wrong sort of Chinese. She had told him that the Chinese term for lovemaking was 'Clouds and Rain', which he found enchanting, but he suspected that the Board members would have employed a cruder term. Most of them were, in origin, expatriate peasants without charm or learning. He took up his post as headmaster on 11 September 1952, having engaged five women teachers, all but one of them pleasant colleagues, well qualified and competent. He had no problems with the school as such. From the start his problems were with the Board who, as soon became apparent, had employed him only as a figurehead and who regarded the teachers as inferior beings, treating them as such.

He was standing one morning with Yap on the veranda overlooking the school courtyard when one of his staff, Miss Brown, strolled across the yard with a leisurely, very African gait. The Chairman turned to him and ordered: 'You dismiss Miss Brown'. 'But why, Mr Yap? She's one of my best teachers.' 'She lazy. See how she walk. That is lazy walk. You dismiss!' Gai made no further comment and ignored the order, but he could see trouble ahead. One day an emaciated Chinese man turned up in the Staff Room. He spoke to no one beyond giving his name as Lin and did not explain his presence. The next time he saw Yap Gai asked: 'Who is Mr Lin and what is he doing here?' 'Mr Lin your Deputy Headmaster' was the only answer he got. So they had placed a spy in the school? No matter, if that was the way they wanted it. But some weeks later Gai realised that he had not seen Lin for a while. 'Mr Yap,' he asked, 'what has happened to Mr Lin?' 'Mr Lin dismiss', he was told without explanation. He tracked Lin down to a miserable room in the slum area of Kingston, half-starved and savage with bitterness. He had been accused of hiding a case of Red Stripe beer under his bed after a fund-raising function with the intention of selling it. There was no doubt that he was prepared to spend the rest of his life seeking revenge. Glad to accept a small donation from Gai—'Just to show how sorry I am for this misunderstanding'—he unbent and explained that he belonged to a different faction of the community to the Board members. He and his friends in the Chinese Benevolent Association would, he promised, destroy Yap.

The Board had appointed Dr Simpson of Wolmers as their Educational Adviser, but he only came to one meeting. He complimented Gai on the work he had done to put the school on its feet, but this was not at all what the Board members wanted or expected to hear. They took refuge in humour—or their notion of humour—and one of them who happened to be wearing a hat jumped to his feet and danced round Gai chanting: 'Misser Eaton getting big head now, head soon too big for hat', and tried to fit his hat on him. Gai exchanged glances with Dr Simpson, who looked appalled. But sometimes it was difficult to maintain his patience. The Board decided to bring twelve boarders from Montego Bay and rented a derelict house adjoining the school. There was not a stick of furniture in it nor did any appear as the time for the boarders' arrival approached. Gai began to pester Yap daily but was always told not to worry, and he soon realised that two members of the Board owned furniture stores, obvious grounds for dispute. On the evening that a bus carrying twelve rather scared boys arrived, a truck bearing twelve iron bedsteads, twelve mattresses and twelve chairs drew up in front of the school. 'You see, Misser Eaton. Why you worry? You real worrisome, Misser Eaton.'

Towards the end of 1952, braving the Atlantic gales aboard a small banana boat, Ruth (now in her early seventies) arrived in Jamaica to spend three or four months with Gai. She took to the Island immediately and she also took to Lola, and she made herself completely at home. She travelled happily on local buses for the pleasure of listening to the market women joking together in *patois* and insisted on being taken to waterfront bars where she charmed Gai's less than respectable girlfriends. She also charmed Evon Blake by writing one of her 'stinkers' to the *Gleaner* regarding the way in which beaches on the North Coast were being increasingly privatised, excluding ordinary Jamaicans, an issue which Evon himself had taken up. He paid tribute to her in his magazine, *Spotlight*, as 'this marvellous English lady with a brave heart'.

'You're the toast of Jamaica', Gai told his mother, indeed she made friends wherever she went. She bought him a new car so that he could drive her around the Island and, in the holidays, rented a beach cottage at Discovery Bay on the North Coast. It was here, while Ruth took a discrete stroll along the beach, that his relationship with Lola was finally consummated. 'You're the last man on earth I'd have expected to be my first', she said. He did not ask her what she meant, although this did not sound like a compliment, but he wrote in the diary: 'She is necessary to me now, but I know both how much and how little this means. I am whole with a woman close to me, a restless fragment without, but does it matter who the woman is provided she is loving and her body is sweet?'

He could not remember ever before having seen his mother so happy and carefree, but in April, 1953, she sailed away while he faced a worsening situation at the school. The Board reduced staff salaries on grounds of economy, Yap complaining that they were lazy and did not deserve to be paid what had originally been agreed. As the months rolled by Gai was caught between his resentful staff, threatening to go on strike, and increasingly hostile employers. He made no secret of the fact that he sided with the staff. One day an article appeared in the evening newspaper, *The Star*, denouncing the management of the school and outlining the teachers' complaints. Since Gai was a regular contributor to the *Gleaner* and a member of the Press Club he was the obvious suspect, although in fact it was one of the teachers who had talked to a journalist. Nothing was said, but he knew that the Board could hardly doubt his involvement, and there was no point in denying it since he would not be believed. He guessed that his days as headmaster were numbered but for several weeks nothing happened. Afraid of provoking a strike and further bad publicity, the Board waited until the end of term when all the teachers had gone home to issue a letter terminating Gai's employment on the grounds that he had only been engaged for one year and ordering him to vacate the school bungalow in which he was living by the end of the month.

He had no intention of doing so and consulted a lawyer who advised him to stay were he was. Fearing that the locks might be changed while he was out, he employed a young Jamaican to stand guard. This lad, Jo by name, had been the school nightwatchman for a short period until he revealed his true feelings. He hated all Chinese and, when a young Chinese man, probably an illegal arrival in Jamaica, had wandered one night into the school premises Jo had given chase, machete in hand, until Gai, hearing screams of terror, had intervened. Now, for £1 a week, Jo was happy to stand at the bungalow door, machete at the ready, eager for an opportunity to chop a member of the Board or, in fact, any Chinese who might approach too close. For the next couple of weeks the Board made no move, while Gai sought out the unfortunate Lin and was taken by him to meet one of Yap's deadly enemies at the Benevolent Association to whom he pointed out the shame that would be cast on the community if he was to expose this outrage in open Court.

Then his electricity was cut off. He borrowed a Primus lamp—the kind that campers take with them—and over-filled it with paraffin. He woke from his siesta to find it was almost dark, left his afternoon companion sleeping, strung a towel round his waist and put a match to the lamp in the living room. Flames rose to the ceiling. In a panic he grabbed the towel from his waist and began to fan the flames. At this moment he heard the tramp of feet and turned to see Yap and several other Board members (all in their best suits) accompanied by a Jamaica lawyer he knew filing into the room and arranging themselves with their backs to the wall. He continued to fight the flames, glancing over his shoulder to shout: 'Sorry! With you in two ticks'. When the surplus paraffin had burned off the flames flickered out and he was able to turn to face his visitors just in time to see the last of them filing out of the room. They had intended to issue an ultimatum, but the sight of their headmaster, stark naked and apparently trying to burn the house down, had suggested to them that this might not be the right moment to do so.

'They thought you were going to set fire to them', their lawyer told him some time later, chortling happily at the memory. 'First time I'd seen Chinese guys really scared.' This was satisfactory, but Gai realised that he could not hold out much longer. The trouble was that he had nowhere else to live and his salary for the previous month was unpaid. The solution came from an unexpected quarter. Flo and Harry had spent some time in the States, where they had got married, and since their return they had both put out peace feelers. Flo had been friendly whenever they ran into each other and Harry, in an article for the *Gleaner*, had praised Gai's acting in a radio play. He poured out the story of the school to Flo the next time they met and, without a moment's hesitation, she told him he must come and live with them. When he found another job he could pay his share of the housekeeping, and Lola, whom she had met a couple of times, would also be welcome. Taking, as usual, the line of least resistance, he agreed at once. Fascinated as always by life's rhythms and by the vicissitudes of time, he found this curiously appropriate. It seemed that Flo was destined still to be a part of his life and he was content with this.

15

C O R A H

'Am I playing with fire?' Gai wrote in the diary. 'But isn't that what I've done most of my life? I feel the cold so easily, you see.' He might have chosen a more peaceful place to park himself, but inner turmoil sometimes prefers a matching environment. Flo and Harry were sparring partners. Harry had never known a woman who did not abuse him, and in him she had an object upon which to vent a profound anger which must have been kindled in her childhood and adolescence. Gai came to live with them as an irritant. One morning, when they returned home from a drinking bout around 4 a.m., he was awoken by Flo's raised voice: 'I could have been so happy with Gai in Cairo'. For once Harry answered her back: 'In that case, why didn't you have the guts to join him?' Not long afterwards he was again awoken in time to hear her shout: 'I'm sleeping with Gai tonight!' A moment later his bedroom door burst open and she flung her considerable bulk onto the bed beside him. Within seconds she was lost in a drunken slumber, but Gai lay awake for a while reflecting on the mystery of time. In Cairo he had thought often that he would be sublimely happy if, just once, he could again lie beside her even without any lovemaking. Now here she was in the present moment, snoring softly, and he was strangely happy, knowing that nothing that happens in the present can spoil what happened in the past. When he awoke in daylight she was gone.

How was he to make a living? He did not know which way to turn and what little he had saved from his school salary was running short. Feeling desperately lonely one evening when Flo and Harry were out, he decided that he could afford one drink at the Glass Bucket. He was bound to see someone he knew there. The club was almost empty, but he recognised a solitary figure seated at the bar. Clem Tavares was the first friend he had made when he came to Jamaica, a tall, strikingly handsome light-brown man with a Byronic air who had gone into politics and was said to be very close to the Chief Minister, Alexander Bustamante. In those far-off days Clem, wearing a dinner jacket and scarlet opera cloak, had taken him to a respectable home in the suburbs and spoken softly to the lady of the house who promptly lined up five pretty girls. 'Which one would you like?' he had asked, but Gai— not yet Jamaicanised—had been too shy to reply.

Clem signalled Gai to join him. 'This is my lucky day', he said. 'This morning I finally persuaded the Chief that we must revive the party newspaper, *The Voice of Jamaica*, and he agreed. But when he asked me who we could find to edit it I was stumped. I've been worrying about that all day, and now you turn up! Want the job, Gai? It's yours if you want it.' Gai wanted it. He wanted it more than any other job he could imagine.

Compared with the politics of other colonies which had reached the stage of internal self-government preceding full independence, Jamaican politics were simple. Before the war, Norman Manley had created the PNP (People's National Party), but Manley was not a man of the people. He was a brilliant advocate who dominated any Court in which he appeared, an intellectual who had little empathy with the common people, more at home with British Labour politicians (who guided him in setting up his socialist party) than with Jamaicans. He needed a rabble-rouser and found one in his cousin Bustamante whom he encouraged to establish a trade union to partner the PNP; this was the BITU (Bustamante Industrial Trade Union). Bustamante had been born Clark but had been adopted by a Cuban whose gardener he had been and had taken his benefactor's name. He and Manley made a good team but, just before the first general election under self-government, Bustamante, who disliked socialism and believed he could do better than 'Cousin Norman', transformed the Trade Union overnight into the JLP (Jamaica Labour Party), roughly equivalent to the British Conservative Party and supported by Big Business. He had gone on to win the election and become Chief Minister.

There were so many stories told of Busta, but one which is almost certainly true illustrates his daring. As a very young man, possessing nothing in the world except for a pair of pearl-handled revolvers, he had gone to Panama where he found the tramways on strike. Presenting himself at the Company headquarters he had undertaken to break the strike in return for a job and a hundred dollars. He had succeeded, then formed his own trade union, called a fresh strike and won it. For Gai this man, who had been his hero when he was a schoolboy and Bruce Barker had shown him the press photograph of Busta on a white horse, was the closest he would ever come to finding a man comparable to his grandfather, the Old Man. Here, he thought, was someone empowered by his heart and by his intuition, fearing no man on earth and contemptuous of danger, moreover here was a fervent anti-socialist.

Gai's hatred of socialism had grown over the years, as had his fear of the all-powerful State. He believed that socialists offered a dangerously beguiling invitation: 'Surrender your liberties to us and we will look after you'. Slave owners in the past had offered no less. Socialism, he believed and would continue to believe, could function only on three conditions: the extension of

State power, the curtailment of individual liberty and the destruction of traditional structures. All three were anathema to him. Moreover people of the Left were usually insufferably self-righteous and therefore convinced that they always knew what was best for those they made their prisoners. He loathed self-righteousness in religion or in politics more than he did egotistical arrogance and he thought it more dangerous.

There was still a problem to be solved. How does one edit a newspaper? Gai went to his good friend Theo Sealy, the *Daily Gleaner* editor, for advice. 'Get in a couple of bottles of rum', Theo said. 'This evening I'll send two of my best men up to the house, a layout man and a typesetter.' They duly arrived and, when dawn came up next morning, the bottles were empty and the Milners' living room carpet was covered in newsprint but Gai was ready to be an editor.

He had not considered a more serious problem. He was required to sell advertising space to pay his own salary and commission together with printing costs. For some months to come this was something of a nightmare and the paper was constantly in debt until the decision was made to change from weekly to fortnightly publication which eased matters, but he was no salesman. Approaching some arrogant businessman or executive he felt like a beggar pleading for alms. His office was in the BITU headquarters and he was allotted a reporter, a junior Party functionary who, he noted in his diary, 'must have been born before the invention of clocks and even of calendars'. He was also given one of Busta's former girls, Kitty, to run errands and make herself useful as required.

The Chief's life was organised by a remarkable woman who had been his mistress and secretary for more years than anyone could remember, known to everyone as 'Miss G' ('G' for Gladys), eventually 'Lady G' when, just before his death, Busta married her. She supplied him with a succession of young girls, chosen with meticulous care. As each of them reached the age of twenty, when she might begin to get ideas above her station and even imagine that she could take over, she was dismissed, 'Miss G' having whispered a few words into her Master's ear. But he always made sure that the Party or Union found a job for his discards. Fairly soon twenty-four-year-old Kitty fell in love with Gai and was fierce in his defence. 'You're such a gentle person,' she told him, 'no one could possibly be nasty to you. If they try they'll have me to deal with'. Gentle as a dove with Gai, she was a terror to any Union official who dared to question his presence there.

He had another protector. Aware that there were those in the Party hierarchy who objected to an Englishman holding such a key post, he left it to Clem to deal with the matter. It was not his concern and, in the event, Clem never troubled him by mentioning the battles he must have fought on his behalf. The advantage of appearing to be someone rather unworldly was that people of a very different temperament tended to look after him. Another of these was Evon Blake, regarded as a dangerous 'Black Nationalist', who was happy to play father figure to a white man. A good friend and a formidable enemy, Evon had offered to pay the Court costs when Gai took on the Chinese School, but the case was abandoned when he discovered that the Board had offered one of the teachers £100 to say that he had tried to rape her. She was the only ugly member of his former staff which made the charge all the more distressing. Evon, whom Kay, when she was in Jamaica, had described as a 'jungle beast' was full of good advice and prepared to guide him through the jungle of human relationships, although he himself was engaged in constant battles with discarded mistresses. He warned Gai against Lola. 'You need a woman who gives you total support,' he said, 'and who builds up your self-confidence. Lola will never do that for you. She'll pull you down in the end. Get rid of her, Gai, and find a woman who offers you unqualified love as Flo did. That's what women are for—to give a man his strength'.

Jamaican men tended to treat their women badly and it was interesting that macho Evon acknowledged his dependence on the women in his life. Gai would always be fascinated by the complexities of the male-female relationship and, long afterwards, he would try to write sensibly and without generalisations about this complexity in the Islamic context, maintaining that the 'human being' was not a man or a woman in isolation but the couple, man-woman. Here and now it was the strength and dignity of Jamaican women that impressed him, and this encompassed the whole society, including those who might have been thought to have sacrificed their dignity. He would always remember a little scene which he had not even mentioned in the diary but which seemed increasingly significant as he looked back on it. The setting was a downtown bar when the American navy was in port for 'R & R' (Rest and Recreation). He was there with a friend, and their attention was caught by a couple at an adjoining table. A drunken young sailor was trying to buy one of the bar girls and, as she seemed reluctant, kept pulling dollar bills from his pocket and piling them on the table. Gai recognised the look of contempt and anger on the girl's face and waited to see what would happen. Instead of trying to woo her, the American, assuming that she was only interested in money, was showing a lack of respect. Finally she came to her feet and sauntered, hip-swinging, over to an impoverished English expatriate drinking alone in a corner. 'Want to come wid me?' she asked. 'Is freeness tonight.' With a final scornful glance over her shoulder at the bewildered American, she led the way up the stairs. She had kept her dignity. She was a Jamaican woman.

It was difficult to know quite where to place Lola in this context. Flo, who was fond of her but was teaching her to drink to excess, taunted her for her English accent, acquired from her mother since she had never been to England. It was a symptom of her confused identity. The diary devotes thousands of words to Lola, trying to fathom the mystery of her character. There was no mystery. She was now twenty-one, a young girl caught up with an older man—Gai, at thirty-two, must have seemed almost middle-aged to her—and unable to break the bond. She was fond of him or loved him (she was too immature to know which), trying to escape from a close but claustrophobic family and finding that she had escaped only to exchange one prison for another. She longed for independence but her lover would not grant her this. Gai had become intensely possessive and, ignoring her youth and inexperience, expected too much of her. She must belong to him, body and soul, and anything less than this was unacceptable. He was puzzled by her failure to conform to the role he had designed for her. If she really loved him she would, he thought, desert her mother and the infant school at which she was teaching in her native town beyond the mountains and come to live with him in Kingston. He was constantly unfaithful to her and made no secret of the fact, exercising an unspoken blackmail: 'This will go on unless you live with me'. It was true that many Jamaican women expected their husbands or lovers to have girls on the side and some might see this as proof of their man's virility, but she cannot have known what to make of the situation.

He himself was still in the grip of ancient insecurities. It seems that there are attitudes and assumptions acquired very early in life which are completely impermeable either to experience or common sense. It might have occurred to him by this time that, on the whole, young women liked him but he still needed constant proof of this, moreover he was convinced that he was uniquely vulnerable because other people appeared to him invulnerable. He thought that he lacked a protective skin which they possessed. Knowing in theory that they must have similar fears, anxieties and self-doubt as troubled him, he could not believe this unless they exposed their weaknesses as he himself tended to do. Anyone who appeared supremely self-confident was, he assumed, exactly as they appeared. As he learned in the course of time, intelligent people can be astonishingly stupid, and his stupidity must have owed much to the fact that, when he had emerged so late from the cocoon woven by mother and aunts, everyone else seemed better adapted to the rigours of living than he was. He sometimes described himself as 'barely viable', whereas he was by nature a survivor and survivors think they have a right to use people in order to survive. So it is that the weak prey upon the strong.

Lola came over to Kingston at weekends and during the school holidays, a two-hour-drive over the mountains and along the narrow winding road which runs between the foaming Rio Cobre and a wall of rock. By the end of April she had formed a kind of feminist alliance with Flo, directed as much against Gai as against Harry. During the years in the Red House he had been obsessed with the desire to be 'in the midst of life' while watching it pass him by in the street, personified by the people he saw only through a pane of glass. Now, in the Milner household, his wish had been granted. 'This involvement with people provides no peace', he wrote. 'Gabriel tells Harry I've told him this or that, Harry tells Flo I've told him such-and-such, Lola tells Flo that Harry has said something critical of her, then Dereck Royston (who's living with us now) tells Lola I've told him something she had asked me not to repeat, Harry pumps me about Flo, and Lola repeats to Flo what I have told her in confidence. The whispers (mostly distorted) go round and round'. He was also in the midst of political life now and, except that it was on a grander scale, it was not unlike life with the Milners.

Busta was in complete control of his Party, the JLP, in fact he was the JLP. All the rest, including his senior Ministers, were satellites revolving around the Chief and fighting each other for the place closest to him. As Gai got to know him he came to appreciate the man's simplicity and modesty. He was indifferent to worldly possessions and still lived in the small house in Tucker Avenue which had been his home for many years. It was here, in the confined space of the living room, that his entourage met, jockeying for position and, like Flo, Lola, Harry and the rest, whispering. Busta was old now and the fire was going out of him, so the most important meetings were held in advance of his making a major speech. If he was to appear briefly as his old self he needed a certain measure of whiskey, but this had to be calculated with the precision that a pharmacist brings to measuring out a dose of medicine. A drop too much and his speech would become slurred, too little and he might not rise to the occasion. On one occasion the precious glass ended up in Gai's hands and he was about to hand it to the Chief when it was snatched from him by someone with more claim to the honour. In fact the whole charade was probably unnecessary. An adoring crowd was the only stimulant Busta really needed.

Since childhood Gai had been fascinated by power and longed to know what it felt like to possess real power over the masses. At the age of thirteen, in one of the first serious entries in his diary, he had decided that power and only power could keep him safe in a dangerous world and, at the same time, enable him to put it to rights. He had decided to 'study the methods of the three great-est men of our time, Signor Mussolini, Herr Hitler and Mr Kamal Ataturk'. Now, for the first time, he was close to a powerful man.

In May the JLP held the biggest meeting since he had been with them. He reckoned there were some 8,000 Party supporters in the square, although he was told by Clem to report a figure of 20,000 in *The Voice*. On the balcony he found himself standing next to Busta in full flow and the intense emotion that rose from the crowd to focus on the Chief embraced also the man standing beside him. He could feel it like an electric current in his flesh and in his bones. He understood for the first time what it felt like when the passions and hopes of the multitude flood out to embrace their hero, and this seemed, in some strange way, comparable to a sexual encounter. The Leader makes love to the people—not gently, but with fierce assertiveness—and the people respond with orgasmic joy. This was a kind of secret intimacy. Each separate individual could feel, 'The Chief loves me', and yet enjoy his union with all those around him. As he saw it, Gai was passing through life tasting experiences in accordance with his childhood ambition. Now he had tasted, albeit indirectly, this delicious flavour.

But there was something still to come, something which probably left a permanent imprint on him. He had to attend all public meetings to report on them and, in June, one was held in the West End of Kingston, the slum area in which white men were advised never to set foot. He was, as usual, seated on a stool in the local bar, ready to make notes when Busta spoke while a series of 'warmers up' performed on the platform; Party functionaries exercising their voices and big women belting out Party songs. On this occasion there was an awkward pause in the proceedings. Someone had failed to turn up. Without warning, two very large men entered the bar, seized Gai by the arms and led—or rather, dragged—him onto the platform, leaving him there to face a sea of black faces. There was no time to think and he dared not hesitate. He would have to depend upon the inspiration of the moment, and it came like a flash.

He began with slow deliberation, assuming the trace of a Jamaican accent. 'You are wondering, my friends—Yes, I know you are wondering what an Englishman is doing on a Jam-ai-can pol-it-ic-al platform.' (*Louder, interrogative*) 'But who is a Jamaican—I ask you, who is a Jamaican?' (*Full volume, dogmatic*) 'A Jamaican is anyone who loves Jamaica and its people!' (*Maximum, ear-splitting volume, both arms held out to embrace the audience*) 'I—love—Jamaica. Am I a Jamaican?' The response came instantly, a roar from the crowd. 'Yes Suh, you Jamaican.' Gai was in ecstasy. He could have climbed Mount Everest, he could have fought a tiger bare-handed, and he knew that he would never again fear an audience. Everyone should enjoy one triumph in the course of their lives and this, he thought, was his, but he realised he could not have done it had he not developed his voice box on the drill square at Sandhurst and learned the art of timing when he was an actor. Above all, he could not have done it had he been insincere, but at that moment he did indeed love Jamaica and its people with a passionate intensity.

After that it was plain sailing. He could denounce the socialist ideology of the PNP with utter conviction, indeed he claimed to have come to Jamaica originally as a political refugee from socialist Britain. 'I have lived under socialism,' he proclaimed at full volume, 'and I know the evil of it'. This involvement in local politics might seem, in retrospect, little more significant than involvement in the affairs of a town council, but that was not how he or others saw it at the time. The year 1954 was still the post-war period, a time of idealism and optimism. It was clear that Jamaica would attain full independence within the next few years, and then the sky was the limit. This small nation whose motto was *Out of Many One People* would be a universal exemplar, an example of racial harmony and communal peace. Nations far away would look to this blessed Island and learn from it. Like Athens in ancient times, Jamaica would be a beacon of light in a murky world.

Some distance from Kingston was a remarkable school, Knox College, where the Headmaster, a Christian Minister, organised weekend seminars for leading politicians, intellectuals, artists and media people. Gai attended one of these to discuss the future and what everyone agreed upon was the glory the future would bring to little Jamaica. There was a terrible irony attached to these hopes. Within ten years of independence the Island would descend into an orgy of self-destruction, a hotbed of crime, senseless violence, fear and malice, so that those who had attended this seminar might well have wept just as Gai had wept after the hurricane. What nature could not do, politics, the drug trade, tourism and an ancient anger, long suppressed, would achieve. Elsewhere, particularly in Africa, there would be similar disasters. De-colonisation was a cynical exercise on the part of the British Government but the administrators had been deeply attached to the people of the colonies in which they served, convinced that they were playing their part in creating a better world. Gai met two of them years later including Lord Caradon who, as Hugh Foot, had once been Governor of Jamaica. They were sad, embittered and disillusioned men.

Among those who attended the seminar was Corah Hamilton, more beautiful than ever in maturity. She had changed since he had last known her, overcoming her deafness by lip-reading and by an acute study of facial expressions. This had had a side-effect. She was now a superb portraitist, bringing out the character of the sitter as no other artist in Jamaica could have done. As he discovered later, she could read faces so accurately that she was never deceived by words and, if she distrusted someone, he would never question her judgement. Masks did not work for her, she could detect falsity at a glance. She told him that she was trying to get a year's leave from her civil service job to study at the Central School of Art in London.

A few weeks later he was passing the Institute of Jamaica in Kingston when she hailed him, running down the steps of the Institute. She had just been granted a year's leave. Gai had no interest in her at the time—or so he supposed—but this picture, like that of the snow maiden Bridgy against the background of the *Jungfrau*, was at once etched in his memory. Her smile dazzled him, he thought he had never before seen such happiness.

Long afterwards and some years after her death in England, Ann, their younger daughter would remark: 'Mummy really could light up a room with her smile when she came into it', and letters of condolence from neighbours in a London suburb mentioned—every one of them—how the writer had been warmed by that smile. Although, that afternoon in Kingston, he never expected to see her again, Gai went on his way marvelling.

He himself had decided to return at least temporarily to England at the end of 1954. Lola intended to take a Froebel teaching course in London and he felt he must hold onto her, follow her and marry her. He could not bear the thought of having to establish a new relationship with a stranger, and the thought of losing Lola was so painful that he concluded that he really must love her. Walking by the sea one evening when they were staying at a small hotel in Runaway Bay he told her he would marry her. 'But you're already married,' she pointed out, 'and still wearing that wedding ring'. He wrenched the heavy gold ring which had once been Ruth's from his finger and flung it into the sea. Next day he wrote to Kay asking for a divorce.

There were other reasons for his decision. Ruth sent him news of Leo Francis whenever he stayed with her. The boy, now nine years old, had told his friends at school that his father was dead. If there was to be a resurrection it must be soon, and it was even possible that he needed his father. According to Ruth he was in danger of becoming neurotic due to his relationship with his mother whom, she said, he often reduced to tears. 'He can be a little demon with her, and she responds by loading him with expensive gifts and becoming hysterical. With real sorrow I see her going rapidly downhill, a thoroughly dissipated woman, quite unaware of the harm she is doing Leo. A few weeks ago when he was with me and she was late picking him up he said: "Oh, we all know where Mummy is. Drinking in some pub". He seems to have made a hero of you and irritates her by asking endless questions about you.' Even allowing for Ruth's bias, Gai thought

287

it was time to see for himself what was going on. Moreover Ruth was getting old and he owed it to her to spend time with her before she died, while letters from his real friends—Chris, Peter and James—told him that they were missing him.

For the moment he was riding high, but he had learned a lot about the precariousness of politics and political friendships. Clem, at one point, said he might persuade Busta to offer him a safe seat in the House of Representatives at the coming General Election, but that too would be precarious. Clem himself was intensely ambitious and expected, one day, to lead the Party as, in fact, he might have done had he not died young. He instructed Gai to publish a flattering profile of him in *The Voice* and dictated the first line: 'Bold and debonair Clem Tavares . . .' Gai's sense of insecurity was heightened by the problem of selling enough advertising space to keep the paper afloat and his own salary covered. It was a hand-to-mouth existence.

One day Clem told him to go to Dossy Henriques, a leading businessman, who was sure to put up £500. He was fobbed off with the Advertising Manager who told him there were no funds left for the current year. He accepted this meekly, but in the afternoon he happened to run into Clem and told him what had happened. That same evening a letter was delivered by hand to Henriques' home. 'Dear Henriques, I understand that, when my personal representative called on you this morning he was shown the door. I always like to know who are my friends and who are my enemies. (Signed) Alexander Bustamante.' Next morning Henriques phoned just as Gai got to the office to say that he was deeply distressed by this misunderstanding, would be happy to purchase space in *The Voice* to the tune of £1,000 and looked forward eagerly to meeting the Editor.

This was fun, but when—he asked himself—would this prolonged adolescence give way to maturity? He was playing at being a rabble-rouser, playing with girls, happy to be a big fish in a small pond, but hardly a day passed without anxiety and even shame because he was neglecting his religion and frittering away his one talent, the talent for writing. Would he have to wait till he was on his death bed before he came to his senses? His Cairo friend, Dennis, now pursuing a successful academic career in Canada, wrote to him: 'Will you never get tired of party-going and frivolity?' True, he believed that every human experience had a significance far beyond its place in the world of appearances. True, also, that he was learning from everything that happened to him, but here and now he was not putting his brief life to good use. Perhaps the shock of leaving Jamaica a second time would bring about a miraculous change in him.

Late in June 1953, Flo and Harry set out for England, leaving the house in Gai's charge. By then they had found a way of living peacefully together. Harry sought comfort in young girls downtown to whom he was both kind and generous, sometimes sharing one or other of them with two English friends, a professor from the University and a teacher from Wolmers. Flo had taken a lover, and she was served by her 'jaggerbats', three or four young half-Chinese who adored her as a mother figure and were in awe of Harry. They had never known such a learned man and marvelled at his flow of talk even if they understood hardly a word of it. At the beginning of September Lola left for London to take up her teaching course and Gai booked a passage on the *Queen Elizabeth*, sailing from New York on 15 December.

Lola's infrequent letters, schoolgirlish in tone, were uninformative, but in October Flo wrote him a long letter about her. 'You will have to be very patient with her. She's going through a silly phase. Under her sister Daphne's pernicious influence she's become rather synthetic and pretentious, and she's hardly bothering with the College.' Flo and Harry had taken her to Paris for a week and she had embarrassed even them by her behaviour, 'prancing around in a pair of imitation leopard-skin tight-foot pants'. There was also an angry letter from Ruth announcing that she would never again have Lola in her flat. 'She behaved

abominably when I invited her to tea to meet some of my friends.'
The outlook for the marriage—if there was to be a marriage—
did not look bright, but the decision was made, and Gai always
felt that such decisions were made for him rather than by him.
Meanwhile he had Kitty to comfort and adore him, boosting his
ego and assuring him that, like her former lover, Busta, he could
do anything on which he set his mind.

Coming as a stranger to a strange land, he had conquered
Jamaica and was ready to take on England however hostile that
cold and uninviting country might be. Clem provided a finishing
touch to this process of confidence building. He organised, not a
simple farewell party but a major JLP function to send him on
his way. After various Party functionaries had paid their tribute,
Clem came to his feet and announced solemnly: 'Gai is the most
popular Englishman who ever set foot in Jamaica'. It was absurd,
it was laughable, but it was wonderful.

On 12 December 1954, on the verge of his thirty-fourth birthday, he flew to Washington, arriving in a snowstorm, to stay with
Lola's brother, a cab driver, before going on to New York to board
the *Queen Elizabeth*. Each day, as the bitter Atlantic winds
penetrated his defenceless body, he could feel the confidence
draining out of him. It was as though he was bleeding from an
open wound and could not staunch the flow. Busta, Clem, Kitty
and the cheering crowds were a dream and had no more changed
him than a dream would have done on waking. Change could
only come from within. He was no better equipped to cope with
England than he had ever been.

Lola met him in Southampton, where the ship docked, and they
spent two nights in a local hotel. He was at once aware of a reversal of roles. In Jamaica he had often treated her as chattel.
Now she was in command of the relationship and dictated the
terms of engagement. This rather seemed like poetic justice. She
would be happy to marry him 'in a few years' time', she said,
keeping him on ice as it were until she was ready. Meanwhile

she intended to have fun and promised to be faithful to him when he was away from her but could not promise the same when he was with her. This might seem a curious arrangement, but he guessed she meant that his possessiveness might provoke her into straying as an escape from a suffocating closeness. She was indeed having fun. James and Daphne were living in Oxford where she spent most of her time and she had been taken up by several very fancy undergraduates. Young members of the upper class liked to demonstrate their superiority to the middle and lower classes who were, for the most part, racist and there was no better way of doing so than being seen with an exotic black girl on one's arm. If the girl in question was pretty and intelligent and knew how to behave, so much the better. Lola was ideal for this purpose but attributed her popularity to her own charms.

It was in a gloomy mood that Gai returned to London to stay with Ruth until he could find a place for himself, and the first priority was to meet his nine-year-old son. He was more nervous than he had ever been before an interview and, to his astonishment, it was Leo Francis—mature beyond his years—who put him at his ease. 'He arrived here at Ruth's flat on Christmas Eve. He's much bigger, of course, but his face is just as I remembered it. A fine, sturdy, boy, quick and intelligent and with a quite remarkable vocabulary. We got on so well, or so it seemed to me; no shyness, surprisingly. I took him for a walk by the river yesterday. "Daddy," he said, "isn't this divorce a nuisance".' That seemed a strange word to use, but then Gai (overwhelmed at being addressed as 'Daddy') realised that he only meant it prevented his father from admiring the decorations which he had helped Kay put up in the Mall Chambers flat while the divorce was in progress. 'In the evening we put on a show for Ruth, Goo and Eleanor with the toy "television" he has been given. This morning we had a long conversation about schools. We were, I think, pleased with each other, so perhaps this justifies my return to this beastly city.'

Lola told him she had a solution to the problem of accommodation. Two young men, Ian and Michael, with a house in a fashionable part of London, had offered her the use of a bedroom in their converted attic when she was in Town. Gai was starting flu and felt very ill. When their taxi drew up at the house she told him to wait while she had a word with their hosts. Only then did he realise that she had not bothered to tell them she was bringing a boyfriend with her. He at once retired to bed and stayed there for three days. On the fourth he staggered downstairs to the living room and suddenly felt so weak that he stretched out a hand for support, grasping a tall dresser laden with plates. It crashed to the floor with a mighty crash. He thought this was probably the most humiliating moment of his life.

A couple of weeks later she took him to the Ritz Hotel Bar to have drinks with three of her new friends. 'Afterwards she told me, "Ian and Richard and Michael are terrified of me". She behaved towards them with a schoolgirlish rudeness that would only have bored them if she had been less exotic. She added that someone or other was dying to meet her because he had been told she was the most beautiful girl in London and, when I laughed, she was cross. Has she lost her sense of humour as well?' She returned to Oxford and Gai began to face the fact that this nonsense could not go on. He had a curious letter from Kitty, curious because he had never mentioned Lola to her. 'Gai, don't let anyone push you around. You are a very quiet person, but that does not mean you should let them take advantage. I am woman and I knows what most woman gives. We all like to know we have a man where we wants him when we don't love him. If we loves a person we always wants to do what they want. Remember a night you said I had been mean to you and I began to cry? That is what love is.'

Daphne found him a cheap room in Linden Gardens in Notting Hill Gate. She told him: 'If I had ever treated James the way Lola is treating you I'd soon have been black and blue', adding that her sister was behaving 'just the way people here expect a coloured girl to behave. I can't control her, and I don't think you can'. James and Daphne invited him to Oxford and there, in the cloisters of Magdalene College, the final act was played out. By agreement, Lola met him around midnight after leaving a party and he thought they were going back to the house. She announced that she was now going to another party and was scornful when he tried to argue her out of it. 'I'm going anyway,' she said, 'take it or leave it. See you later perhaps'. He could not reason or argue any more, but he knew one way and only one way to end the matter. He gave her a light slap on the cheek. 'That's the end', she said. He agreed. 'The end it is.'

He saw her only once more when she called at the Linden Gardens room and told him she was prepared for them to live together 'as pals' provided she had complete freedom to live her life as she wished. He declined the offer but, when she had gone, allowed himself to cry in loneliness and desolation. He could not have foreseen that Lola would be the cause of the deepest guilt he would ever suffer. Not long after their final meeting she met an Irish poet; a very good poet so Gai was told though he could never bring himself to read the poems this Irishman wrote for her. They got married and went to live in Rome where, some six years later, he left her for another woman and she committed suicide, leaving a note to say that she had failed with the only two men in her life. Gai was devastated when James and Daphne gave him the news. He saw, with shame, that in his self-absorption he had never attempted to understand the young girl who had been his lover, never even noticed the troubled child behind the confident face. He had thought her tough, much tougher than he was, self-reliant and invulnerable. When, into old age, he prayed for what he called 'my dead', he would always pray: 'Lord, forgive Lola and forgive me the harm I did her'.

His friends were now his refuge and support. Peter Heyworth, who was making his name as a music critic, introduced him to the people at *The Times*. He wrote an article on the coming Jamaican elections for what is still called the 'op-ed page' (the page opposite the Editorials), as well as two pieces on Caribbean politics for the newspaper's *Colonies Supplement*. There was a suggestion that they might employ him as their TV critic, but he had never in his life seen television and the proposal fizzled out. Enraged by an Editorial in *The Daily Express* claiming that no one in Britain need worry about finding a job, he wrote to the paper and his letter was published under a bold headline: 'Mr Jobless M.A'.

He received a number of letters, one from a man who had 'discovered a foolproof way of making money, and the work is not dirty', another from a former sea captain, equally jobless, who had heard there were good opportunities in Java and suggested Gai might accompany him there. Desperate, he applied to be a shop assistant in a furniture store but was found to be overqualified. Finally he found part-time employment in market research, tramping the streets of various cities accosting women to ask them what magazines they read and classifying their replies according to social class. It was better than brooding in the Linden Gardens room which had no windows, lit only by a skylight. He was paralysed and thought he had reached the end of the road with no hope, no future It never seems to have occurred to him that, had he maintained regular prayer, he might have risen above himself and his troubles five times each day.

James and Daphne offered a refuge. James had a particular talent for conveying affection with a warmth and humour quite free from sentimentality, and Chris Ewert-Biggs, who had returned recently from his latest diplomatic posting, was the 'brother' he had been at Sandhurst and ever since. He and Gai lunched together regularly at the Reform Club. On 4 April 1954, little over a month since Gai had parted from Lola, Chris mentioned casually that he had recently met a Jamaican girl at a dinner party with friends. 'Do you remember her name?' Chris hesitated. 'What was it now? Corah something—Yes, Corah Hamilton.'

'Lead me to her!' Gai said.

16

C O R A H   W I T H   J U D Y

The word 'coincidence' has come to be associated with ideas of chance, pure chance; in origin it has no such implication. Things, roads, destinies coincide, they meet and merge in space and time in relation to an unalterable pattern. Gai thought he had come to the end of the road, finished. Corah too believed she had reached an ending. They were in the same place at the same time.

She was now thirty-four, a few months younger than him, and she could see no prospect of ever marrying or having children. In Jamaica, from the age of twelve (when her dentist had tried to rape her) she had been pursued by men, but they all had one thing in common. They might talk of marriage but they would never marry a woman darker-skinned than themselves however passionate their feelings. In England she had met a handsome young German, Otto, who professed undying love but who, when she joined him for a week in Germany, refused to introduce her to his parents and then made it clear that she should feel honoured by the attentions of a member of the master race. It was time, she thought, to cut men out of her life, accepting with resignation their total unreliability. They were all the same, but she

295

had her art and that must be the sole point and purpose of her life. What amazed Gai as he got to know her was that her humorous cynicism was uncontaminated by bitterness or resentment, sentiments of which she seemed to be incapable. The contrast to Ruth's anger against the world was striking.

Her childhood would, in itself, have provided grounds for bitterness in most people. When she was two or three her father had, after the birth of a second daughter, decamped to America to make his fortune and was never heard of again. Her mother, universally known as 'Aunt Lilah', was a foundation member of Manley's PNP and devoted herself to politics and good works in her neighbourhood. Although often referred to as a 'Coolie woman' (she had Indian as well as African and European ancestry), she was universally admired. Anyone in trouble—with the exception of her daughters—could rely on her help and support, but Corah and her sister were a nuisance and could only expect a box on the ears when they got in her way. The support of the family was Aunt Lilah's father to whom Corah always referred as 'Pappy' with a love and admiration which never faded. He was a master craftsman—in his way an artist—and the only man whom rich families with European antiques trusted to protect and repair their precious furniture. Proud of being descended from freedmen rather than slaves, therefore free from the complexes which afflicted so many Jamaicans, he taught her patience and taught her to use her hands and to love the beauty and aptness of the things that can be made or moulded by the human touch. Another relative, an aunt, struck by the girl's intelligence and potential talents, paid to send her to the best girls' school in the Island.

So, on 6 April 1955, after six years' acquaintance, Gai and Corah met again, this time in the damp basement room she had rented near Ladbroke Grove. She was in bed, recovering from flu, but she had just received good news. Facing the expiry of her year's study leave from the civil service, she had taken advantage of Bustamante's presence in London, where he was to receive his knighthood from the Queen, to call at his hotel and ask him to intercede for her. Although he knew very well that her mother was a pillar of the Opposition party, he had promised to do so. He had been as good as his word. As she was leaving, 'Miss G' had handed her an envelope containing £5, saying: 'Chief knows how difficult it is for a young girl alone in London'. This was typical of Busta. This was why he was loved, whereas Manley was respected as a remote, rather alien figure. Now her extension had been approved and she must plan to stretch her limited funds to last another year.

They talked, or rather Gai talked till he was hoarse, laying out the story of his life without reserve. Amused but sympathetic, she remarked: 'Your cock seems to have led you up a gum tree'. He had met so many pretentious people that her simplicity and naturalness surprised him. There was no mask here, no conceal-ment, no self-protective postures. She was who she was, take her or leave her. Years later this, together with that smile which seemed to issue from the wellspring of all smiles, was to prove her greatest asset. Meeting 'very important people' she treated them as she would anyone else—polite, charming and at ease—and they liked this. There is a photograph of her at a diplomatic function with three prime ministers (British, Canadian and Ja-maican). She is smiling cheerfully into the camera while the three men, including Britain's Harold Macmillan, have turned their heads to admire her. Without even trying she was to be-come a diplomatic wife or, in the jargon of the Service, 'a repre-sentational wife', and the high and the mighty would give her their seal of approval.

She and Gai spent more and more of their time together. 'After a depressing day of market research I went to her room full of complaints but somehow she raised my spirits and made me feel better about myself. She teased me about wanting a nice, sub-missive, worshipping little wife. I hid my face against her body and she asked: "What about Lola then? Does one fire drive out another?"' They were becoming intimate friends but, aware of her determination to have nothing more to do with men on the sexual level, he hesitated to make love to her although one evening some two months after their reunion she remarked tenderly: 'You have such gentle ways, one could so easily . . . ', leaving the sentence unfinished. They both knew which way they were heading but there was no hurry.

On 25 June he wrote in the diary: 'Yesterday, Corah! I did her an injustice in thinking she might shilly-shally when it came to the point. I picked her up at the Central School of Art after lunch and we had tea at Harrods. It was soon obvious that, while I was away in Winchester market researching, she had made up her mind. The way she looked at me, the way she leaned against me and took my hand . . . These things were sufficiently eloquent. Then, in the evening, I took her back to her room and she stood in front of me with an air of extraordinary docility. We kissed passionately and, whenever I drew away from her, she stood motionless, her hands at her side, her great liquid eyes fixed unwaveringly on my face. Afraid of upsetting her landlady (Marcus Garvey's widow) who has promised to help her stay on in England, she said: "If you want me to spend the night with you—as I suppose you do—we'd better go to your place". So we came to Linden Gardens and this Lola-haunted room, dancing—or rather swaying—to radio music. Then we went to bed. I've always liked the Biblical expression for sex, "he knew her". Do a man and a woman ever know each other until they have "known" each other? Waking, we came together again, talking and playing, studying each other's bodies with the minute attention of new lovers. I feel the cobwebs have been swept away, all the silly worries and anxieties, the dust shaken off my heart'.

But the worries were real. His funds were running out, as were hers, and he had applied for more than twenty jobs over the previous months without success. This included what he called 'the two ugly sisters', the BBC and the British Council, both of which had turned him down on a previous occasion. Most of his applications however were for overseas jobs and he hoped successively to find himself working in Turkey, Tripoli, Baghdad, Lahore, Kuala Lumpur and Sabah. Even before he had acknowledged to himself that he loved Corah, the thought of marriage was in his mind. He could not face the prospect of living and working in a strange country alone, starting all over again, seeking a new relationship, lonely and unattached. She remarked once: 'I wonder how long it will be before you unlove me?' and more than once she started a sentence with: 'When you leave me . . .' He was sure he would never leave her but did not say so, believing as he did in the Jamaican principle that a woman should not be allowed to become too sure of her man. At this point pride asserted itself. She believed that all men were the same. Very well, he would show her that he was different, he was superior to those nonentities who had so consistently let her down. His feelings were intensified by a pregnancy which was terminated without any protest on her part. What else could they do, they asked themselves. In contrast to what had happened with Kay, this drew them together and it intensified his sense of obligation to her.

Prevented by Corah from losing hope, he replied to an advertisement in the press for the post of Assistant Information Officer in the LPS (London Press Service) department of the COI (Central Office of Information), the government propaganda agency. He was interviewed and got the job on the strength of having edited a newspaper in Jamaica and having had a book published by a major publishing house. At the time LPS might have been described as a retirement home for ageing journalists and, on his first day, an old Africa hand—reading his mind—assured him: 'Don't worry, old chap, you won't find any civil servants here'. It was true. Nearly all his colleagues, for the most part in their fifties, had tales to tell of wild adventures in far away places, men after his own heart. He was put to work in the West European section (WESCO) with two men who bickered perpetually. Jerome, pompous but kindly, had been the most distinguished British newspaper correspondent in Spain during the Civil War. Unfortunately his colleague, Monty, made exactly the same claim for himself and each tried discretely to enlist Gai on his side.

It would have been difficult to find two more different men under one roof. Jerome, with his fine 'Roman' head, had an almost monumental presence, and his grave pronouncements demanded respectful attention, whereas Monty was restless, bouncy, incapable of sitting still for more than a minute, a mine of misleading gossip and given to boasting about his important friends, frequently promising Gai to introduce him to one or other of them but never doing so. Gai liked them both.

Now, at last, he was in a position to marry. He and Corah discussed the possibility thoughtfully and soberly, without any dramatic undertones. It seemed a good idea. The question was how Ruth would take it, and Gai could guess at the furious outburst it was likely to provoke. He would have to use all his skill to introduce her to the prospect gradually and at least pretend that he was seeking her advice. Then, on 16 March 1956, he lunched with Chris at the Reform Club. After lunch he crossed Pall Mall to where he had parked his car—the same car Ruth had bought him in Jamaica—and grasped the edge of the door with his right hand to close it just as a cab drew close to park in front of him. The passenger opened his door while it was still in motion. The doors of London cabs and private cars are hinged on opposite sides, so the edges of the two doors met on his hand. Feeling no pain he got out of his car, puzzled to see a bloody mess where his hand had been. Ignoring the taxi driver, who was trying to say something, he wandered into the neighbouring travel agency, dripping blood, and told the two young girls behind the counter: 'Look at my hand'.

He may have fainted for it seemed only moments before an ambulance arrived and took him to Charing Cross Hospital where he was put in a wheelchair and, presumably, pumped full of morphine. He gave the staff Ruth and Corah's telephone numbers and relapsed into a happy haze, pleased to be the centre of attention and smiling benignly at everyone. Mother and girlfriend, who had never met before, arrived simultaneously, having been told only that he had had a serious motor accident and expecting to find him at death's door. Overcome with relief on seeing him cheerfully holding court—this was drama, and he loved drama—they fell on each other's necks. A few weeks later Ruth told him: 'I think it would be a good idea if you married Corah, she'll look after you'.

Hands are tricky to deal with and the surgeon who operated on him was, appropriately, called Mr Trickie. The top of his index finger had to be amputated, the middle finger was broken in three places and his thumb was hanging loose, needing only to be popped back into its socket. He was in plaster for three weeks and only when it came off did he assess the damage. People had often told him that he had beautiful hands and, on waking beside Corah the next morning and seeing this beauty destroyed, he wept, pressing his face between her breasts. After that all was well and he had the strange idea that he had somehow paid a debt rather as Japanese gangsters are said to fulfil an obligation by the sacrifice of a finger. The word 'closure' was not in common use at the time, but it would have fitted the circumstances. The book of the past had been closed and he was embarking on a new life. On 17 August 1956, he and Corah were married. Although they did not know it at the time, she was pregnant again despite all their precautions. After a major operation for fibroids three years previously she had been told that she might never be able to have a child, but—so Gai thought—his powerful seed was not to be frustrated.

A friend of hers, the Guianese musician Rudolf Dunbar, found them a tiny flat in a block overlooking Paddington Station and they were happy. His profound need for physical closeness was matched by hers. As he dragged himself out of their narrow bed one morning to go to work she remarked sleepily: 'I can almost hear the flesh tearing apart'. He could almost hear it too. His search for self-loss in the act of love, this too was echoed by her. 'I want to disappear making love', she said. 'I want to break up, not be me any more.' They were indeed happy, and, to his surprise, he was happy enough at work. Jerome offered an almost paternal concern for him, particularly after the accident, and Monty provided constant entertainment. The work itself was undemanding, a simple matter of studying the day's newspapers, picking out any stories creditable to Britain or to the Government—not always the same thing—and rewriting them to be telegraphed to the Information Officers in Embassies and High Commissions overseas who would then try to persuade local editors to use the copy.

The COI at that time was lodged in premises just off Baker Street which had been the secret headquarters of the SOE during the war and from which brave men and women had been dispatched to France to work with the Resistance and, only too often, to die at the hands of the Gestapo. The building was said to be haunted, not by some headless medieval figure, but by a one-legged man, dreadfully disfigured by torture. Gai took his turn doing night duty, scanning the early editions of the newspapers when they were delivered by dispatch rider soon after midnight. On one occasion, alone in the building in the early hours, he was alerted by a strange sound in the distance. It came closer very slowly: TAP-tap, TAP-tap, louder and louder. Then it stopped at the Newsroom door and there was silence. Frozen, unable to move, he waited for what seemed minutes rather than seconds. The door burst open and the ghost announced, in a broad Scots accent: 'Ah've come to work'. Scottie, the sports correspondent for LPS, had lost a leg not, as was supposed, in some heroic wartime action but falling down an escalator when drunk. Now he was very drunk indeed and had lost all sense of time. Gai put him to bed in the secretaries' rest room.

He no longer ached for Jamaica since he held it in his arms and, in any case, the Atlantic had narrowed in recent years. The Caribbean was no longer a twelve-day voyage distant. Early in 1957 Flo arrived in London with a new lover in tow, a handsome young Englishman, Frank, who had served a prison sentence for an act of 'grievous bodily harm'; a violent youth, but Flo was bigger than he was and could deal with him. They were soon followed by Harry accompanied as usual by Alva, friend, chauffeur, valet and absorbent of his interminable monologues. 'I was pleased that she had got in touch with me as soon as she arrived,' Gai wrote, 'and I went round to her flat in the evening. She has recently been re-reading my Cairo letters, and I am glad that she is not one of those people who live on the surface of the present and think the past is dead. As always when she is around, a party soon developed so I went back to the flat and fetched Corah. Flo's adopted daughter Norma, now married and pregnant, was there, so was her former enemy Amy Heron—no enmity ever lasts where Flo is concerned—with a couple of other Jamaicans and, of course, one of the 'jaggerbats' to run errands. Already fairly drunk, she took us all to dinner at a Chinese restaurant and, hugging Frank, proclaimed for the thousandth time that love alone made life worth living, and she gave Corah a little lecture on how to cherish me. Interesting to note how Flo dominates any company in which she finds herself. I rejoiced in the flood of affection I felt for her. Nothing to regret, ever'.

After that it was the waiting game, waiting for the baby—due on 20 March—fussing, worrying, wondering. The 20th came and nothing happened. There was a false alarm, a dash to the hospital and still nothing. At 11.30 p.m. on the 27th Gai wrote up his diary: 'It's a girl. This afternoon Corah phoned me at the office. There had been a show of blood and pains. Home in ten minutes.

Got her to the hospital at 6 o'clock. They wouldn't let me stay with her so I went to Ruth's flat, pretty shaken. Waited till 11.15 to phone, thinking it was going to take the whole night. Baby had been born at 9.40, weight 8¼ lbs. All well. Thank God'. Next day: 'Corah is well. Judy Layla Ruth is well. All is well, but no thanks to St Mary's Hospital. Excitement over having a daughter—the answer to so many dreams, including the longing to have a sister when I was seven or eight—has been overlaid by anger, rage over the unnecessary pain Corah suffered, the unnecessary risks. She knew the birth was proceeding with uncommon speed. Ignorant and arrogant idiots at the hospital wouldn't believe her, thought they knew better. Doctors! Then of course there was panic. As the baby started to come Corah gave one great yell and was rushed into the delivery room. Nothing was ready, the midwife did not even have time to put on her uniform, the gas-air machine wasn't working. Within minutes Judy was out in the world, looking around her—so Corah says—with evident disapproval'.

This was a good baby. Everyone said so. Almost from the start she slept through the nights in perfect peace. Awake she was unfailingly cheerful and, having overcome her initial distaste for the world into which she had been catapulted, she seemed to like the place. Gai was obsessed with her and thought that this must be the first time he had experienced unselfish, undemanding love for a human creature. In the office his eye turned repeatedly to the wall clock, counting the minutes till he could be with his wife and child. On Sunday mornings, when he had the habit of going out briefly for a coffee, he could not bear to be without Judy for fifteen minutes, bundled her into the car and took her with him. The confined space of the flat was an asset since it reinforced the closeness of the three of them, his family in his nest. When Leo Francis came round, as he did frequently during the school holidays, the circle was complete. 'These are my people,' he told himself, 'my tribe, my world, all mine'. Ruth boasted to her sisters: 'Gai does everything for that child except give milk from his breasts and he'd do that if he could'. He failed to detect the implied criticism of Corah, but he basked in the approval of his childless aunts. Life could not get better than this.

Black winter came, damp and slushy rather than cold. One evening, when she was three months old, Judy became sick, at one moment her bright self, at the next limp, listless, whimpering. A junior doctor from the practice came round, prescribed a medicine for gastro-enteritis and said she would return in the morning. Soon afterwards the child began to bleed from both ends. Gai might have waited, but not Corah. She telephoned the practice and was reminded that there was a flu epidemic raging and she had been told to wait till the morning. Now her Jamaicaness asserted itself and, in icy fury, she commanded that the doctor come at once. The woman who came within thirty minutes had the air of a doctor who has had enough of over-anxious mothers but her expression changed very quickly. It was the first time Gai had seen someone's complexion turn from pink to white in seconds. 'I've never met this condition before,' she said, 'but I think it may be an intussusception', explaining that this was a process in which a section of the bowel telescopes like the finger of a rubber glove turning in on itself. She telephoned the local hospital. It was just before midnight when they got there.

Staff took the child away to examine her and, within minutes, a doctor came to explain that the diagnosis was correct and the only hope of saving Judy's life was an immediate operation. The appropriate surgeon had been telephoned at his home in the suburbs and was already on his way to the hospital. The doctor had spoken in a soft voice and Corah had heard nothing of what was said. She stood there, the very image of patience, motionless and expressionless. Determined to control himself, Gai turned to her but was seized with such a fit of sobbing that he could not speak. She waited while he hung onto her as though his life depended upon her support. Still she waited, asking nothing. Then he told her. Now they understood why their own doctor been so shaken. Had they followed instructions and waited till morning, the baby would have died. Later, Gai asked if the condition had any hereditary element and was assured that it did not. In due course they would have two more children and both developed intussusceptions at the same age, but by then they were overseas and the doctors did not hesitate to accept Corah's diagnosis.

Next morning in her hospital bed Judy—a wizened, wounded creature—lay between life and death, but after that she made a quick recovery and the flat was again a happy place. 'I think it would have killed you if she'd died', Ruth told Gai. With her granddaughter she was soft and tender, but with no one else. She was now seventy-six, but the fires of anger still burned with a dark flame. She had lost her old friends, complaining to one or other of them about her son but, when on a subsequent meeting they asked her, 'How's that wretched son of yours?' banishing them from her sight for ever and then telling Gai: 'That foul woman has been abusing you'. MEO, who had been such a good friend first to Gai and then to his mother, was one of these casualties. The aunts, of course, knew better than to take her seriously, but they too had cause for complaint. For as long as Gai could remember and from long before he knew what the word 'rape' meant, he had heard her say with savage relish that any woman who had never had a man 'should be raped by the troops, a sack over her head if she's ugly'. Perhaps she had picked this up from Major Dick, the friend of her youth, and she had always liked to shock, but now she had taken to saying this in the presence of her virgin sisters, Rose, Violet and Eleanor. They were not pleased. Far worse was the fact that she made contemptuous references to Lesbianism to Eleanor, who had shared a bed with Goo for the past thirty-five years. It was almost as though she wanted to break all human bonds.

Not only was her apartment too big for Ruth but a new Rent Act meant that the rent would soon be raised beyond her means to pay and she might be banned from taking lodgers (with whom she always quarrelled). Corah had the solution. It was unthinkable for a Jamaican that an ageing parent should be left to live alone and Jamaicans always preferred to buy a property, however humble, rather than rent one. Corah suggested that they purchase a house together, Ruth putting down the deposit and Gai paying the mortgage, which would come to no more than they were already paying in rent for their flat. Eventually they found a house in Wandsworth Common and it was divided into two self-contained flats. In the Spring of 1958 Gai and Corah moved in with Judy, and he was happy that Leo Francis seemed to feel this was his home too and marked out a part of the garden for his private use.

Ruth joined them late in the summer, full of plans to improve the house. For three weeks all went well. Then, one day, they were in a store called Arding & Hobbs, purchasing small items for the house. Ruth was in her Lady Bountiful mode. 'I'll buy this for you, Corah; I'll get you that'. Corah did not like to be patronised, she did not like to be indebted. Her face took on a thunderous expression while she said nothing. Ruth turned on her with the speed of a snake striking, denouncing her for gross ingratitude, cursing her. They drove back to the house in silence and, by the next morning Corah was 'that black devil' and 'that beggar on horseback'. She had forgotten her role which, in Ruth's eyes, was to be the successor to the nurse-maids who had taken care of Gai when he was a child.

The following evening he wrote in the diary: 'Ruth came to my darkroom to look at some of the pix I had printed. She began to abuse Corah again. I refused to listen but talked pompously about my art as a photographer. She continued, bitter and sarcastic. Her eyes became small, hard, like little, shiny stones yet somehow reminiscent of an angry, frightened animal. I'm numbed by the suddenness and finality of the blow to all our happiness and peace of mind. Her mere presence seems like a malevolent haunting of a previously clean and happy home. I could eat nothing at dinner and Corah asked what the matter was. I told her and spoke of Ruth as I have never before spoken of her to anyone. She took it calmly, having overcome her own anger after a sleepless night and after steeling herself to face what more may come. Bright side, if it can be called bright. I'm released from any obligation to Ruth to stay in this country. If this had been a happy house and Ruth had been happy with us it might never have seemed right to take a job that would keep C., Judy and myself abroad for years. God knows, I understand Ruth. There is so much of her in me, but I am not going to sacrifice our happiness to this mother of mine who has, sooner or later, turned on everyone close to her. She has lived too long. In the past she often spoke with approval of the Eskimo practice of leaving aged parents on an ice floe to die peacefully from hypothermia and suggested I should do the same with her when she became a nuisance. But where am I to find an ice floe.'

For many weeks the atmosphere in the house was thunderous and it seemed to have affected Judy, who was becoming fractious, no longer sunny. Then Corah became pregnant again and there was the added worry as to how all this might influence the child in her womb. Returning from the office, Gai spent more and more time in his darkroom. He had had a passion for photography ever since, at Charterhouse, he had learned to be a competent printer, and a settlement of £800 for the injury to his hand had recently enabled him to buy a good camera and the necessary equipment. This passion was another case of trying to stop time in its tracks rather than fly with it. Now he thought that, if he could have his life over again, he would be a professional photographer, preferably a photo-journalist, combining his two talents. It would, in fact, have been the ideal career for him. As Corah often pointed out, he was not temperamentally suited to being an employee. He should have been his own man, self-employed and independent.

It was too late for that. In spite of repeated failures in the past, it was now essential to find a job abroad. By law the Colonial Office and Commonwealth Office were obliged to advertise Information Officer posts overseas in the COI. Everyone knew that this was a mere formality and the posts had been filled even before the advertisement appeared, but Gai applied for every one, was interviewed and duly received a printed note informing him that he had failed. In May of 1959 he was interviewed for a post with Colonial Office in Lagos. This time there was no note. It was more than two months before he heard anything and then he had a telephone call at the office from one of the senior officials who had interviewed him, a man called Noakes. 'Afraid you haven't got the Lagos job, old chap. Sorry.' Gai began to have a feeling of unreality, sensing that something very strange was happening. 'When we saw you,' said Noakes, 'you talked a lot about Jamaica'. 'Afraid I did, Sir.' 'Yes. You liked Jamaica, didn't you?' 'I did', Gai said. 'I believe your wife is Jamaican, isn't she?' Stranger still. He agreed that she was, and then there was a pause in which he could feel his heart thudding. 'I wonder,' said Noakes, 'how you would feel about going back there as Director of our Information Office?'

For moments afterwards Gai wondered if he was going mad. Could this be some kind of auditory hallucination? He knew that Monty always listened to private conversations and asked him: 'Did you hear what I said on the phone just now?' 'Gai, you know very well I never listen to people's phone calls', Monty said. 'I know that, but I thought you just might have heard me say this . . . and perhaps that?' Monte acknowledged that he might, by accident, have overheard something of the sort. Assured that he was not mad, Gai sat back in his chair, stunned. Noakes had warned him to tell no one for the time being. Four or five people were being moved around, a complicated operation, but, if everything went according to plan, the job was his. A week or so later it was in the bag. A colleague in the Newsroom came up behind him and started rubbing his back vigorously. 'Just hoping some of the luck might rub off', he said.

He went round to Colonial Office for a long talk with Noakes. What had happened was that one link in a chain had failed, upsetting all their plans. A number of colonies were fast approaching independence and the Office was setting up UK Information Offices in each of them. To Jamaica they had sent one of their best men, Frank Morgan, and he had established a functioning office in record time, finding accommodation, engaging an efficient local assistant and an excellent secretary. The man they had sent to Uganda, according to Noakes, was 'sitting under a Banyan tree complaining about his housing and doing nothing'. He had to be replaced quickly, and who better to clear up the mess than Morgan? That left the Jamaican post vacant and it had to be filled by early October. Where could they find someone suitable without delay? It was at this crisis point that Gai had appeared before the interview Board, rather as he had appeared in the Glass Bucket at the very moment Clem was looking for an editor for *The Voice*. He might not be ideal, but they had to take a gamble on him. At least he would be stepping into a functioning office and he knew the Island well. There was an added bonus. He would also be responsible for Belize, the primitive and mosquito-ridden Cayman Islands, and the Turks and Caicos (a sub-colony of Jamaica), an excuse to travel whenever he wished.

Still trying to assimilate his good fortune, Gai had given no thought to the status of the job. When they met, Noakes stunned him a second time. 'Don't let the Governor try to interfere', he told him. 'The Governor represents Her Majesty the Queen. You will be representing Her Majesty's Government. Two quite different functions.' In those days colonial governors were thought to stand on the right hand of God. They were magnificent potentates in plumed hats and splendid uniforms. 'Me, an independent power base?' Gai asked himself, and he remembered those stories in the *Thousand and One Nights* in which a beggar beachcombing by the sea wakes up one morning to find himself on the Sultan's throne. Noakes continued. 'If you play your cards right, you'll be taken over by Commonwealth Office after independence. It's likely that Commonwealth Office will soon be amalgamated with the Foreign Office so, if you can get yourself established, you'll end up in the Diplomatic Service. As I'm sure you know, the French call it, not 'a career' but 'the career'. Up to you from here on, old boy.'

There were arrangements to be made, including the renewal of his passport. The form he received included a new question in accordance with the 1949 Nationality Act. He was required to give his father's place of birth as he himself had been born in Switzerland. What father? His father had never been born, never having existed. He took the problem to Noakes and, soon afterwards, was interviewed by three senior government solicitors. He had told his story often enough to friends and they had found it romantic, but these men had no romance in their souls. He tried to make a little joke but their faces remained stony, without a trace of a smile. When he had finished they conferred quietly between themselves, after which the senior man told him: 'So far as we can see, you are a stateless person. You could, of course, apply for naturalisation'.

The prize had been snatched from him, the COI would probably no longer employ him and he would be lucky, from now on, if he could find a job as a shop assistant. As for these lawyers, these grey bugs, he felt as Ruth would have felt and wished he could stamp on them and squelch them under his heel. He left the room seething with a mixture of rage and despair. Briefly, he thought of his real father as 'that silly old man' for not having foreseen this, but how could Francis have foreseen a time when a British government would dare to inquire into someone's ancestry? Post-war Britain would have been a foreign country to him, more like Tsarist Russia or Germany under the Kaiser. His generation would never have tolerated the theft of basic liberties, the interference of the State in private lives, the proliferation of laws and regulations binding the populace hand and foot. But that was socialism.

In 1959 Gai himself could not have foreseen that, by the end of the century, this process would have accelerated to a point at which the British would have forgotten their ancient liberties, hastening down a primrose path paved with good intentions, concerned only with 'fairness', security and health. No one would bear in mind the warning given some 150 years before by a great American (perhaps the greatest), Benjamin Franklin: 'Anyone who would give up a measure of freedom to gain a measure of security deserves neither security nor freedom'.

Not even Corah, heavily pregnant, coping with a small child and a hostile mother-in-law, could find anything hopeful to say. She provided tenderness and understanding, indeed her disappointment was no less than Gai's, but there was nothing she could do, nothing he could do either except wait for some kind of miracle. If only he had been true to his religion.

17

M A U R I C E ,   A N N   &   C O R A H

He thought this was the worst of times, the worst ever. He could not have foreseen that the best of times was just round the corner since none of us can see round corners. He consulted anyone and everyone, finding some relief in recording each step in this desert landscape. 'Three hours today talking to people at the Passport Office. First man I saw thought I was probably Swiss, second man said he had phoned FO and recommended granting of a passport (on what grounds?), after this a helpful woman suggested that 'Charles Eaton' might be regarded as an alias used by Francis Errington (he'd have loved that)'.

In retrospect, the 1949 Nationality Act might be seen as a defining moment. Until then 'Britishness' had been, as it were, a state of being, immediately recognisable even if ill defined — you could always pick out the 'Brit' in a group of 'foreigners' — and closely identified with the battles of an island people against the continental giants, first France and then Germany. Now, since Nazi racial theories had made it unacceptable to associate nationality with 'blood', a new definition had to be found and this could only be a legalistic and bureaucratic definition. The Passport Office was obliged to employ guards to protect them against elderly men, apoplectic with rage, who could trace their ancestry back to the Norman Conquest but who were told that they were not British because they and their fathers before them had been born in India.

In the midst of all this, Corah gave birth to a boy in a Catholic hospital in Wimbledon. Diary, 11 August 1959: 'Maurice Le Gai born 11.50 last night, 8.4 lbs. Corah says he did most of the work in labour, "popped out rearing to go". Her pains had only begun at 11.20. Unlike the wretched staff at St Mary's, the good nuns (Ursulines) acted quickly and there were no problems. Saw Corah this morning, tired but not too battered, and the boy is obviously eager to meet and perhaps challenge the world'. A few days later: 'I took Judy and Leo Francis round to the hospital. Judy not allowed in the ward, so I held her up for C to see her and tears poured down her cheeks. When we got home Leo did a strange thing. I had told him that Peter Heyworth and I were no longer good friends. Without a word to me, he picked up the phone and called Peter: "Daddy's here. Would you like to speak to him?" Peter and I had a good talk'.

Nine days after the birth Corah was home with the baby. Having inspected her brother critically, Judy seemed to approve. She said she would buy him and lend him to Dingding, her teddy bear. 'Are you sure Dingding won't eat him?', Gai inquired. She thought not. It soon appeared that Maurice had brought with him a gift of good fortune, perhaps the miracle for which his parents had hoped but which they had never dared to expect. Noakes phoned. 'Come and see me. It's just possible I may have good news for you.' Unreported in the press, Parliament had just passed an Act legitimising children born out of wedlock if their parents had subsequently married. Gai's guardian angel clearly had influence in high places but there were still obstacles to be overcome. The Act would not come into force until the end of the year so he would have no claim to British nationality until then. He had to be in Jamaica by mid-October at the latest, and the

Colonial Office were not going to have their plans disrupted once again. Although nothing was said, Gai could guess that Noakes would have to find someone else for the post if he was not available in time.

The Home Office was responsible for questions of nationality, and the Home Office was—and probably still is—the most timid of the great Departments of State and therefore the most rigid, swathed in red tape and incapable of going beyond the letter of the regulations by one iota. The automata who staffed it were terrified of responsibility and therefore incapable of making decisions outside the rule book. The Colonial Office, having governed a large part of the globe until very recently, was the exact opposite. It believed in personal responsibility, used the rules and regulations when they were useful, ignored them when they were not. To some extent it still lived in an earlier century when orders to its servants overseas could take weeks in transit by sailing ship. It chose its man, dispatched him to some distant colony and left him to get on with the job. If he made a grave error such as starting a local war he might be reprimanded, but he was probably dead before the reprimand arrived. This was a virile department, prepared to trample on red tape if the 'exigencies of the service' made this necessary. With the gleam of battle in his eyes, Noakes told Gai: 'We'll take this to Under-Secretary level if we must'.

Ruth now had something more important than her resentment of Corah to occupy her. Like it or not, they were on the same side. Having destroyed the letters which would have been conclusive, she spent days searching for any scrap of paper that might serve to prove Gai's parentage. 'I suppose this is my fault', she said, but she returned at once to cursing Francis, that 'evil old man'. Gai thought it was indeed partly her fault. Much as she had loved him, she had never, from the time of his birth, given a thought to his future except as a reflection of hers. On 5 September he wrote: 'The worst five days I can remember. Tuesday I phoned

315

Passport Office to make sure there were no problems about my
nationality at that end. Told someone would call me back, then
the Deputy Chief Passport Officer phoned. There was no way he
could issue me with a passport under present circumstances, he
said. I asked him if I could come and see him but he told me there
was nothing to discuss. I asked colleagues for advice and they
suggested I write to someone called Webb in Nationality &
Treaty Department at the Foreign Office. Webb phoned me after
getting my letter, said I had been misinformed. Home Office had
come to no decision about my nationality after the Act came into
force and I was still stateless. Patrick Lacey, our senior diplomatic correspondent, promised he would try to see the Home
Secretary on my behalf. Bless him, but what's the use? I'm sunk,
feel like a character in one of Kafka's novels. How can anyone
take on this vast, stinking bureaucratic machine whose
members should, in Ruth's opinion (and mine), be put up against
a wall and shot?'

Someone could and did take it on. Noakes, with the support of
his seniors, went into action, much as his predecessors in the
Colonial Office might have dealt with a recalcitrant African tribe.
Words passed at a level of government never seen by the general
public. Ten days later Gai was informed that his birth had been
re-registered at the British Consulate General in Geneva as the
son of Francis Launcelot Errington and, soon afterwards, he received his passport, three months before he was entitled to it.
The enemy fort had fallen and he was Jamaica bound. That was
great, but where was he bound for in the longer term? He would
soon be forty. He had been graced with certain spiritual insights
or so people said, but these had been overlaid with a life entirely
out of keeping with what, at heart, he knew.

'Have We not opened up thy breast [heart]', says the Quran,
'and lifted from thee the burden that weighed on thy back and
raised thee in status? Truly, with hardship cometh ease . . .'.
Gai's easement was complete, his mind clearer than it had been

since he had finished *The Richest Vein*. Ever since his adherence to Islam in Cairo, the diary had been concerned only with the turbulent surface of life. Whatever might have been going on at a deeper level was ignored since he himself was unaware of it. Throughout these years, however, he had been reading the books which would determine the future course of his life, digesting them, assimilating them. As Frithjof Schuon's books appeared, one by one, he read them first in French and then, when they were translated, in English, finding in them truths that satisfied his hunger. He met a young clergyman who had converted to Islam after reading only one of them and who explained: 'After every paragraph I sit back, wipe my brow and exclaim, "Phew! That's it".' It was Schuon's function to answer, subtly and with profound insight, the questions modern man asks concerning the very nature of things, questions which most people think unanswerable. He cut through the undergrowth to reveal what now became self-evident. For those who were intellectually attuned to his perspective he satisfied the deepest of needs; the need to know and to understand.

But Gai's appetite was omnivorous and he had packed into an expandable mind and memory a great variety of seemingly contrary ideas, happy to leave them to cook like the components of an exotic stew until they merged together. In particular he was once again fascinated by the writings of the thirteenth-century Sufi, Ibn Arabi. Gai, like others before him, was told that he would never understand the Master's work and the complexity of his spiritual insights, yet this did not really matter. Here was a vast treasury from which such a busy magpie as he was could snatch jewels which seemed to radiate light. Amidst the apparent obscurities of the Sheikh's writings, a phrase here—a few lines there—struck home, evoking in the reader a gasp of recognition. Gai never doubted that there was an absolute Truth, inexpressible within the limitations of human language and inaccessible to the unenlightened human mind, yet within reach of the human being as such. It seemed to him that he had lived with this conviction since childhood. Perhaps he had been born with it, and nothing that he did could destroy it, just as none of his fevers and follies could destroy a nameless certainty to which as yet he dared not give the name of 'faith'.

Now, with a degree of security he had never known before, a stable marriage and a growing family, the moment had come to start thinking again or rather to discover what it was he had been thinking over the years while his attention was focused elsewhere. That meant writing, and he began to make notes for what would eventually provide the basic material for a book. In doing so he made an astonishing discovery. He was writing as a Muslim, he was writing as a believer, he was converting himself—or re-converting himself—to Islam. Something had been going on at a level of his being unnoticed by consciousness, waiting only for an opportunity to formulate and express itself. 'I never knew I knew that', he told himself, 'I never believed I believed that, I never thought I thought that'. The result was that, when the book came to be published (*King of the Castle: Choice and Responsibility in the Modern World*), much of it read like the work of a stranger, one with whom he was in enthusiastic agreement but a stranger none the less.

At the same time, he was learning to fit his private passions into a religious—primarily Islamic—framework, taking advantage of the fact that, in Islam, there can be division between the spiritual and the mundane, between religion and politics. Ruth had consigned the civil servants who had almost ruined his life to the fires of hell. His approach was more subtle. In this book he would try to undermine the very basis of bureaucracy in modern society by spiritual and moral arguments regarding the nature of human responsibility. Obedience to any human authority as against obedience to God and to conscience became the supreme sin. By implication, he would be equating the mousy officials who had questioned his nationality with Nazi bureaucrats sending millions to the gas chambers, but only by implication. This technique worked, and the leading newspaper columnist of the time (Bernard Levin) would, when the book was published, hail him as an outstanding libertarian. He had succeeded in making his hatred of authority appear both reasonable and respectable. But here and now more immediate political considerations might, he realised, still prevent his return to Jamaica. Preoccupied with the passport question, he had forgotten the hostility of the Manley family.

Norman Manley was now Chief Minister of Jamaica, Bustamante's JLP having been defeated in a recent election. Manley had two sons, Michael and Douglas, the one dazzling, a born leader, and the other an embittered academic living in the shadow of his brilliant brother. Corah, of course, had known both since infancy, and, in September of 1956, soon after he and she had first got together, Gai had recorded in the diary an encounter she had with Douglas. 'I have had a startling insight into the PNP's attitude to me. I could not have guessed that my going to work for Busta had been so sensationalised. Over a farewell drink with Corah, Doug Manley (who is returning to Jamaica) warned her that, if she told me what he said and I used it against him, he would personally see to it that she was ruined. He told her that I had been the power behind Bustamante's throne; the most vicious enemy the PNP had, the centre of a web of evil intrigues. If I had not had the sense to see which way the wind was blowing and left Jamaica when I did, they'd have "fixed" me. This is madness. I always suspected that Doug had a screw loose. I don't know whether to be flattered or appalled.' Now, three years later, he was appalled. Had Douglas been reflecting his mother's view of the 'traitor'?

Edna Manley, a talented artist, might have been described as a typical left-wing 'Hampstead' intellectual and, like most of her kind, she assumed that all intelligent people must be socialists. If they were not, this could only be due to some malignancy in their character. When he had first arrived in Jamaica and after the publication of *The Richest Vein*, she had taken Gai into her circle. Hating argument, he had never mentioned his right-wing beliefs to her and so, when he went to work for Bustamante, she could only assume that this was from the darkest of motives. He was a traitor to her, to socialism and to decency as such. This was a dangerous woman, a dangerous enemy, and, even at this last moment, it would be in her power to prevent his return to Jamaica. When he asked Noakes if Manley was aware of his appointment he made the question casual, but he knew that his future might depend on the answer. 'Yes, of course,' said Noakes. 'As Chief Minister he had to be consulted before it was finalised. He had no objection.' There was only one possible explanation for this. Manley was fond of Corah and it must have been for her sake that he had approved the appointment. 'Watch your step', Gai told himself. 'Watch your step very carefully.'

Two weeks to go, and he could hardly believe that all the traps had now been sprung and the way ahead was clear. The Office had arranged for him to fly to Kingston via New York, but Corah and the children would follow three or four weeks later by sea with the baggage. He did not worry about leaving her to Ruth's tender mercies — she would soon be free — but he worried intensely about leaving Judy from whom he had never been parted for more than a few hours. She was now two-and-a-half, old enough, he thought, to understand if he could find the right words. He sat down with her again and again explaining. 'Daddy going on airplane. Then Judy, Mummy and Maurice come on big ship, cross sea, find Daddy.' She repeated what he had said over and over. She seemed to have got the point, but what he had not foreseen was that the 'big ship' would call at seven ports in Latin America before reaching Kingston and she would be looking for him in each. With Kay, he took Leo to Marlborough College where he was starting his first term and it was agreed that he would come out to Jamaica for his summer holidays the following year. That left the problem of Ruth, but she had, after all, four sisters with whom she could make her peace if she so chose.

8 October 1959. 'Thought I'd begin at last to believe it once airborne, but I'm not sure I do even now, two hours into the flight. How can I be sure I'm not dreaming? [Ten hours later] Had a good night, dozing. Headwinds have forced us to put down at Gander, Newfoundland. Red and orange sunrise over Gander Lake. I've left the old world and all its troubles behind me in the night. But I wish Judy was beside me saying 'Jelly sweetie please, Daddy'. After another ten hours he reached his destination, tired, unwashed and unshaven, to be greeted by Frank Morgan whose impeccably laundered white shirt dazzled him. Frank was every inch the Director, every inch the diplomat. They shook hands, then shook hands again for the benefit of the press photographers and a third time for television. This must be a dream.

On the second evening Frank gave a party to say farewell to Jamaica and to welcome his successor. Towering above everyone else, Bustamante was there as were many of Gai's old friends but, after a while, the guests dwindled down to a hard core of British businessmen, some of whom he had met when selling advertising but most of them unknown to him. He soon discovered that he was not unknown to them and he was astonished by their cordiality. This was explained when one of them took him aside and told him in conspiratorial tones: 'You're a clever bugger, you really are! We never suspected. None of us ever suspected. We thought you were a Commie or something, letting the side down. Well, 'nuf said, Eh?' The man actually put a finger to the side of his nose and winked.

The notion that Gai had been a secret agent sniffing out subversion in the Colony was on a level with Douglas Manley's conviction that he had been the centre of a web of political intrigue. Five years before, blundering through life in Jamaica under the protection of Clem Tavares, Evon Blake and Theo Sealy, he had thought himself innocent as a lamb and never asked himself how others saw him. Now he knew. He had been both a Machiavelli and a James Bond. As it was, denials could only confirm his secret identity so he smiled, exchanged wink for wink and held his tongue.

It was not long before an old friend, Elsie Benjamin—the leading woman journalist in the Island—started telling her friends that she had been converted to a belief in miracles. 'Well, what else can I believe,' she asked, ' now that I've seen a miracle with my own eyes? I've seen the most indiscreet man in Jamaica return here as a model of discretion. Isn't that a miracle?' After a few days Frank left for Uganda with his family and Gai took his seat at the big desk under a portrait of the Queen, assembling his staff of five for a pep talk and assuming, not for the first time nor the last, a new identity, a new mask. Far beyond the horizon was the grey land he had left behind, a place of shadows bleached now by the tropical sun. A long letter from Corah written on the eve of setting out on the long sea voyage was followed by a classic 'stinker' from Ruth, seething with anger and abuse both of Corah and of himself, steam almost visibly rising from the paper. Her invective could no longer wound him but he could not have guessed that, within eighteen months and at the age of eighty, she would board a small banana boat and come to Jamaica, the steam blown away by the Atlantic gales and the anger cooled.

He waited now to make his peace with the PNP and, specifically, the Manley family. An exhibition of paintings at the Institute of Jamaica gave him his opportunity. Edna Manley would never miss such an occasion, so he set out for the Institute with a pounding heart and an uneasy belly. She was standing at the top of the main aisle, the centre of a small group of admirers. Gai walked very slowly towards her, aware that the people on either side had stopped talking and had turned to watch him. He stopped a few yards from her to wait meekly for an acknowledgement of his presence. Her timing was perfect. Having kept him waiting just long enough for him to feel awkward she took a few steps towards him, leaned forward and kissed him on the forehead. 'Kiss of peace, Gai', she said. Soon afterwards he was invited to Drumblair, the Manley home, cleansed, purified and shriven by Edna's kiss. This reconciliation would be confirmed later in the year when Edna sent her official photographer to create a Madonna and Child image of Corah bending tenderly over baby Maurice for the Manleys' 1959 Christmas card; black mother with near-white infant symbolising the Jamaican multiracial ideal.

Gai's formal interview with the Chief Minister, however, was delayed until the Big Man, the Chief Information Officer in charge of Gai and his colleagues throughout the British West Indies, arrived from Trinidad. Bill Morrison was a tough Highlander who did not suffer fools gladly and whose likes and dislikes were conclusive. He liked Gai, and the feeling was mutual, an attraction of opposites but also between two men who shared the same rather quirky sense of humour. In due course they would become firm friends and, when they travelled together in Central America, Gai would laugh more than he had ever done before in his life or ever would do again. Faced with pretentiousness or pomposity, they would be obliged to avoid catching each other's eye if they were to keep straight faces. That was in the future. Here and now, having decided that Gai was up to the job, Morrison relaxed and his parting advice was characteristic. 'Sometimes', he said, 'you're bound to get tiresome letters from London. Don't worry! Just think of those poor sods in their dusty offices watching the rain pissing down outside the window. They're under the illusion that we spend our time sitting by a pool sipping rum punches. Such nonsense!' After that they returned to watching the pretty girls diving into the Myrtle Bank pool and sipped their rum punches in companionable silence.

Gai was still not entirely clear as to what his job involved, apart from issuing press releases, showing films which glorified Britain and giving parties for a hundred or more guests (this would be Corah's department). Morrison filled in the blanks, filled them with the images of some very important people. An astonishing number of British politicians, including Ministers of Government, were seized each winter by the need to embark on fact-finding trips to the West Indies at the taxpayers' expense. It was as though the first frosts triggered a need to seek information about Caribbean affairs and, in some cases, about Jamaican or Trinidadian night life. It would be Gai's duty to welcome, entertain and inform these eminent visitors. He was still fascinated by power in all its manifestations. Politicians might be dull as individuals and they might be hypocrites, but that was irrelevant. They were the people who made history, and that was what was so fascinating, as were the secrets they might divulge after a third or fourth drink. To shake hands and exchange words with a prime minister or a president was to step into the great stream of events or to have a walk-on part in a Shakespearean drama.

That was how Gai felt when he was summoned to King's House to talk with the Colonial Secretary, Iain Macleod. This was no ordinary politician. His acute intelligence put him head and shoulders above his colleagues and, after his premature death a few years later, he would be known as the Lost Leader, a man who—had he lived—would certainly have become leader of the Conservative Party and reformed it in his own liberal image. His job now was to lead a bundle of colonies to independence and to pretend (although he probably believed this) that, with their traditional patterns of government in ruins, they would flourish under an imposed Westminster model.

Before leaving Gai alone in his study with the Secretary of State, the Governor placed a stiff whiskey at his elbow. He did not need it. The fact of being closeted with a history-maker and invited to advise him was sufficiently intoxicating, but his brain was scarcely engaged. He did not have to think in order to talk about Jamaican politics, and his mind wandered. He remembered that windowless room in Linden Gardens, tasted in recollection the loss of hope, the loneliness, the blighted future, no chink of light at the end of any imaginable tunnel, and he marvelled. Muhammad is reported to have prayed: 'Lord, increase me in marvelling', and Gai was thankful that he had retained a child's capacity for wonder at the world's strangeness and the strangeness of human destinies. As he talked he studied the face of the man who sat in the armchair facing him and asked himself: 'What's it like to be Iain Macleod and to hold the fate of millions in those pudgy hands?' In some obscure way and through a leap of the imagination, he knew the answer to his own question.

Although fascinated by people, those mysterious beings seen only beyond the window-pane when he was a child, he had no skill in deciphering hidden motives. When the Colonial Office had made their travel plans he had not asked himself why they had insisted on Corah travelling by sea. Not until long afterwards did it occur to him that they wanted him to settle into the job free from family concerns. After seven weeks on his own, old friendships had been renewed, new relationships established and he was comfortable in his new role. He was ready. 'In a week's time they'll be here, I hope. Letter from Corah posted in Curacoa to say the ship is spending an additional two days there, but they might make up time in Port Limon. She has had a hell of a voyage, Judy with a heavy cold and Maurice with prickly heat, no facilities for children on board. Poor little Judy—'She expected to find you in Trinidad, and now she thinks you are in every aeroplane that passes overhead'. Now it looks as though I might have got a house by the time they arrive. The owner had turned down my offer of £55 monthly rent, then phoned accepting because she "liked my disposition".'

It was night-time when they arrived on 17 November 1959, and one of Gai's most vivid childhood memories was resurrected as he looked up at the tall ship from the bustling quayside. Above the hubbub he heard a high-pitched cry from an upper deck, a cry that somehow triumphed over the surrounding uproar. Judy, held up in Corah's arms, had seen him. 'I had a permit from Customs to go straight aboard. Corah, looking smart and pretty, was a delightful stranger compared with the household drudge I left behind. Judy a wreck, twisting her hands together, chewing the hem of her skirt while her eyes darted from side to side. Maurice plump and placid in his basket.' They returned to the cabin to pose as a family for the press photographers, a family yet to be completed as it would be by the birth of a second daughter, Corah Ann, two years later; the 'littlest one', the only true Jamaican. She would be a particular comfort to him in his old age, patient and understanding.

It was very late by now but time did not matter and neither Gai nor Corah was touched by weariness. To save money he had moved from the expensive hotel into which Frank Morgan had booked him into 'Miss Ivy's Guesthouse' on the Hope Road, an old wooden building which creaked and groaned in a friendly way, and it was here that they came at midnight. 'Judy slept at the bottom of our bed, untroubled by the complaining springs, and Maurice on the floor beside it, both sleeping the sleep of total exhaustion while we found each other again, crying out and babbling of love, telling each other incoherently of giving and taking in a frenzy of renewal.' Next morning they set off downtown, leaving the children with Miss Ivy. To the visitor bound for some bland, hygienic tourist resort, Kingston was a sordid city with no redeeming features, but this was their city. They could feel its pulse and they knew some of its secrets, dark as they might be. Where else but in Jamaica and in the 'wickedest city in the world' could the predecessors of Gai's present employers have appointed the most celebrated pirate of the age, Captain Morgan, as Governor of the Colony?

They strolled along Harbour Street in blazing sunshine. For Gai this shabby street was a highway of memory. More than ten years before, on his first arrival in Jamaica, he had come this way to swim in the Myrtle Bank pool where he had met a girl who, soon afterwards, introduced him to her brother. This brother was Clem Tavares, and it was so that the chain of events which led to the present moment had begun. Without Clem there would have been no editorship of *The Voice*, without that no job at the COI but for which there would have been no marvellous return to the Island. It was down this same street that he had walked with Flo early one morning past men working on a building site. One of them had called out: 'T'ink you can handle her, man?', and Gai had replied triumphantly, 'Sure, man, I can handle her'. Here too he had been approached by the hit-man eager to kill Harry Milner for a fee and, at the wrong end of this same street, the slummy end, Frenzie Fook still presided over Shanghai Lil's bar. Memories crowded in on him, happy memories because they led to this joyful present.

Corah slipped her arm through his and told him, 'Now you've got a new girlfriend. I'm your new girlfriend'. It was true. She was a young girl again, rejuvenated by happiness, and Gai was a new man, all the troubles of his bad beginning behind him. Although they would never have dared to hope for so much, they had twenty-five good years ahead of them.

As the shadows close in and age takes its toll, I am free to wonder where they are, the couple who strolled arm-in-arm down Harbour Street more than forty years ago, for of this I am sure. Nothing is lost in time, and we are told that a moment will come when the past, preserved in the divine knowledge, the universal memory, becomes present again. What can one do but marvel? There is no end to marvelling.

EPILOGUE

PACKING UP

When the hothouse atmosphere at Charterhouse became oppressive and I needed solitude I used to cycle down the hill to the village of Compton and make my way to the little Norman Church built, it was said, by a crusader influenced by Islamic architecture. It was always deserted so this became my private place, a perfect sanctuary. Here I would sit for a while listening to the ticking of the Church clock, the grandfather of all grandfather clocks, sonorous in the confined space. I sensed the seconds of my life ticking away with a sacred solemnity. The church itself seemed to me so ancient that it partook of eternity, yet its silence was punctured by the passage of time, the inescapable ticking of that clock.

Now, more than seventy years later, time is a cascade. Days, weeks and months pass almost before they can be counted. I am breathless trying to catch up and to register their passing. In a few weeks, God willing, I shall be eighty-nine and I cannot quite believe that so many years have passed since a little boy began to record the trivial events of his life. The twinkling of an eye, no more. I neither know nor care what the life expectancy of an eighty-eight-year-old smoker is supposed to be but it cannot be long and I have purchased an agreeable plot in a Muslim cemetery. The Angel of Death is so close that that I could almost stretch out a trembling hand and stroke his cheek in greeting and expectation. But the mystery of time fascinates me still as it fascinated that little boy. The ticking clock has devoured all the men and women who peopled my story. Martin Lings died four years ago at the age of ninety-five, active to the last breath, and, while writing this, I learned from a *Times* obituary that James Michie has died of cancer, witty and stoical to the end. I feel, sometimes like a bubble tossed on the surface of that vast ocean of the dead into which I shall soon be absorbed. After birth, un-remembered, death is the only universal human experience of mankind.

I never expected to live so long and I am not even sure how one is supposed to feel as an old man since I never meet other old people with whom I might compare notes. Most people want to live as long as they can, preferably longer, and the medical profession conspires to support them in this. To those who con-stantly monitor their health and who fear that smoking one cigarette might shorten their lifespan by a month, I have to say that I cannot entirely recommend old age. The American saying that 'old age is not for sissies' hits the mark when periods of enjoyment give way to periods of endurance. Thibon says some-where that, in youth the body is our slave whereas, in old age, we become its slave—'reversed in creation' as the Quran puts it—and disabilities pile up. I have almost forgotten the joy it must have been to run or jump or climb a hill. Could I grasp a sword in my hand? I would drop it. Could I ride a horse? I would fall off. And if a nubile young woman were presented to me on a golden platter, what use would I have either for the girl or the gold?

Perhaps the greatest deprivation is not being able to drive any longer. I had always hoped to die before that happened. An im-portant liberty is lost but that goes with increasing dependence on my children. When I was young I would have been horrified to think I might end my days in London of all places but my children, apart from Leo, are here and I cannot do without them. Nor am I fit to travel. If I long for tropical beaches or Swiss mountains, now that my legs are unwilling to carry me more than a short distance, memory serves very well. If I dream of more adventurous journeys, imagination provides a comfortable means of travel. And then certain Quranic verses provide a *vade mecum*. 'He is with you wheresoever you may be' is a reminder that it matters little where we happen to be so long as awareness of that presence endures. The true loss, the ultimate deprivation would occur if one were to lose that awareness.

I look around at the myriad of people in supermarket or street and reflect with astonishment that not one of them existed when I first came into this world and, in a whisper of time, a hundred years perhaps, not one of them will still be here. Such is our evanescence. The clock ticks and only God can stop it. Then, of course, there is the question of sexuality or its absence in old age, a subject on which no one would be so indelicate as to question me with the exception of my Parisian friend who suggests I should contribute to a book she means to write on this mystery. Echoing, as I recollect, a Greek dramatist of ancient times, a well-known actor remarked recently that he felt himself finally 'unchained from a lunatic'. It is often difficult to recall or imagine what it was like to be so possessed, so enslaved, so crazed. Only very occasionally is there a tiny flicker from the dying embers. Then I understand and am again bewitched.

But am I inwardly the same person I once was? I think so, and I think we all have a sense of continuity in the midst of change which is not entirely dependent on the brittle thread of memory. In Islamic as in Christian doctrine this continuity extends beyond earthly life. Otherwise the idea of the Last Judgement would be meaningless. What is most to be feared is the decay of spirit and mind in the last days of earthly life. I used to excuse

my father for the will which Ruth saw as an unforgivable betrayal on the assumption that a man in his late eighties was no
longer entirely responsible for his thoughts or actions. Now that
I am in the same age bracket I would not wish to excuse anything
I think or do on grounds of age. There was, I suspect, some deep
fault-line in his character which cracked open when he was old.
This may happen to any of us and may happen to me if I live too
long which is why, when people wish me 'many more years', I beg
them not to do so.

Then why, at this late stage, take up an offer to publish the story
of my early life? When it was completed I made a feeble effort to
find a publisher but did not persevere. I have tended throughout
my life to follow W. C. Field's advice: 'If at first you don't succeed,
give up'. I thought also that it would damage my 'image' as,
indeed, it may do. I have been honoured by my fellow Muslims
and praised beyond my deserts. Do I want to imperil my reputation? Above all—and this is what really matters—would I be setting a bad example? Some years ago I was invited to Los Angeles
to receive an award for 'services to Islam' and the Muslim students at UCLA invited me to speak to them. Typically the function started late and went on for hours after I had said my piece
so, by the time the students took me for dinner, we had to drive
round the city to find a restaurant still open. Finally three of them
drove me back to my hotel and asked if they could come in and ask
me something. I was exhausted and jet-lagged but could not
refuse. Their question boiled down to this. They had read the
autobiographical Introduction to one of my books and wanted to
know if they could misbehave as I had done and survive spiritu-
ally intact. I gave what I still think was rather a good answer. If
you choose to walk a tightrope over the abyss, I said, and you then
step off it safely you must thank God but you must never encourage others to do the same. They might not be so fortunate.

And still I want to see my story published. An American poet,
deciding to ignore the advice given him, published something he

had written several years before because it seemed like an un-born child burdening the womb. He needed to be free of it and pass on just as I need to be free of the story of my early life, rid myself of it and prepare, as must everyone of my age, for the final summons. Friends however have urged me to add an epilogue or afterword since my life did not end in 1959 and the story there-fore needs some kind of conclusion however difficult it may be to condense the experiences of fifty years into a few pages. So let me cast my mind back to that happy couple rejoicing in the tor-rid heat of Jamaica long, long ago.

*

We stayed on in Jamaica for five years. There must have been bad moments, there must have been problems, but in retrospect it seems like a time of unblemished happiness. Until 1962 when Jamaica gained independence I myself was independent, free to do as I chose since my 'boss', Bill Morrison, was a thousand miles away in Trinidad and was, in any case, my good friend. With a generous entertainment allowance Corah and I developed a talent for giving successful parties, cultivating friends and enter-taining VIPs from London including those sun-seeking parlia-mentarians. If I needed a change I could always fly over to Belize, a ramshackle little wooden town that I came to love, returning by way of Miami. It was, indeed, the good life.

This was the period of Britain's hasty and irresponsible with-drawal from the burden of Empire. One day an official from London turned up to warn me of the proposed Commonwealth Immigration Bill. I was to tell the Chief Minister, Norman Man-ley, confidentially that the Bill was aimed, not at West Indians who were British to the core but at those 'hordes from South Asia who threaten to invade us'. In retrospect it might be seen as a singularly ineffectual Bill. The 'hordes' came none the less, the majority my fellow Muslims; something of a time-bomb since

Islam is not only a religion, it is a civilisation, and you cannot expect radically different civilisations to cohabit comfortably.

In 1962 Jamaica, intoxicated by the dream of becoming an Island Utopia, was granted full independence with Bustamante as Prime Minister and a High Commission was established with Sir Alexander Morley as High Commissioner and myself as First Secretary (Information). The Foreign Service had a tendency to send the wrong man to the wrong place, something of which I was bitterly aware remembering how my friend Chris had been sent to his death as Ambassador to the Irish Republic; as a former Head of P.U.S. Department in the Foreign Office which supervises the Secret Intelligence Service he was inevitably regarded by the IRA as a 'spy master'. Morley was a sophisticated intellectual of finicky tastes who would have been more at home in a major European capital. We were invited to his dinner parties more often than we might have wished because all his best jokes were in French and my function was to initiate laughter at the right point. Contrary to most of his staff, I liked him.

The constraints imposed by Commonwealth Office were irksome but there were compensations. I was told that our home was not a 'representational' house and invited to find something grander. It was Corah who found something beyond our dreams. This was a former Bishop's Palace, a big old house with wide wooden verandas on the upper floor giving an uninterrupted view of the Blue Mountains, extensive grounds and even a servants' cottage. By this time our third child, Corah Ann, was already a year old and soon we were joined by a creature we described sometimes as the 'fourth child', a beautiful Siamese cat whom we named TamTam and who would eventually come to be known as 'the most travelled cat in the world', leaving her progeny on three continents.

This was all very well, but what about the future? I was not 'established' (permanent and pensionable) and the Foreign Service was unwilling to take on relicts of Colonial Office who were suspected of having 'gone native'. I needed some special advantage and this, I think, was acquired through a chance encounter. Duncan Sandys, Churchill's former son-in-law, was by then Commonwealth Secretary and he had a reputation for destroying the careers of civil servants who displeased him. When Morley announced an impending visit from this menacing figure at the weekly office meeting faces around the table fell. Various members of staff were designated to take Sandys here and there. 'The Secretary of State intends to spend a day relaxing in Montego Bay and would like someone to accompany him. Any volunteers?' My colleagues looked down at their shoes. Ignorant of the risk I raised my hand, meeting with looks of pity from my new colleagues. A week later I flew over to Montego Bay.

Sandys was in holiday mood and his new wife, an enchanting Frenchwoman, enchanted me. We swam together, enjoyed an excellent lunch and chatted as though we were friends. In due course Morley received the usual thank you letter: ' . . . and please thank your staff, particularly Gai Eaton', three words that were worth their weight in gold; no, in diamonds. In December that year there was an open competition for 'establishment' but with only one post available. The Office was obliged to fly candidates over to London wherever they might be and, although I saw no possibility of success, the chance of a free trip, a week staying with Ruth and doing my Christmas shopping in London was irresistible. As expected I received a note a few weeks later telling me I had not been successful, but soon afterwards an official who had been on the five-man interview Board turned up in Jamaica and told me to persevere. I had been the Board's second choice.

The following December I was again invited to an interview. I was on a visit to the Turks and Caicos Islands, marooned on South Caicos by a storm, but the Administrator radioed a passing private aircraft which put down on a muddy field, picked me up and took me to Miami. Once again I received a rejection note and decided that our future was clearly in Jamaica where I would find work as a local journalist and the children would grow up as good Jamaicans. Then the High Commissioner sent for me. The Board's first choice had been rejected on security grounds. I had again been their second choice so now I was duly 'established'. He expected me to be over the moon and was astonished to see a look of dismay on my face. I knew this meant a final parting from my Island, my adopted home. When, a few months later, I received a letter appointing me to the Deputy High Commission office in Madras I sat under a bush in the garden and wept. Corah, however, was thrilled.

We sailed from Port Antonio on a banana boat in September 1964, spent a few days in London and then flew to Madras. Everyone I know who has been to India has been captivated and fascinated. I was fascinated but never learned to love the country. It was not Jamaica and there were too many people, a suffocating human multitude. The combination of self-righteousness and corruption among politicians and officials depressed me, and, with three small children in tow, the prevalence of every kind of deadly disease kept us in a state of constant anxiety. I myself fell ill with hepatitis, attended by a former army doctor, a dipsomaniac Irishman who claimed to have cured his CO of the same disease by a liquid diet of Champagne. Meanwhile Corah had to manage a cohort of nine servants, settle disputes between them and act as a kind of den mother when they were in trouble. On arrival I had suggested to the Office that we did not need an assistant cook as well as the chief cook and a 'cook's boy' but it was pointed out to me that a whole extended family probably depended on his meagre earnings.

Culture shock was inevitable. The office car park also served the local Catholic Church and a dozen or more lepers squatted every day on either side of the entrance gate hoping for donations from good Christians. Driving into the compound it took skill to avoid crunching rotting limbs. I was advised to adopt one of them so that the others would not pester me and I chose a young man with glossy, flowing black locks. One day I could not see him and, as I looked around, the others burst out laughing and then pointed to a bald man. He had sold his hair. No doubt it would eventually become a handsome wig for some fashionable lady in Paris, London or New York. Others made a bare living by smuggling liquor under their rags as the police were afraid to search them.

It is sometimes suggested that the spiritual dimension of India is a myth. There are, of course, plenty of false 'gurus', hypocritical priests and questionable ascetics, but that is of no consequence and ignores the sprawling tolerance of Hinduism which cheerfully embraces both the true and the false, the saints and the clowns. There is perhaps an awareness of the fact that a false 'guru' might in spite of himself lead a disciple to enlighten-ment. We need to be constantly reminded that with God all things are possible. But Corah and I were granted an audience with the exemplar of all that was best in the tradition, the Shankaracharya of Kançi, the supreme religious figure of South India. There were humbler exemplars: the father of a friend of ours who had been a successful businessman was now a simple *sanyasin* meditating daily in the temple, his face adorned with the signs of Shiva, his wealth dispersed and the world forgotten.

As Information Officer I was free to visit newspapers, of which there were said to be over a hundred, in the vast area of the four southern states and I had a car and driver at my disposal. I had my favourite destinations, chiefly in Kerala which often reminded me of Jamaica, but in the deep south was a very spe-cial city. One would have to be singularly obtuse to be unmoved by the great temples of Madurai decorated with a riotous profu-sion of what I saw as the masks of God, multitudinous to match the multiplicity of the cosmos yet transparent to the light of the One which would blind us if unveiled. The contemporary world might be darkened and vulgarised but here the sacred was in the very air, an everyday reality that mantled the city. On another tour however I got my driver to stop at a little white mosque in the village of Seringapatam and, encouraged by a group of four old men who sat talking together, I climbed the minaret and was moved to rededicate myself to Islam. It was the beginning of a real return (not that I had ever left the Faith but hitherto it had been marginal rather than central in my life).

Later, in Hyderabad, I met a group of elderly Sufis who took me under their wing; gentle undogmatic men who would have seen today's radicals as a disgrace to Islam and who had an almost palpable sense of angelic presences sharing in their prayers. I visited them when I could. In Madras itself there was a sizeable minority of Muslims, in particular an extended family of twenty or more who lived in a compound behind high walls. My first friend among them came daily to recite the Quran at my bedside when I was ill, refusing to accept his taxi fare from me. 'I want to walk,' he said, 'while this music is sounding in my head'. Eventually I met the patriarch; very old and very serene. He spoke good English and when I was introduced to him as a convert he looked at me with a wry smile. 'You must be mad', he said. 'Mad to join us when we are so fallen, so decadent, so untrue to all that is meant by Islam', adding that the Arabs in general were completely degenerate. I cannot count the number of times since then that I have been asked: 'What is wrong with us?' as though a western convert, coming from afar and therefore objective, might have the answer.

I was away from the office a good deal and early in 1965 we flew to England on extended leave, taking with us our admirable Anglo-Indian Nanny to whom the children were devoted, so I did not see much of my 'boss', the DHC (Deputy High Commissioner). I said earlier that everyone I have known had been captivated by India, but there was one exception. The DHC had an almost visceral dislike of Indians and utter contempt for their religion and their customs, another case of the wrong man in the wrong place; nothing in the country would improve, he claimed, until the women gave up wearing their 'silly saris'. So far as my job was concerned, he regarded Information work as a complete waste of time and money. He never asked me what I was doing or why and, when an Inspector arrived from London for a routine inspection, he recommended that my post should be abolished.

One Sunday morning the young Immigration Office burst in on us to let off steam. He had gone to the office to collect his tennis racket and had been shocked to find the DHC sitting at his desk examining the contents of the desk drawer in which he kept his private papers. I remembered that, exceptionally, I had left my diary at the office; it contained damning comments on this man for whom I had no respect. I would never know whether he had read it or not although I thought that he looked at me rather strangely whenever we met, a look in which malice and a kind of secret amusement were mixed. In any case he got his wish and my post was duly abolished. In October 1966 we set off back to England sailing on a P & O liner, the *Orsova*, an eighteen-day voyage calling at various ports including Aden, Naples and Lisbon; a free cruise with all the comforts of First Class, spoiled by the fact that the children were unwell through much of the voyage. Corah, however, was far from sorry to leave India. There seems to be a kind of instinctive antipathy between people of African origin and Indians. She had never felt at home in Madras.

Back in London and shivering in the unaccustomed chill I went for an interview with Head of Personnel Department without any presentiment of disaster. It was a horrible interview comparable to the meeting with Major S. more than twenty years before. The DHC's report on me had been subtly damning, subtle in that it was not bad enough to justify an appeal but bad enough to ensure that I would never be promoted. The Personnel man suggested grimly that I had made no effort to do a decent job and there was nothing I could say, knowing that any criticism of my former boss, let alone a suggestion that he might have read my diary, would only make matters worse. Seething with rage, I listened in silence. When I got home and told Corah she was even angrier than I was and said that, if I felt I should resign, she would go out and scrub floors until I could find a job. With three small children, resignation was obviously out of the question but I had lost any sense of loyalty to the Service, thinking that in future I would get as much out of it as I could and give as little as was strictly necessary.

References to 'the Service' require a word of explanation. It had been known for some time that the Commonwealth Office was to be amalgamated with the Foreign Office to the distress of old Commonwealth hands who were placated by the assurance that the FO was also being abolished and an entirely new joint department would be created. A high-powered (and highly paid) committee was set up to decide on a name for it and, after long deliberations, came up with a proposal which they must have thought imaginative. The new department would be entitled the Foreign and Commonwealth Office (FCO). Such are the ways of Whitehall. I was posted to the East Africa Department and given the Uganda 'desk'. This was the time of General Amin, the ugly tyrant, so my job was, to say the least, interesting. I had my first encounter with SAS (Special Air Services), an elite unit of derring-do officers, when I attended a meeting to discuss what was to be done if Amin threatened the British community. Two young men from SAS were present and they came up with a fabulous scheme. They would be dropped by parachute, their faces blackened, some distance from Kampala, make their way to the capital and assassinate the dictator. The idea of these hulking white men pretending to be Africans as they passed through a number of villages on their way to kill a well-protected monster had a certain charm.

Meanwhile we had bought a house in Purley, a suburb some twenty miles from London, mainly because two former colleagues from the COI lived there, and I began to share Corah's passion for gardening. The time had come for my 'positive vetting' and I was interrogated by an agreeable young security officer. The naiveté of the interrogation astonished me. Even the most incompetent spy or traitor could have sailed through. At one point however, leafing through my file, the man looked up and said: 'I see you are a Muslim'. I said that I was, expecting further questions, but he returned to the file and remarked: 'I see you are a keen gardener'. I realised that this balanced the oddity of my

being a Muslim. Gardening is such a very British passion that
one might be sure no gardener could be a traitor. However my
friends and acquaintances were questioned about me by Special
Branch and one of them, Stan Godfrey, told me afterwards about
the interview. The policeman had asked him: 'What can you tell
me about his relations?' Knowing quite well what was meant,
Stan pretended to misunderstand and said I had an aunt in
Bedford. 'You're a wag, Sir, indeed you are', said the policeman.
'I mean his sex-u-al relations.'.

Having been cleared I was put in touch with SIS (the Secret Intelligence Service), and I attended a two-day course to learn how
they operated. Ever since then I have been irritated by the readiness of the press to use the term 'MI6', a deliberate deception
designed to imply that the organisation comes under the Ministry
of Defence rather than the FCO. In those days SIS seemed like a
last refuge for the upper classes. Spying was a gentlemen's sport
and members of the Service were to be found relaxing in the best
London clubs. They were usually charmers with formidable social skills, essential if they were to seduce important targets and
persuade them to reveal their secrets.

The children, meanwhile, were adapting themselves to this new
environment and attended a local school although, with an overseas
posting likely, Judy was sent to a boarding school in Brighton when
she was eleven. This was customary in the Service but distressed me
none the less. We were quite unaware of the problems faced by the
other two. Maurice frequently turned up on the doorstep having run
home from school to escape bullying but never told us the reason
and it was only many years later that Ann confessed that one of the
teachers had told her she was an 'abomination' on account of her
racial mix. To this day I do not know why they said nothing to us.
With Maurice perhaps it was a matter of pride and Ann would
always be rather a private person. Had we known what was going
on we would have descended on the school with fury. But we were,
in any case, preoccupied with the problem of Ruth. She was now ap-

proaching ninety. The ground floor flat of the house we had once occupied jointly was now rented to a single mother for a nominal rent
in return for keeping an eye on her and attempts to find a nursing
home which suited her led nowhere. One day she fell all the way
down the flight of stairs in the house, relieved, as she fell, to think
that death had come for her at last, but she suffered nothing worse
than mild concussion and a few bruises. Distressed to find herself
still alive she began, I think, to turn her face to the wall, ultimately
taking refuge in senility.

Late in 1969 we were posted to Ghana, the country in which,
as a child, I had believed I would die of Yellow Fever. Leaving
Judy behind we sailed for Accra in a small ship, four of us and
TamTam, in January the following year. Our arrival was a shock
for the High Commissioner, Horatio Matthews. He had warned
the Office that an impending inspection was likely to result in
the abolition of the Information post for reasons of economy and
advised them to delay our departure but the warning had been
lost somewhere in the bureaucracy. The six months we spent in
Accra were not a happy time although Maurice and Ann, both
expert swimmers, enjoyed the beaches and, at Easter, Judy flew
out to join us. We had not been there long when I became ill with
a low but persistent fever and physical weakness. Perhaps it was
psychosomatic or perhaps it was some obscure West African bug
but it dragged me down. Then the Inspector arrived. By a weird
coincidence this was none other than the man who had been my
nemesis in Madras. With evident glee he abolished my post and
I was told we would be returning to London.

This spelt disaster. An overseas posting always involved initial expense which was more than compensated later by special
allowances but we were still out of pocket and had nowhere to
live, having rented out our home. To my surprise the High Commissioner wrote to London saying that he had never before
known anyone so badly treated by the Office and urging them to
find us another overseas posting. And then—'with hardship

cometh ease' says the Quran—I was given a telegram which is still pasted between the pages of my diary. 'Please inform Eaton that his next appointment will be First Secretary (Information) Port of Spain. He should arrive there before his predecessor leaves 22 June.' There was nothing I could say except: *al-Hamdu li'Llah*, Thanks be to God. I had enjoyed other strokes of almost miraculous good fortune in my life but this seemed the greatest. Packing up all our belongings had been a chore in the past but this time it was a joy. When we boarded a plane for New York on 11 June my illness, whatever it was, vanished.

Arriving very early in the morning in New York I left Corah and Ann to relax in the hotel while, with renewed energy, I took Maurice for a short walk wondering whether, in later life, he would remember this moment, this city, this happiness. Next day we flew to Trinidad. Years before when we were in Jamaica a former colleague from the COI had come on a brief visit to the Island and had been astonished to find me a changed personality from the person he had known in London; more alive, more joyful, more outgoing. Now, on the plane, it was almost as though I could feel myself changing in the way that a character in a film may change, by a technical trick, into someone else. A West Indian personality had been resurrected.

I had visited Trinidad several times in the old days to confer with Bill Morrison so this was familiar territory, a kind of homecoming. Trinidad is a fragment torn off from South America, lush, orchidaceous (the best orchids flourish there) and physically less rugged than Jamaica just as its people are less rugged than Jamaicans. I could never choose between the two although my roots were in Jamaica. I rejoiced in both islands. We stayed three years in Port of Spain. I liked and respected the High Commissioner, Roland Hunt, and, after an uncomfortable start, Corah got on well with his wife, Pauline, which was just as well because the wife of a Head of Mission determines whether the staff wives are happy or unhappy. Wives in an overseas post are members of the team and their husbands are in trouble if they forget this. The wife of a junior member of staff objected to acting as an 'unpaid waitress' at official parties. She and her husband were on the next plane back to London. Corah, of course, served cheerfully and probably received brownie points for this. Above all she was painting again and had a successful exhibition opened by the Prime Minister of Trinidad.

The question arose as to how I could make discrete contact with the Muslim community. One of the local secretaries was a pretty girl called Zayda who appeared to be a typical short-skirted Trinidadian, unlikely to be pious. I found an excuse to call her to my office and remarked casually: 'You have a Muslim name'. Her response has remained with me all these years because of its warmth and passion. 'But I am Muslim,' she said, 'and I love my religion'. It was a heartfelt declaration of love, unexpected and moving. Her father turned out to be one of the leading figures in the community and the family welcomed me. Then I became friends with a local TV personality, in this case a 'lapsed' Muslim, who took me to meet his parents in a village some way from Port of Spain. Driving there on the day of the festival which ends Ramadan I was seized with a joy so intense that I said to myself: 'So this is what people mean by 'faith.'

It used to be said that life in Trinidad was a perpetual party. Certainly the annual Carnival was the summit of the year and the poor often went without many essentials to save up for a splendid costume. We too were party-givers and, thanks to Corah's skill in organising these occasions and mine in selecting compatible guests, we made quite a splash. Luck contributed to this. At one time the diplomatic fraternity was troubled by the fact that the Commander of the Army (such as it was) regularly turned down their invitations. Could there be a political reason for this? Was he perhaps planning a coup against the Government? I happened one day to attend a function in the Officers' Mess and got talking to a pretty woman from Guyana. On the spur of the moment I invited her to a party we were giving a few days later and was promptly surprised by a hefty slap on the back. 'We'll be glad to come', said the Army Chief who had overheard me. 'I won't go any-where unless she's invited.' This, unknown to all of us, was his current mistress. After our party the High Commissioner asked me: 'How on earth did you persuade him to come?' A moment later the German Ambassador took me aside to ask the same question.

In 1971 we had an unexpected visitor. Eleanor, the youngest of the aunts, was by now eighty, lonely but uncomplaining after the death, the previous year, of Goo, her lifelong companion. She had never until then been in an aeroplane but, with Judy who was coming for the Easter holidays as her escort, she embarked on what must have been a great adventure for her. One day a close friend, my opposite number in the American Embassy, Bill Gresham, rented a boat and invited us to join him and a dozen of his colleagues for a trip along the coast. We anchored in a creek and, to the amazement of the Americans who made a great fuss of the old lady, Eleanor joined the children for a swim in the warm and welcoming sea. The water of that sheltered creek must have reflected the surrounding jungly greenery which pressed upon it but, in memory, it is sky-blue and the children, three of ours and three Greshams, are for ever young. That evening she said to me: 'This has been the happiest day of my life'. I could only think she meant the happiest day since Goo died but I had, as so often, a sense of wonder at the permutations of human destinies. Here was a woman who had been a dominant figure in my childhood and a disapproving presence in my youth but whose total approval I now enjoyed and who revelled in being invited to diplomatic parties.

I guessed that Goo must have left Eleanor comfortably off—I had no idea of how comfortably—but money was a taboo subject for her generation and I never questioned her. I was not surprised however when she offered to pay for all of us to have a short holi-day in Tobago, then off the tourist track and entirely unspoilt, a gem of an island with marvellous beaches and fine coral reefs. This too was a wonder for her and I had never seen her so happy. In the summer we went to England for the three months' leave due to us, stopping on the way to spend a few days in Jamaica. The worst had not yet happened but there was already a sinister change in the atmosphere. Driving somewhere one day we had a puncture and a black man came over to see what was wrong. He then held up a car driven by a white man and told the driver: 'Come and help your white brother'. White brother? Such racial stereotyping would have been unthinkable in the old days.

Ruth was by now senile and confined to the geriatric ward of a big hospital. When I visited her she was unresponsive until a moment when a claw-like hand seized one of mine and her almost sightless eyes focussed on my face as though seeking an answer to an unanswerable question. For me she was already dead. There was nothing here that related this functioning corpse to the mother I had known so well and loved so much. It was a relief when she died the following year aged ninety-two. I was more affected by a visit to my aunt Dolly who had been persuaded to give up her little house in a Sussex village and move into a residential home to await death. Her delight and excitement at seeing me were heart-breaking yet I hurried away to pick up Ann who had been left with friends and I have felt guilty ever since, haunted by the image of that forlorn figure waving farewell. She died soon afterwards. It was a joy after this to return to my sun-drenched West Indian world.

345

Not for long. My three-year stint in Trinidad came to an end in July 1974 and, after a flurry of farewell parties, we flew to St Lucia to board a small banana boat, the *Geest Star*, with only eleven other passengers and sail back to England knowing that this was likely to be our last overseas posting. I had talked to the High Commissioner about the possibility of taking early retirement and seeking a job in Geneva. This seemed a remote hope until a very senior official from the FCO had come to inspect the post and, when I drove him to the airport, had asked if there was anything he could do for me. I thought he meant for the Information side of things but he said: 'No, I mean for you personally'. He had promised to see what openings there might be with the UN agencies in Geneva. So I was optimistic on the two-week voyage while Ann, by now a pretty twelve-year-old, was fussed over by the ship's officers and Maurice was allowed onto the bridge to steer the ship for a few minutes. We docked in Liverpool (where Ruth, heavy with child, had landed fifty-two years before) and made our way home to Purley. It seemed like the end of an era and so it was.

*

While we were in Madras I met several people who knew of Martin Lings and who also knew about the Sufi Tariqah to which he belonged. He was now living in Croydon, having been thrown out of Cairo with my other colleagues at the University, and he had by now published several important books on Sufism. I contacted him soon after we returned to England. He never reproached me for my long silence nor did he ask the reason for it but, almost as soon as we met again, he suggested that the time had come for me to enter the Tariqah and, although I prevaricated for a while, this made sense. The following year he received me into the branch of the *Alawiyyah* Tariqah to which he belonged and, soon afterwards, I went to Lausanne to meet his Sheikh or Spiritual Guide. This was none other than Frithjof Schuon whose books had provided my spiritual and intellectual nourishment ever since the publication of *The Transcendent Unity of Religions*. So I was 'born in Lausanne and reborn in Lausanne', as his wife remarked. In joining a Tariqah one is reborn into a new family, taking on a spiritual ancestry which stretches back to the Prophet himself, every name in this 'chain of transmission' being known and recorded.

This is not the place for an essay on Sufism usually defined as 'Islamic mysticism' although there is nothing inherently mysterious about it. It carries Islamic devotional practices to their logical conclusion or to their culmination which is why many Muslims prefer to call it the '*ihsāni* tradition', the way of excellence, which places it firmly within the contours of normative Islam. There are fairly minor differences between the *turuq* (plural of Tariqah) but the basis is always the remembrance of God—what Christians call 'the practice of the presence of God'—through invocation, called *dhikr*. The method of invocation taught by Sheikh 'Isa (whom I shall refer to as Schuon without any disrespect) is in its way unique. It turns upon a series of meditations on the revealed Name of God, *Allah*, pronounced with deep concentration either silently ('in the heart') or aloud. During the invocation the Name may be a holy refuge from the evils of worldliness, a blow struck against these same evils within ourselves, a centre of peace or a powerful current of love and longing; the permutations are limitless. Beyond this lie meditations upon the divine transcendence which reduces us to nothing but a seeing eye and then upon the divine immanence in which the Name as such replaces the human ego or, in other words, fills the heart leaving no room for selfhood. I said that this method is unique but it has been approved by Sufi Sheikhs in the Muslim world and is within the tradition.

Equally unique is the delicate balance exemplified in Schuon's many books between our respect for forms, that is to say for each of the traditional religions in which God has revealed himself, and our universalism which embraces all that is truly traditional since no single form can accommodate the infinite. This is not an easy

347

balance or, indeed, an easy concept for most people to grasp but it is particularly timely. Marx dismissed all religions because they appear to differ irreconcilably. This is a common belief today and for more than fifty years I have been convinced that Schuon has provided the most effective antidote. We can only pursue one path-way—or high road—in a lifetime but, if only from the corners of our eyes, we perceive and respect those other routes to God. 'God,' wrote the poet Rumi, 'is not a King for whom a single herald would suffice. If all the atoms of the universe were his heralds, they would have been incapable of making him known adequately'.

Schuon, who died in 1998 at the age of ninety, was a controversial figure as are a number of Sheikhs, particularly among those living in the West. Perhaps he saw too much and saw too deeply. So far as his teachings are concerned, not only those in his books but also in the great number of texts written for his disciples, it would take a comparable intelligence to fault him and I have never met anyone of comparable intelligence.

In any case I was and am content with the path I chose and have tried, clumsily and often negligently, to follow it for the past forty years. The practice of our *dhikr* supported me in Ghana and delighted me in Trinidad. Now, on our return to Britain, I had Martin Lings (whom we always called Sidi Abu Bakr) to instruct and support me as a plodder on this path. No doubt the invocation assuaged my obsession with the passage of time, the ticking of the clock, for the only escape from time is in the timeless and, in principle, the invocation is beyond time since its focus is eternity. Whether or not we are truly aware of this is unimportant because subjective feelings are not the issue here, just as the ritual prayer of Islam is valid whatever feelings we bring to it, as is the Catholic Mass.

So the four of us returned to the cold country, the grey country, soon joined by Judy on her school holidays while poor TamTam languished in quarantine. I was given a desk in the Commonwealth Co-ordination Department of the FCO, concerned mainly with briefing Ministers. Now I was enmeshed in the bureaucratic process, with occasional moments of satisfaction. One day I was required to produced a particular brief in haste. I wrote a single A4 page. My Head of Department added a couple of paragraphs, the superintending Under-Secretary added his own contribution and the Permanent Undersecretary contributed a few lines. As the brief was needed urgently I was asked to take it by hand to the House of Lords. The Minister concerned glanced through it, frowned and said: 'Much too long'. He took a red pen from his pocket and, after making deletions, handed it back to me. 'Isn't that better?' he asked. What remained was my original brief. 'Yes Sir,' I said, 'much better'. Finally, in 1977, I was given the early retirement for which I had hoped, seeing no future in the Service.

There followed several months of severe financial anxiety although my pension, such as it was, started at once. I learned the hard way how ready Arabs are to make promises they cannot fulfil. A distinguished Syrian academic assured me he could persuade his friends in the government of the United Arab Emirates to open an Information office in Geneva with myself as

Director but, as the months passed, omitted to tell me that nothing had come of this. The book on which I had been working on and off for several years was published by The Bodley Head: *King of the Castle: Choice and Responsibility in the Modern World*. It might so easily have sunk without trace but Bernard Levin, the principal columnist on *The Times*, was bowled over by it and wrote, not a simple review, but an article on the op-ed page which went beyond anything I would have dared to write about my own book. He hailed me as a fellow libertarian and, after several quotations which were the very ones I might have chosen, added: 'These cannot convey the breadth or the power of his case, nor the vigour, clarity and wit of his prose. Nothing but reading his book can do that . . .'. Visiting London's leading bookshop a few days later I found a whole table laden with copies of the book. What more could I have asked of life?

I had made friends with a leading Islamic scholar, an Egyptian who had lived in London for many years, Zaki Badawi. He was a man who acted rather than promised. One day he telephoned to say that he had been appointed Director of the Islamic Cultural Centre, the administrative wing of the recently completed Regent's Park Mosque. I was to start at once as his assistant and as Editor of the Centre's journal, *The Islamic Quarterly*, working in my own time three days a week which would leave me free to pursue other activities. I began regular broadcasting, particularly on the BBC World Service, and doing occasional TV interviews. My book had helped to establish my credentials but my position as the only Englishman attached to the principal Islamic institution in the country served to guarantee my authenticity.

I spent twenty-two years at the Centre, quitting only when health problems prevented me from driving any longer into London. I had found a niche that suited me and, having lingered for so many years on the sidelines, I was now immersed in the affairs of the *Ummah* (the community of Muslims). Zaki Badawi was forced out by the Saudis (who held the purse strings) after three years but went on to become an adviser both to the Prince of Wales and to the Government on relations with the community. I stayed on although the Centre had become an essentially Saudi institution though with Egyptian imams in accordance with its charter. This was an odd situation since the Saudis are officially followers of the Wahhabi version of Islam and are therefore totally opposed to Sufism. Few would have heard of the sterile Wahhabi creed had it not been for the world's appetite for oil, the black muck which oozes out of the desert sands and which the Arabs called 'Satan's fire' before its value was known and which was described to me by a contemporary Syrian academic as 'Satan's urine'.

The Arabs however tolerate eccentrics and tend to prefer 'the devil they know' to any stranger. I was apparently irremovable and visitors who came to the Reception desk saying they wanted to learn about Sufism were simply told: 'Room 7. Mr Eaton'. Here I had a comfortable office overlooking the courtyard of the Mosque and here also people who found it easier to talk to me than to some of the imams came after Friday prayers seeking advice, usually on family problems, occasionally on Sufism.

The Prophet is reported to have said that, out of a herd of a hundred camels, you are lucky to find one good riding beast. This obviously applies to the adherents of any religion and it is therefore misleading to judge the religion by the behaviour of the majority of its official adherents. Human nature does not easily adapt itself to the requirements of faith or, indeed, to the requirements of truth. Among the people I met at the Centre the proportion of 'good riding beasts' was, I think, much higher, but these were people who frequented the Mosque and were mostly sincere in their faith.

And then, of course, there were the 'political' Muslims. It is a truism that, in Islam, politics cannot be separated from the religion as such. But here we have a uniquely modern phenomenon: Islam as an ideology. Once Western power had crashed into the closed world of the Muslim *Ummah* (in 1798) leaders of the community reacted initially by subservient imitation (top hats and all). In the twentieth century, the century of ideologies, imitation took a new form. Communism, Socialism, Nationalism and even Fascism all became fashionable and all failed to restore the greatness of the *Ummah*. After that there was nothing left but to transform Islam into an '-ism' and men who had not an ounce of piety (let alone humility) in their makeup and who disdained spirituality became fanatical 'Islamists'.

One day when there was turbulence in the Mosque after the Friday prayers, raised voices and fist-waving, I wandered amongst the tightly packed congregation trying to find out what the fuss was about. One youth, his face contorted with fury, almost knocked me over in his excitement. An elderly worshipper came up to him and said: 'Please, Brother, couldn't you demonstrate outside? Some of us want to pray'. The response was as inappropriate as it was ill-mannered: 'You can go and pray somewhere else'. This demonstrated an extraordinary reversal of priorities. It also demonstrated a complete lack of *adab* and here we have the surest sign of decadence. The word is usually translated as 'good manners' but it has a deeper and more universal meaning. The principle of *adab* is at the heart of Islam. It signifies in the first place good manners towards God including gratitude for the gift of life, for the food that nourishes us, for the light of day and even for the air we breathe. Secondly we must show good manners in all our dealings with our fellows, even our enemies, respecting the dignity of the human condition. But this is not all. The animal creation also is to be treated with courtesy and compassion (as the Prophet demonstrated on several occasions), and no tree or plant which feeds man or beast is to be abused. The environment as such is sacred.

Since fate had given me a voice and, as it were, a 'pulpit', I had an obligation to speak my mind when speaking to Muslim groups and, particularly one evening each Ramadan, when I addressed the congregation in the Mosque while they awaited the breaking of the fast. One day I said to the Chief Imam (a good friend and supporter): 'How is it that I get away with saying things which, if you said them, you would probably be stoned? I suppose it's because Muslims still have great respect for age'. He laughed. 'It's because you have a white face', he said. I saw nothing wrong in taking advantage of this privilege to say things that needed to be said. I heard that one young radical had told his friends: 'Someone should take Mr Eaton by the ear and lead him out of the Mosque', but there were no volunteers. The Chief Imam, trained in Islamic Law at al-Azhar University, was himself constantly in trouble. In one of his Friday sermons he told the congregation that many ordinary British people behaved more like good Muslims than did the self-proclaimed faithful. This did not go down well. When people came to him, demanding to be told if some intended action was permissible or forbidden and expecting a cut-and-dried answer, he would explain the differences of opinion among the jurisprudents only to be accused of ignorance. They were not interested in subtleties. They only wanted to be told what to do as though they had no minds of their own nor any responsibility to use their God-given intelligence.

So the years passed pleasantly enough. I had my place in the Muslim community. In a different identity, walking from my Club in Pall Mall to the Houses of Parliament to attend regular meetings of an inter-Faith group, I could reflect with an inward chuckle that I had become an improbable member of the Establishment, respectable at last, fully legitimate. In the summers there was the glorious freedom of the open road when we drove each year to camp in the South of France with the children squabbling for space in the back of the small car—like a nest of rats as Corah put it—till they fell asleep in a heap. All was well or seemed so.

There is a scene permanently engraved on the tablets of my memory. It is the morning of Corah's fifty-eighth birthday. Half awake, I watch her as she stands by the bedroom window examining her breasts as she does regularly. She rejoins me in bed saying quite casually that she seems to have a small lump in her right breast. There is a twinge of anxiety, no more. We relax and make love. Nothing to worry about.

A few days later she went on a routine visit to her doctor. The doctor did not seem worried but gave her a sealed letter to the Royal Marsden Hospital, the leading cancer hospital in Britain. We steamed the letter open. It referred to a 'suspicious lump' in the breast. It is so that a single word can strike terror in the heart. 'Suspicious' could mean malignant and that, after a series of tests, was what it meant. A mastectomy followed soon afterwards but there was no follow-up treatment and I have always assumed that Corah was in a test group to be compared with others who were given radiotherapy or chemotherapy. Regular tests however over the next two years suggested that all was well. I was able to make a pilgrimage to Mecca and to pray for her with my forehead pressed against the wall of the Ka'ba. Someone said to me once that cancer is a 'tease', raising hopes, dashing them again, raising them once more until the blow falls. A day came when Corah complained of a pain in her arm. The hospital thought it was arthritis and it was a while before they admitted, almost unwillingly, that she had bone cancer in her spine.

There followed what seemed endless tests followed by radiotherapy and a mild form of chemo. As though to make the place less frightening I familiarised myself with every corner of the Marsden during the long waits for attention (like a cat exploring a new home), pleased when a nurse invited me to lunch in the staff canteen. The disease moved around in Corah's body, seeming to clear up in one area only to reappear in another, but she was well enough for us to holiday one summer on Lake Como and in Minorca the following year. After that there were no more holidays. Towards the end—aware as she was of my selfishness— she told me that I had done better than she would have expected. I did not do well. Those close to a cancer victim are urged to maintain an appearance of cheerfulness, but I was never much good at hiding my feelings. One day when I had stopped the car to go into a shop she watched me as I walked back, desolate and distraught. 'If you go and die on me now,' she said sharply, 'there'll be two deaths on the same day'. On another occasion she remarked that she was glad it was her, not me who had been afflicted. For my part I could almost envy her. At least she had me. When my time came I would not have her.

The end came in December of 1984. The Marsden took her in, supposedly for a week, to see if they could do anything to alleviate the pain. I asked the nurse in charge of the ward if I should alert Judy, who was on a trip around the world, to return by Christmas and was told gently that Corah would not last so long. When I got home Ann said: 'Mummy will be home on Tuesday won't she?' I burst into tears and, when she hugged me waiting for an answer, told her that the end was close, responding to her murmurs of comfort by gasping: 'So the child becomes the parent'. Late on the Monday evening the hospital telephoned to say I should come at once. Maurice drove Ann and myself into London, careless of speed limits. We were too late. Death had come twenty minutes before we arrived. Now Maurice and Ann took charge, pulling me away from the empty body before it became cold and taking charge of everything after that. On a bitter winter's morning she was buried in a country churchyard, far from our Caribbean sun.

I had always kept Corah short of money. Now she had died too soon to enjoy even a few crumbs from the table of a new-found prosperity. Eleanor had died a few months earlier at the age of ninety-two. Only now did I learn that she had inherited twelve small houses in South London from Goo, who had specified in her will that these should come to me in due course. The couple's closest friend for fifty years had been a cousin of Goo's, Elsie, who, when the will was published, wrote Eleanor a cruel letter containing the dread word 'Lesbian' and claiming that the houses were family property, hers by right. There was no legal foundation for the claim but Eleanor, appalled by the letter, gave Elsie six of the houses 'to get rid of the woman'. She had not discussed this with me although the neighbours who had been her main support in recent years begged her to do so. The Muddock family had never been sensible over money. Neither had I, but now I was relieved of financial worries and, for some while afterwards, whenever I saw something in a shop that Corah would have liked, I had a twinge of sadness thinking that I could have bought it for her. I had never even given her an engagement ring.

For the next two years until her marriage Ann lived with me. I had another companion as well. Towards the end of her life Corah had asked me to get her a small dog to keep her company when I was in London and she had spent happy hours choosing the breed she wanted. Her choice was a West Highland Terrier and we found a joyful puppy whom we called Hamish. Soon afterwards he needed a minor operation and had an adverse reaction to the anaesthetic. He was blind. I overheard Corah saying to him: 'Little Hamish, I'll be your eyes and you can be my ears'. But he was deaf too. Given Corah's condition at the time this was almost unbearable, a tragedy within a tragedy. He recovered completely after a few weeks, but this incident had endeared him to us immeasurably. He lived on for twelve years, was followed by another of the same breed and finally by a Jack Russell whose little brown face I see on the adjoining pillow when I awaken in the bed that Corah and I once shared. I wonder sometimes how anyone can live without an animal companion, particularly nowadays when most of us are completely cut off from the non-human creation. It is, I suppose, a sure sign of old age that when I pass a pretty girl in the street who has a dog with her I turn round to look, not at the girl, but the dog.

Elderly widowers are not the happiest of God's creatures but I still had some good years. In 1988 I offered to pay for Judy, a skilled scuba diver, to take a diving holiday on the Florida Cays and she suggested I should go with her. I snorkelled among the waves while, far below, she explored the still depths. The father of a beautiful daughter finds himself remarkably popular among younger males in the vicinity, moths attracted to the flame. One in particular, a boat captain who took us out to the reef, was my ideal American, a free spirit, untouched by conformity (the flaw in so many of his countrymen) who went everywhere with his pet parrot in his shoulder. When we were leaving he handed Judy a letter to be opened on the plane: 'You came into my life like a bright star over the ocean . . .' Each summer until the end of the century I put the car on a train to Avignon and stayed for a while with friends who lived in a converted farmhouse high in the hills of the Drome before driving through the mountains to Lausanne to stay with a couple from the Tariqah.

I have often been asked why I never revisited Jamaica (though my Blessed Isle has left me with a memento in the form of skin cancer). I took the advice of a friend, Cedric Lindo, who wrote: 'Keep your dreams and your memories intact. Your Jamaica is history and you would be bitterly disappointed'. However, I have always loved coincidences. Cedric's wife had been Ruth's closest friend when she visited the island. After his wife's death he answered an ad, 'Lodger required'. His landlady was Flo who, after Harry's death, took occasional lodgers to make ends meet. The two old people lived peacefully together until Cedric himself died.

I had been commissioned to write a general book on Islam. This was published in Britain and the United States soon after Corah's death and is still selling after all these years. *Islam and the Destiny of Man* made no pretensions to being a work of scholarship based upon serious study. It was a very personal exploration of what it was that appealed to me in the Faith and, as such, it had a very personal impact. I had been writing primarily for non-Muslims but the book's appeal has been primarily to young Muslims in the West who have found their parents' understanding of Islam either unappealing or incomprehensible and perhaps it echoes that Trinidadian girl's passionate exclamation: 'I love my religion!' A work of love, then, but in more senses than one. It was written while Corah was dying and, often, she sat beside my desk while I was writing. Did this, I have sometimes wondered, give the book a particular emotional intensity which touched the reader on a subliminal level? I cannot tell. But it has sold some 85,000 copies and led to many invitations to speak to Muslim audiences here, in America, Pakistan and even in Peru, where my friend and mentor, Seyyed Hossein Nasr, organised a traditionalist conference.

Remembering the occasion long before when I had been dragged onto a soapbox in Jamaica and drawn a response from the crowd, I understood that one has to be in love with one's audience, however briefly, to make personal contact with them and I was so happy talking to people, whether a hundred or a thousand, that a wave of affection always caught me up in its warm flow. I had, after all, once been an actor, and actors must be possessed by the required emotions while on the stage. Whether such feelings are sincere or superficial hardly matters if they facilitate communication. There were two high points in this period of my life. The first was at a meeting of the World Parliament of Religions in Chicago when I was one of five people chosen to address the final Plenary. I have no idea what I said, but I was intoxicated by the presence of an audience of some six thousand and rode the crest of a wave. Afterwards I was mobbed by American women hugging me or patting me on the back. The second occasion was when I received an award in the Moses Room of the House of Lords and rejoiced in the presence of my family in the front row of a responsive audience. A standing ovation at the end of my speech left me feeling a little dizzy and, as Jamaicans would say, 'in my ackee'; on top of the world as I had been fifty years before.

I complained once to Sidi Abu Bakr (Martin Lings), the most truly humble man I have ever known, that being praised to my face embarrassed me. He responded to this false humility by exclaiming: 'I love to be praised!' I remembered an occasion when, responding to a young man who had praised my 'wonderful' book, I had said: '*Astaghfiru 'llah*', God forgive me, meaning that I sought forgiveness for the self-satisfaction I felt. He had told me sharply: 'You should say *al-Hamdu li'Llah* (Thanks be to God)' and now I saw the point. It is a basic principle of Islam that whatever we say that is good, whatever we do that is good, comes from God, not from our creaturely selves. When we are praised it is only He who is praised. We have no excuse for self-congratulation, only for thankfulness. It is just so that, in a different context, an Arab beggar given a coin by a passing stranger does not say to his friends: 'See what this man gave me'. He says: 'See what God has given me'. It was said by a great Sufi Master of classical times that there is no greater obstacle to spiritual progress than popularity. To avoid this obstacle it is essential inwardly to redirect praise to its proper object. But we are human and may still be permitted to enjoy what is enjoyable so long as thankfulness surrounds and penetrates this pleasure.

The time had come to embark on a new book and I was minded to write something on religion and politics, a self-indulgent exercise. I wasted months making notes until I realised that the extensive research necessary for such a book would be quite beyond me, realised also that the book would be little more than an angry rant, a howl of anguish, over the loss of liberty in our time. A lost cause. Social changes in the West have radically altered the priorities of political policy. A passion for liberty, so well expressed by Benjamin Franklin's dictum that those who prefer security to liberty deserve neither, was essentially an aristocratic principle. The vast majority of people have always, of necessity, been preoccupied with their daily needs and the struggle for survival, therefore with security for themselves and their families. Liberty has been a luxury, low in their order of priorities. This is now the prevailing mindset of our rulers although some vestiges of the libertarian principle may have endured in the United States where the citizen's right to bear arms witnesses, if only symbolically, to a healthy suspicion of State power. In Europe the State is now a fostering mother as well as a protecting father and no one would think it necessary to be armed against it.

In the end I wrote a book called *Remembering God: Reflections on Islam* (published in the year 2000) but, with the excuse of dealing with Islamic principles of government, I sneaked into it some of my political preoccupations. I know something about the lust for power. As a teenager I was possessed by it, always from the best of motives. To set the world to rights I needed untrammelled authority. Such was my benevolence in this recurrent fantasy that only the very wicked could possibly oppose my rule and they would have to be eliminated, probably—in my mother's favourite phrase—'put up against a wall and shot'. The thought saddened me, but how else could I deal with such wickedness? So, when it comes to considering what the Islamic tradition has to say about political power, I rely upon a particular *hadíth* (saying of the Prophet). A man came to him asking for the governorship of a recently-conquered region only to be told: 'As you want it you are not fit for it'. This seems to me to have tremendous implications for an age in which we are governed by men and women of ruthless ambition whose lust for power is overwhelming. The early history of Islam is full of stories of men who, from a deep fear of God, did all they could to avoid being appointed to positions of authority.

Sidi Abu Bakr maintained that the best form of government would be rule by a 'principled autocracy'. He did not suggest how this might be achieved. Looking back to British politics of an earlier age it now seems to me that government by an hereditary ruling class might come closest to offsetting the evils of rule by power-hungry politicians who will always try to increase the monstrous authority of the State. I have lived to see the removal of the hereditary peers from the House of Lords in the name of 'democracy', a further erosion of liberty. The peers were, in the words of an eminent journalist, 'the reserve troops of common sense' and a kind of 'hereditary jury of the nation'. They were a bulwark against a torrent of ill considered and restrictive legislation, mitigating the tyranny of the majority. This is not an expression of the sclerosis of old age. I would have taken the same view in my twenties and, if it smacks of 'elitism', I must ask what is wrong with that except that it conflicts with the current egalitarian ideology? One should always question fashionable ideologies that are taken for granted by the majority since, historically, the majority have usually been mistaken or misled.

Remembering God however was not really the place to express my personal prejudices. These would have been better suited to the diary. That 'childhood-to-death' diary still continues but for many years it has become less personal, more concerned with the lives of my children. Theirs have, on the whole, been happy stories. Leo married an American girl he met while wandering in Mexico and has a son now in College. He was described to me by an authority on film-making as 'one of the finest documentary producers in the States'. Until my health stopped me short I used to visit him every year, first in Texas and later in Maryland. Judy qualified as a physiotherapist, following in Eleanor's footsteps, and has her own clinic in Brighton. Maurice, married to an Irish girl who has truly been another daughter to me, is a highly qualified petroleum engineer. Ann, after some years in the advertising business and after qualifying as a psychotherapist, has devoted herself to bringing up two small children. Respecting their privacy I need say no more beyond the fact that they have been at the centre of my life ever since Corah died. This private world has also been enriched by two singularly beautiful women, one French and the other German, who have enlivened an old man's days (not, I hasten to add, his nights).

I celebrated my eightieth birthday in Cairo where there was an assembly of members of the Tariqah led by Sidi Abu Bakr. Six months later I had a stroke. This was a strange experience; damage to the mind's instrument, the brain, in full awareness of what was happening. I had been to the local shops and, on returning home, almost tumbled out of the car overcome by weakness. I sat down in the kitchen for a cup of coffee, then climbed the stairs on all fours, tried to fling myself onto my bed but fell on the floor, banging my head against the wardrobe, hauled myself onto the bed and phoned Maurice. The following day Judy accompanied me to the local hospital where I spent a month in the hands of the dilapidated NHS, a sclerotic socialist system in which the British persist in taking pride to the derision of other western Europeans.

My memories of that time are mainly of the other victims—I mean patients—who shared the same ward. Opposite to me was a man probably younger than myself but in a much worse way, partially paralysed and incontinent. He was due to be discharged since nothing could be done for him and I listened while the doctor advised his wife, a tough working-class woman, that he should be put into a 'home'. 'No', she said, 'We've always been a couple and we'll stay that way to the end'. She then sought instructions on how to care for him. A hospital is a good place to observe human nature, sometimes admirable and sometimes shameful but stripped of falsehood, unmasked.

I received no treatment but at least I survived the lack of hygiene and the slovenly care which seem to be characteristic of National Health hospitals today. The only lasting effect of the stroke has been a weakness of my legs, a constant inconvenience; this however did not interfere with my public speaking even if I have had to be helped onto the platform by willing hands. Now, finally, I am quite glad to keep my mouth shut. I would be asked questions about 'Islamic terrorism' and I have no easy answers to that. I completely misunderstood the significance of what is now called '9/11', joking to my secretary at the Islamic Centre that this could not be the work of 'our people' since they would be incapable of such efficiency. Remembering the *Blitz*, particularly that morning when Peter and I walked back from St Paul's and nothing could be seen around us but smoking ruins, the destruction of the twin towers seemed no more than a pinprick. As for 'terror', I wonder if people have forgotten so soon the true terror of the nuclear threat at the height of the Cold War. No threat we might face now from 'terrorism' can compare with that and yet people went about their business knowing that their lives — all our lives — might be hideously ended at any moment. We are indeed strange creatures, scared by trifles, untroubled by a sword hanging over our heads by a very loose thread.

If you live long enough you must prepare to be astonished. Ruth implanted in me her prejudices against the English (the Scots were exempt), but even so I would have respected their wish to be as they were; narrow-minded, according to Ruth, culturally ignorant, obsessed with class, and rabidly anti-foreign. Later I came to appreciate their virtues and even their cosy insularity, but I could never have believed that eventually they would accept a peaceful invasion by people of a different race and different cultures or submit to edicts imposed by a European authority. They had expended blood and treasure to prevent the unification of Europe first under Napoleon, then under the Kaiser and finally under Hitler. Perhaps, exhausted by their victories, the fire went out of them with the loss of the Empire. But it is certainly astonishing.

With my grandchildren in mind I wish I could be more optimistic about a future which I shall not live to see, but here the beliefs to which I have held firmly for sixty years take precedence. For me swift change has been, not a sign of progress, but a symptom of instability. The civilisations which have endured the longest — China and India for example — have been static therefore or, in terms of contemporary opinion, 'stagnant', as was Islamic civilisation for a thousand years until disrupted by the impact of the West. In youth rapid change may be a characteristic of growth, in old age it is the harbinger of death. Given the vertiginous speed at which western civilisation is changing, I cannot believe that it will survive much longer. There is, moreover, the nightmare of overpopulation. We have become parasites on the face of the earth instead of its guardians. There are too many of us. Far, far too many. The irony, perhaps, lies in the efforts we make to save and prolong human lives in the belief that this present life is all that we have. Given that belief, a craven obsession with 'health and safety' is natural enough, but it only intensifies the problem as the homeland, the earth, is increasingly overburdened and poisoned while the animal creation cries out for living space.

I am reminded of an episode in a popular TV series a few years ago, *Star Trek*. The hero, Captain Kirk, is kidnapped by an alien civilisation which has conquered disease and prolonged lives so that their planet has become virtually uninhabitable and they have to steal his bacteria and viruses to reduce their population. An absurd fantasy, but it makes a point. Various traditions, including that of the native Americans, speak of a Great Cull, a 'Day of Purification', the levelling of the cities, times of almost unimaginable destruction which precede the final closure. Certainly the Quran speaks of the destruction of many past civilisations which had departed from the straight path. It is pointless to speculate as to how such a holocaust might come about, whether by human agency or by an 'act of God', but I fear that it must come.

But, if night is approaching, we may still enjoy the day. The Prophet's advice to live at one and the same time as though we would live for ever and as though we faced death on the morrow is applicable to humanity as a whole as it is to the individual. There is still music in the air, beauty in field and forest, splendour in the rising of the sun and in its setting. Love still triumphs over the vicissitudes of time and reaches out beyond itself to the timeless because all human love is, by devious ways, directed to God to whom 'all matters return', as the Quran constantly reminds us. I have been haunted as have others (including T.S. Eliot) by that saying of the medieval mystic, the Lady Julian of Norwich: 'All shall be well and all manner of thing shall be well'. It is a mystery why these seemingly banal words carry such power, but they do. Obviously this holy woman was not thinking of our worldly affairs which terminate in the dust but of the scheme of things entire, the whole in which all the fragments come together in glory. This is why, whatever our condition and whatever the future may hold, we are forbidden to despair and encouraged to give praise.

*

So that is it. I am fascinated by my own story, as must be only too obvious, but then I am fascinated by all stories. I have heard so many. The frustrated novelist? At least this has made me a good listener. Tell me your story and you have at once a captive audience, waiting eagerly to hear how it works out. I marvel at the variety, the complexity and the drama of human destinies, all the more because each is, in Ibn Arabi's terms, a glimpse of the divine self-disclosure, as are the splendours of the natural world. Penetrate the surface of the everyday and we discover meaning even if we cannot articulate what it is that we discern. And then there is the fascination of what may be revealed in human faces, 'mirrors of the soul'. I look into the faces of old people I pass in the street, wondering about the destinies hidden behind these ruined features. It is seldom that I see serenity or happiness, such as I perceive in the faces of certain elderly Muslims whose piety has overcome all disorders or in those of elderly monks and nuns. This, surely, is a terrible reflection upon our culture. Despite our prosperity, our ease, joy such as may be found even among simple, impoverished peoples around the world has fled from here.

Judy asked me once if I felt my life had been a success. What is success? Long ago I read somewhere that the only failure in life was the failure to achieve sanctity, in which case I have failed miserably. For that I seek forgiveness daily in my prayers, having wasted my assets, my talents. The hope of forgiveness is the balm that assuages distress. As for worldly success, it might have destroyed me and, perhaps, others. Behind the evident mildness, the unwillingness even to hurt a fly let alone confront an opponent, I detect a vein of ruthlessness which few people have discerned since I have had few opportunities to display it. 'The child is father of the man', so it has been said, and my schoolboy fantasies of power are sharp in my memory. Because I wanted it so much, I could never have been entrusted with real power.

From a completely different perspective, every human life is successful because each is what it is meant to be in terms of the destiny 'written' for us on the tablet of divine knowledge before ever we came crying into this world. In Islam we are commanded never to repine over what passes us by since it could never have come our way. Vain regret is the most pointless of emotions. In that transcendent knowledge past, present and future are a single moment, an eternal plenitude. There, indeed, 'all is well', and if we understand that or at least sense it, however dimly, we can be content with what is and must be. So I take my leave, exempt from regret and thankful for what has been my life experience. *al-Hamdu li'Llah*.